Dear Pa

On the occasion of yo[...] 10.

You were one of these [...]

much love Barba[...]

Gentlemen
of the Raj

Gentlemen *of the Raj*

The Indian Army Officer Corps, 1817–1949

Pradeep P. Barua

PENTAGON PRESS

PRAEGER

Westport, Connecticut
London

Library of Congress Cataloging-in-Publication Data

Barua, Pradeep.
Gentlemen of the Raj : the Indian Army Officer Corps, 1817–1949 / by Pradeep P. Barua.
p. cm.
ISBN 0–275–97999–7 (alk. paper)
1. India. Army—Officers. 2. India—History, Military. 3. India—History—British occupation, 1765–1947. 4. Great Britain—Armed forces—India—History. 5. India—Politics and government—1857–1919. 6. India—Politics and government—1919–1947. I. Title.
UB415.I4B75 2003
355.3'32'095409034—dc21 2002044987

British Library Cataloguing in Publication Data is available.

Library of Congress Catalog Card Number: 2002044987
ISBN: 0-275-97999-7

First Indian Edition 2008

Praeger Publishers, 88 Post Road West, Westport, CT 06881
An imprint of Greenwood Publishing Group, Inc.
www.praeger.com

Printed by Ritomate International, Noida Special Economic Zone, India. www.ritomate.com

PENTAGON PRESS
206, Peacock Lane, Shahpur Jat, New Delhi-110049
Phones : 011-64706243, 26491568
Telefax : 011-26490600
www.pentagon-press.com
email: rajan@pentagon-press.com

Contents

Tables

Introduction

In the first half of the twentieth century the colonial Indian army underwent a dramatic transition during which a glorified colonial police force was transformed into a relatively modern army, complete with its own institutionalized officer corps. This impressive achievement was the culmination of a complex, if cautious, program of social, political, and military reforms. Although these changes dramatically altered the character of this army, and perhaps even the nation to which it belonged, they practically have been ignored by the historiography on the colonial Indian army. Even the scant work done so far tends to underplay this crucial development. This book analyzes some of these institutional and organizational reforms. In this case, institutional reform refers to the development of a professional officer corps along with the training establishments that sustain such a cadre; organizational reform refers to the structural and doctrinal evolution of the colonial Indian army.

Scholars including Stephen P. Cohen, William Gutteridge, Andrew Sharpe, Jeffrey Greenhut, and David Omissi see the slow progress made by the British to establish an institutionalized Indian officer corps as evidence of British racism. They argue that "Indianization" (the replacement of British officers by Indian officers) was a low priority for the British because the British perceived no benefit in it for British rule in India. These scholars overemphasize the influence of Indian nationalist politicians, whom they credit for pressuring the British into any reform.[1] A similar view is held by Mark Houston Jacobsen, who also analyzes the organizational modernization of the colonial Indian army.[2] A. Martin Wainwright has distanced himself somewhat from the dependency writers by acknowledging that considerable advances were made in modernizing the colonial Indian army and the adjoining military industries (but only during the Second World War).[3] Both Jacobsen and Wainwright, however, fail to explain British motivations for proposing radical military reform. Their monocausal explanation of military reform being dictated by the needs of imperial defense is inadequate. Indeed, all of the aforementioned scholars appear to favor the world systems school of dependency theory that sprang up in the mid-1970s. According to this school, the developed world forms the core of a world system economy that exploits the peripheral underdeveloped world, extracting its resources.[4] The Indian army is often seen as a resource of the periphery (India), which is being exploited by the core (Britain). The end result has been the veil of information that shrouds a unique and remarkable event in the history of colonial military modernization.

My work seeks to analyze India as a historically specific case and not as part of a generalized evaluation of colonial military modernization. My study will demonstrate not only that the dynamics of colonial military modernization in India involved a complex process of interaction of external (British) and internal (Indian) factors, but also that the role of being the modernized and dependent partner in the relationship changed rather dramatically in the course of these reforms. I will show that it is misleading to lump the Indian army in the periphery of an imperial world system. I then seek to remove the colonial Indian army from the structures in which the modernization and dependency theorists have placed it. I seek to untangle the study of the colonial Indian army from the intellectual straitjacket in which these theorists have placed it and identify and analyze the players and actors within it, including the British viceroys, civil servants, and Indian officers. It is their perception of modernization and their interaction with each other, British with Indian and British with British, that ultimately determined the course of reform in the colonial Indian army.

The first chapter seeks to establish the organization and composition of the postmutiny (1857) colonial Indian army on the eve of the Great War (which is also the starting point for the modernization period). This is essential in order to understand the intellectual and strategic origins of the Indianization program. Chapter 2 analyzes the dynamics of the organizational politics in the postwar period. The politics and debates of this period ultimately resulted in the establishment of the Indian Military Academy at Dehra Dun, thus initiating the institutionalization of the Indian officers corps.

Chapter 3 examines the first phase of the Indianization process—the military and social education of the Indian officer cadets at Sandhurst and the Indian Military Academy. It examines the social and ethnic backgrounds of these officers and compares and contrasts cadet life in Sandhurst and the Indian Military Academy at Dehra Dun. Chapter 4 analyzes the careers of the Indian officers in the Indian army proper. It examines how the Indian officers were accepted into the British-dominated army and their own reactions to the treatment they received. It concludes with how the war helped the Indian officers' program and Indianization.

Chapter 5 analyzes the doctrinal evolution (the second leg of the modernization program) in the post-1919 era. It examines how changing perceptions of the Indian army at home and in England not only transformed it into a relatively modern fighting force, but also enabled Indian military doctrine to evolve in a more realistic and coherent way than its British counterparts. Chapter 6 examines the emergence of the modern Indian army in the Second World War. It begins with an analysis of how Commonwealth armies led by the Indian army and not the British army, emerged with a winning tactical doctrine in the war. It concludes with an examination of how a professional Indian general staff emerged from the ranks of the rapidly growing Indian officer corps during the war.

Chapter 7 examines the overall impact of the modernization program on the armies of independent India and Pakistan. Relying mainly on confidential reports of British military advisers to the U.K. high commissioners in India and Pakistan, the chapter examines closely the performance of the two armies' officer corps in the first half-decade after independence. In doing so, it demonstrates how it was the Indian army and not the Pakistani army that emerged as the main beneficiary of the partition of the armed forces.

Finally, the conclusion examines the evolution of the Indian officer corps in the postindependence period. It analyzes how the independent Indian officer corps developed with both striking continuity and discontinuity with its colonial past. Among the issues examined in this chapter are the continued doctrinal evolution of the officer corps; the ethnic, sociological, and economic composition of the corps; and civil military relations. The chapter ends with a commentary on the overall effectiveness of the Indian officer corps, especially in comparison to other developing world officer corps.

NOTES

1. Stephen P. Cohen, *The Indian Army: Its Contribution to the Development of a Nation* (Berkeley: University of California Press, 1971); William Gutteridge, "The Indianization of the Indian Army 1918–1945," *Race: Journal of the Institute of Race Relations*, vol. 4 (May 1963); Andrew Sharpe, "The Indianization of the Indian Army," *History Today* (March 1986); Jeffrey Greenhut, "Sahib and Sepoy: An Inquiry into the Relationship between the British Officers and Native Soldiers of the British Indian Army," *Military Affairs* (January 1984); David Omissi, *The Sepoy and the Raj: The Indian Army, 1860–1940* (London: Macmillan, 1994).

2. Mark Houston Jacobsen, "The Modernization of the Indian Army 1925–1939," Ph.D. dissertation (University of California, Irvine, 1979).

3. A. Martin Wainwright, *Inheritance of Empire: Britain, India, and the Balance of Power in Asia, 1938–55* (Westport, Conn.: Praeger, 1994).

4. See Immanuel Wallerstein, *The Modern World System* (New York: Academic Press, 1974).

Abbreviations

AA	antiaircraft
ADC	aide-de-camp
AFNEI	Allied Forces Netherlands East Indies
AFRC	Armed Forces Reconstruction Committee
AG	adjunct general
AHQ	Army headquarters
ALFSEA	Allied Forces South East Asia
APCs	armored personnel carriers
ASC	Army Service Corps
BL/IOR	British Library/India Office Records
CA	Commonwealth Affairs
CAB	Cabinet Office
CCPA	Cabinet Committee on Political Affairs
CENTO	Central Asia Treaty Organization
CID	Committee for Imperial Defence
CIGS	Chief of Imperial General Staff
CO	commanding officer
COS	chief of staff
CRA	chief of Royal Artillery
CRE	chief royal engineer
DCGS	deputy chief of general staff
DMO	director of Military Operations

DSO	Distinguished Service Order
ECIOs	emergency commissioned Indian officers
ECOs	emergency commissioned officers
EIC	East Indian Company
FOs	forward observers
GC	gentleman cadet
GHQ	general headquarters
GOC	general officer commander
GOC-in-C	general officer commander in chief
GS	general staff
GSO	general staff officer
HLI	Highland Light Infantry
HMSO	His Majesty's Stationary Office
HQ	headquarters
IAC	Indian Armored Corps
IAF	Indian Air Force
IAOC	Indian Army Observation Corps
IAVC	Indian Army Vehicle Corps
ICC	Imperial Cadet Corps
ICOs	Indian commissioned officers
ICS	Indian Civil Service
IDC	Indian Defence College
IDR	Indian Defence Review
IEF	Indian Expeditionary Force
IMA	Indian Military Academy
IMRs	Indian Military Records
INA	Indian National Army
JCOs	junior commissioned officers
JDC	Joint Defence Council
JUSII	*Journal of the United Services Institute of India*
KCIOs	King's commissioned Indian officers
KCO	King's commissioned officer
KGVO	King George the Fifth's Own
LMG	light machine gun
LOC	lines of communications
MC	Military Cross
MGO	master general ordnance

MS	military secretary
NCOs	noncommissioned officers
NDA	National Defence Academy
NILF	Native Indian Land Forces
NCS	National Security Council
NWFP	North West Frontier Province
OBE	Order of the British Empire
OTC	Officer Training Course
PLA	Peoples Liberation Army
PMO	prime minister's officer
POW	prisoner of war
PWIRIM	Prince of Wales Royal Indian Military
Q-2	second-class grade
QVO	Queen Victoria's Own
QVOLI	Queen Victoria's Own Light Infantry
RAF	Royal Air Force
RAPIDs	Reorganized Army Plains Infantry Divisions
Retd.	retired
RHA	Royal Horse Artillery
RIASC	Royal Indian Army Service Corps
RIN	Royal Indian Navy
RMA	Royal Military Academy
RMC	Royal Military College
RUSI	Royal United Services Institute
SEATO	South East Asia Treaty Organization
TOT	time on target
VCOs	viceroy's commissioned officers
VCP	visual command post
WO	War Office

1

A Cathartic Debate: The Indianization of the Indian Army Officer Corps, 1817–1919

The dynamics of colonial military conquest rarely have been the subject of significant academic debate. Most scholars agree that the conquest of the non-Western world by the West was primarily a case of the advanced state organizations with superior military technologies overrunning the inferior ones. The most frequent depiction of a battle of colonial conquest is that of a few well-disciplined European troops holding their ground and overwhelming the hordes of the *native* armies. This scenario also has been accepted largely in India's case. Scholars such as Geoffrey Parker, Bruce P. Lenman, and Randolf G.S. Cooper attribute India's collapse to its inability to catch up with the West in terms of military organization and tactics.[1] Their analysis is based on the assumption that everything the Indians did was in reaction to the West. However, recent research has shown that the British succeeded not so much because of the inability of the Indians to adopt completely the Western military system, but because of the ability of the British to adapt rapidly to the changing military situation in India.[2] It is only by acknowledging the fact that the wars of colonial conquest in India were, in military terms, at least a contest among equals that one can begin to form an understanding of motivations behind the British attempts to modernize their colonial army in India.

The debate on the postconquest era has been monopolized by dependency theorists. Many of these scholars found the affair of the so-called martial races fascinating. Briefly, the "martial races" were certain categories of peoples from the subcontinent whom the British considered to be particularly suited, physically and mentally, for inclusion in the Indian army. Scholars, including Nirad C. Chaudhuri and David Omissi, have adopted the view that the martial races were in effect a conspiracy by the British to "divide and rule" India,[3] and thus theorize that the British employed certain minority communities like the Sikhs and the Gurkhas to suppress the larger Hindu community. Again, recent research has indicated that the martial races were the culmination of a prolonged process by the British to classify the peoples of colonial India. As a result of early anthropologists-cum-administrators' pseudoscientific conclusions, the British officialdom for much of the nineteenth and early twentieth centuries actually believed that certain Indian ethnic groups were more suited to military life than others.[4]

The belief that the Indian army was merely an exploitative tool in the hands of the British has deflected the attention of researchers from a key aspect of the modernization of the Indian army: the Indianization of the officer corps. Scant years after the revolt of 1857, the British had, on their own initiative, begun a process that ultimately would pave the way for the complete transformation of the colonial Indian army into a modern national army. Yet before we investigate the dynamics of this change, it is imperative that we have a clear understanding of the organization and composition of the Indian army on the eve of these reforms.

THE FRONTIER ARMY

In the years of incessant fighting in India from 1750–1850 the East India Company army proved itself to be a major military innovator. It was not uncommon for techniques that were learned in the Indian campaigns to be utilized by British troops in their European campaigns. Experience of the Anglo-Sikh wars in particular greatly affected the development of British tactics. At Chillianwallah and Gujerat, for example, the British used for the first time a combination of line and column infantry formations.[5] At Chillianwallah it was the stunning defeat of the British cavalry that prompted the adoption of the inversion drill for cavalry formations by entire divisions rather than by threes and twos, as had been the regular practice. As one scholar notes, "It required the Chillianwallah debacle, a far greater strain on the British cavalry than the charge of the Light Brigade, to ensure . . . [that] inversion was permitted."[6] Artillery went through a similar process of reform. During the battle of Gujerat—the final battle of the Sikh wars—the British, in reaction to the excellent Sikh artillery, deployed no less than 100 guns, the largest artillery concentration by the British to that date. The Sikh wars convinced the British that artillery was the answer to reduce infantry casualties.[7] However, once India was firmly in British hands, the military emphasis changed from a dynamic conquest to a more mundane policing effort.[8]

After the revolt of 1857, control of the Indian army passed to the crown. A commission of inquiry was appointed immediately to investigate the causes of the mutiny and to propose changes in the army's organization. The chief recommendation of the Peel Commission (headed by Secretary of State for War Jonathan Peel) was that the proportion of Indian to British soldiers in India in the future should not be greater than three to one.[9] As a result of this recommendation, the number of British soldiers stationed in India trebled in comparison to premutiny levels, placing a tremendous burden on the British army. The Cardwell system, while maintaining the ratio in favor of British troops, sought to neutralize some of the pressure on Britain. In the process of a far-reaching reform of the British army, the Secretary of State for War Edward Cardwell, introduced a twelve-year standard service to be split between active and reserve service. According to this system, short-service commission soldiers who came to India (or elsewhere in the empire) had to be at least twenty years old. They had to serve with the coloured at least six years, after which they could return to England on reserve status.[10] In practice it was never possible to keep anywhere near an equal number of battalions at home, and units were unable to maintain regular drafts. According to Brian Bond, the home units became little more than training battalions for their sister battalions overseas. One contemporary British military critic of the system, Colonel G.F.R. Henderson, went so far as to declare that the real army was in India.[11] Ironically, the Cardwell system was ill-received in India, too. The government of India resented the expenditure imposed by the system (the cost of passage to and fro for the recruits) as well as the fact that India essentially had the job of training raw recruits for Britain. The government of India noted, "It was no consideration for the efficiency of the army in India that evoked the short service system, and its suitability to the conditions of Indian requirements had been gravely questioned on more than one occasion."[12]

In July 1879 the army in India was comprised of 6,602 British officers and 60,341 British and 123,254 Indian soldiers.[13] That year the specially appointed Eden Commission, whose mission was to examine the army's organization and expenditures, warned of the dangers in persisting with the presidential armies. The commission proposed the establishment of four regional corps located in Bengal, Madras, Bombay, and the Punjab. It also concluded that it was not possible at that time to reduce the army (the presidential armies were abolished by General Sir Frederick Roberts in 1895 in favor of a single army headquarters).[14]

It was under the energetic and ambitious Lord Kitchener that the Indian army experienced dramatic structural and doctrinal reforms prior to the Great War. Kitchener's primary aim was to deflect the Indian army from its increasing emphasis on internal security duties. Ever since the revolt of 1857, the deployment of the Indian army had been based more on internal than on external security concerns. Kitchener began by forming the army into nine divisions, divided between two commands—Northern and Southern—the latter having four divisions and the former having five. The regiments were renumbered and deficient ones were eliminated. The old designations of Madras, Bombay, and Bengal that had persisted through

Lord Roberts' reforms were dropped from the regimental titles. In 1905 Kitchener established the staff college at Deolali, later moved to Quetta. Kitchener undoubtedly hoped that the army would absorb the lessons of the Boer War, just as the British army was attempting to do at their own staff college at Camberley. It was his experience of fighting Boers with high-powered Mauser rifles that led Kitchener to reequip the Indian army with the Lee Enfield .303 magazine rifle. He also introduced the 2.75in mountain screw gun. The screw gun fired a ten-pound shell about six thousand yards and broke up into five mule loads for transport, making it a highly effective mobile support weapon.[15] The officers of the newly created mountain batteries were not from the Indian army, but came from the Royal Artillery and spent several years in India. Whatever reservations Kitchener may have had about institutional military reform (Indianization), he did contribute significantly to the establishment of a small and highly trained frontier army.[16]

Although it was Kitchener who streamlined it for frontier fighting, the army had been engaged in frequent conflict there long before his arrival. With few exceptions, warfare against the northwestern Pathan tribes was mainly a midlevel insurgency operation. A lot of time was spent on endless patrols and garrison duties in some forgotten hilltop or valley. Prevention of an uprising was preferable to a battle. To this end, intelligence was vital and primarily gathered by tireless political officers and their agents. Since the tribes rarely confronted the British in open battle, it became vital to guard from ambush all lines of communications (LOC) to garrisons and outpost ambushes. This often entailed the establishment of high posts to protect and support advancing troops and convoys. The 2.75in. screw gun was the lynchpin of most of these posts, the forerunners of the firebases found in Vietnam. Punitive offensives launched usually ranged from battalion-to brigade-level formations.

The unique requirements of a frontier army had an impact upon the British home army as well. At a 1906 meeting to coordinate the practices of the home and Indian armies, the majority of the army council rejected the army corps' formations of the British and Continental armies in favor of large divisions as seen in India, which were regarded as more flexible and better suited to the imperial requirements of the British army.[17] The disorganized state and lack of modern armament of the northwest and Afghan tribes allowed the British to control them with a small but highly professional army.

The system of recruitment reflected both the highly selective requirements of such an army and the workings of the "martial race" system. Soldiers already in the regiment typically brought in relatives and friends to apply for entry. After a medical examination and interview with the Indian non-commissioned officers and the adjutant of the regiment, they usually were placed on the *Umedwar*, or "hopeful," list, to be called upon when vacancies opened. Training of the new recruits usually was done within the regiment itself. Toward the close of the nineteenth century, as martial race selection became the norm, recruiting officers would rove a particular district to look for the right kind of recruit to be presented before the British officers. The elaborate process of selection was influenced heavily by pseudosciences like "anthropometry" (race determination by physical measurements) and ultimately led to the creation of a series of recruiting handbooks that conveniently highlighted physical and mental traits of a particular martial race. These handbooks, which were regularly updated, became the bible of the recruiting officer.[18]

THE DEBATE

It is only within this context of a highly specialized army that we can comprehend the unprecedented reforms that the British were trying to implement within the Indian army. These reforms are remarkable not only due to their controversial nature, but also due to the fact that they were being discussed long before the consolidation of British rule in India had become a reality. The issue of the Indianization of the officer corps is not a twentieth-century phenomenon; rather, it can be traced back to the early nineteenth century. Sir Thomas Munro, a prominent administrator in Madras (governor of Madras from 1819–1827), writing in 1817 on the subject of granting commissions to Indians in the army stated, "No elevation of character can be expected among men who in the military line cannot attain any rank above that of Subadar [NCO—noncommissioned officer], where they are as much below an ensign as an ensign is below the Commander in Chief."[19] In a relatively farsighted report that predated similar conclusions about Indian soldiers in the Great War, Munro was pointing out the obvious lack of initiative that characterizes soldiers of colonial armies. Munro added, "Our government will always be respected from the influence of our military power; but it will never be popular while it offers no employment to the native that can stimulate the ambition of the better class of them."[20] Here Munro raised a political issue by pointing out that it would be better to rule with the support of the "better class" than with the use of force alone. In 1842 another prominent British administrator in India, Sir Henry Lawrence, concurred with Munro and stated that, unless higher positions were open to sepoys[21] of "better education, [and] superior character," it was quite possible that their energies and talents could be turned against the British.[22]

The views aired by Munro and Lawrence are amazing, for they came at a time when British rule in India had not yet been consolidated. In 1817 the remnants of the Maratha Confederacy in western India and the Sikh Kingdom in the Punjab were still independent of British control. The Sikhs in fact were only "subdued" after a decade of bloody warfare in 1849. The rationale behind the views of Munro and Lawrence lies in the unique brand of Utilitarianism they espoused in India. Munro and his fellow Utilitarians in India believed in pragmatic government. Their common aim was to preserve as much as possible the original institutions of Indian society rather than change them completely. To this end, the Munro school was prepared to support liberal measures like the admission of Indians to higher posts in the civil service and the army. Unlike such Utilitarians as James Mill, they did not believe in the ability of government to illuminate or educate the people. As far as Munro was concerned, the task of the government in India was paternal protection and little more. Change, if and when it came, would do so from within Indian society itself and could not be imposed from the outside.[23] Almost Machiavellian in concept, their writings on the subject nevertheless provided a convenient precedent for the liberal British officials and generals who in the late nineteenth century launched a concerted effort to introduce Indians into the officer ranks of the army.

The revolt of 1857 dampened further talk of reform (at least at an official level) until Sir George Chesney, first as military secretary and later as member of the Military Department, took a sustained interest in this issue. On 16 April 1884, Chesney, in reference to a proposal to confer an honorary commission upon the nawab of Mandot, wrote, "It would be sound policy to open a definitive military career to natives of the higher classes giving them not only honorary commands but substantive ones."[24] Sir Chesney went on to propose a trial experiment with a "native" regiment. Although this scheme was rejected by General Wilson, a military member, on the grounds that native princes would not take to continuous military service, it was revived in January 1885 by Chesney on the basis that the position would be open on grounds not of wealth, but of good birth, education, and physique. This proposal piqued the interest of the Commander in Chief General Sir Donald Stewart, who, along with Sir Chesney, sent a joint proposal on 21 March 1885 to Lord Kimberly. In it they recommended the raising of two special native regiments—one cavalry and one infantry—to be officered entirely by Indians (this was to meet General Wilson's plea about the painful isolation of the Indian subaltern in the British mess).[25]

Lord Kimberly reviewed the proposal on 15 April 1886 and deemed it expedient to obtain the views of senior officers, thus opening the first large-scale official debate on Indianization. The outcome was surprising. The vast majority of the soldiers polled supported the plan, while the most potent objection came from a civilian. The reasons given for supporting it and objecting to it are equally interesting. Those who backed the plan did so on political grounds and offered generalized explanations. General Sir Neville Chamberlain (no relation to the future prime minister) felt that British rule would benefit from incorporating Indian elites into the army. Field Marshal Lord Napier of Magdala stated that the time had come to match the civilian service in opening the higher posts of the army to "distinguished native gentlemen of suitable character."[26] This group backed the plan on the grounds of principle rather than fact, and their occasional dissent to the plan was based more on minute technicalities. General Sir A. Taylor, for example, objected to part of the proposal that would reduce the number of officers with new regiments below the number allowed to European regiments.[27]

On the other hand, the dissenters, though few in number, appeared to have logic on their side. Among other things, they questioned if such a move actually would increase the efficiency of the army. They wondered if the Indian officers would lead another mutiny. They questioned if there was evidence of any demand for military employment among the Indians. They wanted to know if British officers would ever be placed in a subordinate position to an Indian.[28]

Last-minute attempts to revise the scheme were unsuccessful.[29] They were firmly put down by Lord Roberts, who had succeeded Sir Stewart as commander in chief of India. In his minute of rejection Lord Roberts declared:

> Though a policy which would improve the prospects of the native officers of the Indian army and open to men of superior military qualities opportunities of rising to positions of trust and responsibility is one which has my warmest sympathies, I am unable to support the proposal that Indian gentlemen should be appointed to the commissioned ranks of the army in the same grade as Europeans. I am convinced that however well-educated and clever an Indian may be, and however much he may distinguish himself, he would be never looked up to by the British soldier in the same way that the latter looks up to the British subaltern.[30]

Without the support of the commander in chief, all hope for reform in the near future died, and the government of India decided to drop the plan on "financial" grounds.[31]

In 1888 Sir Chesney reopened the issue by proposing the creation of a military school, since he felt that education was the key to higher military posts. Sir Chesney had discarded the plan to advance existing native commissioned officers and had instead reapplied an earlier proposal of the Army Reorganization Committee of 1879. Although this scheme had the support of the civilian members of the India Council, Lord Roberts rejected the proposal, and it too was shelved during the council discussion on 13 June 1888.[32] But, to Lord Roberts' chagrin, the issue refused to die, and in 1890 Colonel Holroyd, director of public instruction in the Punjab, submitted a scheme for creating a military section in Aitchison College, Lahore, for native officers of good birth, who, after passing a course in the college, could be appointed to native regiments. At the same time, the duke of Connaught's memorial committee, based in Poona, put forward a similar scheme. Sir Chesney immediately supported these plans, but Lord Roberts, rejecting them, declared, "Once you introduce anything but regimental training, on however limited a scale, you are on the highroad to an Indian Sandhurst."[33] As if finally to squash the issue, Roberts added that he doubted if Indian officers could be impartial like the British in handling rival claims of jealous native soldiers.

The issue of commissions for Indians arose again in 1897, this time in England. The maharajah of Cooch Behar pleaded to the Secretary of State for India Lord George Hamilton that his sixteen-year-old son, then studying at Eton, be allowed to join a British regiment. Noting the War Office's opposition to such a move, Lord Hamilton wrote to Lord Elgin stating, "The War Office have destroyed their own case by admitting Dhuleep Singh into a cavalry regiment."[34] A committee led by Field Marshal Sir Donald Stewart had noted in December that the "occasional" admission of sons of "Indian Princes and Gentlemen . . . would be politically very desirable," which Hamilton pointed out.[35] In his reply of February 1898, Lord Elgin stated that he and his India Council felt the proposal would do little to secure the goodwill of the Indian nobility. They also believed that the men who would send their sons to England would not be among those with influence in India. Like the dissenters before them, they considered Indian custom and caste to be a major consideration to the chiefs of the strongest race (martial), and were thus prevented to send their sons to England.[36] Lord Lansdowne, writing to Lord Hamilton that same month, expressed that the request of the maharajah must be turned down, for the reforms, once begun, would have no foreseeable end.[37]

The momentum for reform, however, was gathering pace. Sir Alfred Lyall, the Anglo-Indian chairman of the Political Committee, was determined to make a beginning. Part of his strategy was to embarrass the War Office by portraying its opposition to Indians as a policy based primarily on the grounds of color. Lyall also addressed the fears of the War Office that reform would result in a flood of Indians; he assured them that this would not be the case, as the secretary of state would nominate selectively only a limited number of Indians for officer training. He added, "Nor is it to be anticipated that more than a few Indian youths will really desire to enter a service which offers little or no emolument, and involves long absence from their native country." Sir Lyall cautioned the War Office about its fears that the Indians with military service would prove dangerous by stating, "The danger lies rather among those who have been educated as Europeans, and have not been employed."[38]

Another potential problem arose when Sir Arthur Wilson, the legal adviser to the secretary of state, pointed out that special legislation would be required to admit the sons of native Indian chiefs. The settlement of 1790, which formally placed the crown on the Hanoverians, also contained a clause forbidding any person "born out of the Kingdoms of England, Scotland, or Ireland, or the dominions thereunto belonging . . . , except such as are born of English parent," to hold office or place of trust, civil or military.

Wilson added that, although this rule had been relaxed in favor of naturalized persons, it otherwise remained in force.[39]

As Lord Hamilton and Sir Wilson pondered ways to sidestep this constitutional hurdle, Secretary of State for War Lord Lansdowne delivered a death blow to the latest reform attempts. Late in 1898 he came out in full support of Lord Elgin's view that those who would send their sons to England would be "natives of advanced opinion" with a veneer of British civilization. Lansdowne considered all non-Europeans as unsuitable candidates. In the case of Dhuleep Singh, Lord Lansdowne pointed out that the prince had to leave the regiment, as he could not pass the riding school, and that he had set a bad example for the other cadets with his extravagant ways.[40]

LORD CURZON AND THE IMPERIAL CADET CORPS

After carefully studying the debate on reform, Lord Curzon, the new viceroy, declared that most of these reform schemes had accomplished nothing simply because they lacked careful planning. Although Curzon saw some validity in Lord Roberts' contention that most native Indian officers were quite contented, he did feel that "from [his] own experience . . . manifest and undeniable," he was aware of pleas from the aristocratic ranks to obtain entry into the officer corps. Lord Curzon felt that this demand grew as educational opportunities grew. He mentioned specifically the prestigious Chiefs Colleges—Mayo College, Ajmer; Aitchison College, Lahore; Rajkumar College, Kathiawar; and Daly College, Indore—and stated, "I hold, therefore, that the problem of finding some military opening for the cadets of princely and noble families, not merely exists, but that it is yearly becoming more acute."[41] Curzon also brought attention to an obvious flaw in Lord Roberts' argument that the move to create an Indian officer corps could prove dangerous, as it would create a class of military adventurers. As Curzon noted, this belief undermined the theory of Indians being destitute of military aptitude.

Curzon instead proposed the establishment of a Viceroy's Corps (later to be known as the Imperial Cadet Corps [ICC]) consisting of twenty to thirty young men from princely and noble families, selected solely from the four Chiefs Colleges. These youths would be eligible at age seventeen to twenty and be selected according to family, conduct, and knowledge of the English language. They would be brought to Calcutta and placed under a prince or noble of high birth, exemplary character, and military attainment. In Calcutta they would live a simple life in the *maidan*, or park grounds; associate with young English officers; be taught to dress, ride, and perform other physical activities; and then proceed to Delhi for further military drill. They would then be sent home for the summer, and those still keen could return for a definite course of military training. The nature of the commis-

Table 1
List of Native Officers Holding British Rank in 1898[42]

NAME	RANK	HISTORY/UNIT
1.Nawab Of Jaora	Honorary Major 27 April 1881	Central India Horse
2.Rana of Dholpur	Honorary Major 8 February 1882	Central India Horse
3.Maharaja of Kuch Behar	Honorary Major 22 February 1883 promoted to Hon. Lt. Col.	6th Bengal Cavalry Lord Kimberly said this should be done only under very special circumstances.
4.Nawab of Mandot	Hon. Lieutenant 25 March 1885	Attached to 2nd Punjab Cavalry.
5.Maharaj Dhiraj Sir Pertab Singh of Jodhpur State.	Hon. Lt. Col. 21 June 1997 Hon. Col. 20 January 1898	Proposed by Secretary of State for assistance to Tirah Expeditionary Force.
6. Rissaldar Major Mohammed Aslam Khan	Hon. Major 25 March 1885 Hon. Lt. Colonel 18 January 1890	5th Bengal Cavalry Recognition of services with Afghan Boundary Commission. Services with the Black Mountain Expedition.
7. Maharaj of Jammu & Kashmir	Ho. Colonel 21 January 1888 Hon. Major General 22 January 1896	37th Bengal Infantry For raising it. For valuable services of men and state during the Chitral operations 1895.
8. Raja Jai Chand Lambagraon	Hon. Major 21 January 1888	37th Bengal Infantry (Dogra)
9. Muhammed Ali Beg Nawab Afsar-i-Jang Bahadur A.D.C. to his Highness Nizam of Hyderabad	Hon. Major 16 May 1888	3rd Cavalry Hyderabad Contingent
10. Bir Bikram Singh Son of Maharaja of Sirmoor	Hon. Lieutenant 4 September 1889 Hon. Captain	1/2nd Gurkha for drill and instruction. Approved bu Govt of India.
Nawab of Rampur	Hon. Captain 6 February 1895 Hon. Major	9th Bengal Cavalry
Maharaja of Gwalior	Hon. Colonel 21 May 1898	For Assistance to Tirah Expeditionary Force, 1897-98.

sion (a key issue that would in the future almost wreck the reform effort) would be left to discussion.[43]

The ICC held its first course in April 1902. It had two seasonal locations; it wintered in Meerut and spent the summers in Dehra Dun. Curzon's unrelenting efforts to allow Indians into the officer corps have cast him as the great pioneer in the Indianization effort.[44] In reality, the ICC was far from a realization of that goal. The object of the corps, according to the official statement, was to provide "military training for selected members of the aristocracy of India, and of giving them such a general education in the imperial army as British officers, they may never lose their character and bearing as Indian gentlemen."[45] The camps at Meerut and Dehra Dun were geared more toward producing educated Indian "gentlemen" rather than Indian officers.[46] The popular perception in those days was that Indian princes and aristocratic youth were an indolent and licentious group. The ICC course appears to have been designed, initially at least, as a disciplining camp. Great emphasis was placed on the "moral" aspect of the cadets' character. The rules of the ICC stated clearly that "immoral" and "unmanly" practices would be sternly suppressed.[47] It is also evident that the cadets were to represent a "martial" standard for the rest of the Indian princely community. There are indications that the camps were little more than princely boarding schools; each cadet, for example, was allowed to bring with him a personal attendant and cook.[48] The ceremonial uniforms worn by the cadets were probably among the most colorful and expensive worn by any military unit in India. It was comprised of a turquoise turban with a gold hang. A gold cockade and a gold ornament completed the striking headgear. The white coat had elaborate embroidery on the collar, the cuffs, the shoulders, the back, and the front. The *kumerbund*, literally "stomach wrap" was blue with red embroidery. The breeches were white and joined by black patent leather boots up to the knees. Solid brass spurs completed this elaborate ensemble. The cadets also received a lot of equestrian training to conduct themselves flawlessly in ceremonial parades.[49]

After the cadets successfully completed the three and half–year course, they obtained a second lieutenant's commission into what was known as the Native Indian Land Forces (NILF).[50] This, however, was an extremely limited commission, for its holders could only command "native" Indian officers and soldiers. Failing this, they were assigned to the staffs of general officers.[51] This is precisely where the majority of the cadets ended up. Their inferior status vis-à-vis their British counterparts left them in a very awkward position. General Sir Edmund Barrow, commander in chief of the Southern Army, noted in March 1912 that two of his ICC aides-de-camp (ADCs), Lieutenant Aga Casim Shah and Lieutenant Kanwar Amar Singh (whose diary I make extensive reference to above, see n.44), were "naturally not altogether pleased with their present position and prospects."[52] Barrow, usually a staunch opponent of Indianization, was sufficiently moved by the plight of the two Indian officers to suggest that they be given probationary postings to regiments.[53]

The first commission under Curzon's new system was granted in July 1905. Indians commissioned in this system, however, were not employed in ordinary regimental service.[54] With the momentum for the introduction of Indians into the officer corps becoming irresistible, senior officers like General Sir O'Moore Creagh (who succeeded Kitchener as commander in chief in 1909) also called for steps to give further responsibility to native officers. Unfortunately, even Creagh's qualified suggestion was strongly opposed by General Kitchener, who in September 1908 issued a powerful memorandum. Arguing along lines similar to those of previous dissenters such as Lord Roberts and Lieutenant General (and later Field Marshal) Sir Charles Brownlow, Kitchener contended that such a policy would be detrimental to the continuation of British rule. Yet, perhaps cognizant of the majority view in favor of reform, Kitchener added, "Nevertheless I myself do not think that we should remain for ever stationary, and completely bar against natives of India all paths for further military advancement except those now open to them; though I am convinced that we must move slowly and on well considered lines."[55] Kitchener also noted that he did not recall meeting men of good education among the Sikhs, Pathans, and Marathas whom General Creagh had described. He also deemed the ICC a failure (started a year before Kitchener's 1901 arrival). Although the ICC had made a promising start by filling its quota of twenty-four cadets in July 1902, enthusiasm for the corps and enrollment dropped rapidly thereafter, never to reach the twenty-four mark again. One of the cadets, Amar Singh, noted that by 1904 no Rajputs (one of the vaunted martial races) were entering the corps.[56] Kitchener correctly identified the establishment of the corps as a political move and not a military one. He proposed instead a military college to train Indian *jemadars* (King's commissioned second lieutenant) as a reward for loyalty, but would not lay down anything definite for promotion. He added, "I would sweep away the racial disability, but I would not confer any absolute rights, leaving each case to be considered on its merits."[57]

Fortunately, Kitchener's reservations did not have the same effect as had Lord Roberts' several decades earlier. In February 1911 the War Office informed the India Office that it was willing to give two commissions to selected sons of Indian chiefs in the Household Cavalry and Foot Guards, provided they passed Sandhurst. Later that year, the Indian general staff put forward the most cogent commitment to Indianization yet by laying down a tentative guideline for the process:

a. The administration of Indians to the full rights of King's Commission is a step of greatest importance for it is on its officers as a body that an army depends for success in war. Any distinction between the two races as regards to conditions of service or relative rank will militate against whole-hearted cooperation and good comradeship, and Indians should therefore, be in all respects on exactly the same footing as their British brothers-in-arms.

b. Indian gentlemen of best birth and position alone will be suitable to hold commissions. Therefore there will be strict selection by nomination.

c. Early education must be in England.

d. Military education must be carried out at Sandhurst where a certain number of vacancies (Indian cadetships) will be reserved for Indians who obtain the minimum qualifying marks.

e. They should go through the whole curriculum at Sandhurst, the same as their British counterparts.

f. Indians for the present will be posted to the Indian army where vacancies will be reserved for them.

g. Promotion, pay, army and regimental rank will be on the same term as those of British officers of the Indian army.

h. After obtaining their commissions Indians should be attached to a British unit in England for a year.

i. Indians will be eligible to serve in all units of cavalry and infantry of the Indian army and should not be relegated to a special corps.

j. Three senior officers of the regiment should decide if retention of the young Indians is desirable after the first three years of service.

k. Though twenty commissions a year might eventually be given it would be advisable to limit the number to ten until this scheme has proven its feasibility.[58]

The recommendations of the general staff were largely accepted in 1911 by Lord Crewe, the secretary of state for India. There was, however, an important exception: the establishment of a specially formed "native" regiment in India to absorb these officers. This would ensure that Indians could not command British officers in India.[59]

During the following years, the proposals were subject to constructive criticism. Major R.L. Ricketts, the commandant of the ICC, declared in 1914 that few of the cadets were fit educationally. He doubted if there were any desire among these "top" families to go to Sandhurst. In October the same year, Viceroy Hardinge noted that the Indian middle class would reject the plan, for it was restricted to the ruling class. Like Major Ricketts, he felt it was useless to pursue commissions for the disinterested princely classes. Lord Hardinge thought that a military academy must be set up in India along the lines of Royal Military College (RMC) at Sandhurst. In a pointed note to dissenters, including Roberts, Lord Hardinge stated, "it is not the British *soldier* who would be unwilling to receive orders from the Indian officer, but the British *officer*."[60] Hardinge received indirect support from Sir Harvey Anderson, lieutenant governor of Burma, who in September 1915 stated, "Indian officers in this war lacked initiative to command, because they have never been taught to do so. Therefore they must be given opportunities of advancement."[61]

Opposition to the proposals came from the Commander in Chief General Sir Beauchamp Duff, who, in the best tradition of Lord Roberts and other dissenters, also considered Indians as lacking any leadership ability. He feared that British NCOs and men would not take direct orders from Indian officers (a suggestion rejected by Lord Hardinge). General Duff also concurred that the proposal should be dropped, as it would prove incompatible with the efficiency of the army. Sir Benjamin Robertson, chief commissioner of the Central Provinces, expressed concern over potential problems that would arise when Indians were in a position to order British officers.[62]

In January 1917, Austen Chamberlain, the secretary of state for India, urged the War Cabinet to come to a decision. He asked the cabinet to sanction an announcement that it had decided to accept, at least in principle, the appointment of Indians to the commissioned ranks in His Majesty's Army. In subsequent letters in June and July, the secretary complained to the War Cabinet that the War Office was holding up the entire scheme by its unwillingness to concede the principle of giving Indians command over Europeans. Secretary Chamberlain pointed out the difficulties in supplying sufficient officers of a pure European descent for the Indian army and the effect the racial bar would have no recruiting. Chamberlain was convinced that the time had arrived for the principle of granting King's commissions to Indians to be admitted. Nonetheless, in July 1917, a War Office letter to the India Office stated:

> I am commanded by the Army Council to inform you that after the most careful consideration they have come to the conclusion that to grant commissions to natives of India would entail a great risk from the military point of view, in that it involves placing native Indians in a position where they would be entitled to command European officers. For this reason the Council are not prepared to take the responsibility of advising such a step.[63]

The "great risk" that the War Office was referring to was explained in 1918 when they noted that granting King's commissions to Indians

> cannot fail to have a very harmful effect upon the recruitment of British officers for the Indian army. The measures already taken in this direction have rendered parents and guardians and young men themselves suspicious, and it is submitted that such a sudden and large measure as the above would more than confirm their ideas on the subject.[64]

Despite the War Office's misgivings, in August 1917 the War Cabinet formally agreed in principle to the appointments of Indians to commissioned rank in His Majesty's Army.[65] The only stipulation the War Office placed was that all candidates be subject to competitive exams in a course through Sandhurst, nomination after service in the ranks, or to completion of the Officer Training Course (OTC) through Sandhurst. Ten Indian candidates would be nominated per year.[66]

The War Cabinet's decision brought to an end decades of internal debate within the upper echelons of the Indian government and the Indian army on the question of Indianization of the officer corps. Much of this debate had been carried out within the ranks of the liberal reformers themselves. Outright dissent in the manner of Kitchener was the exception rather than the rule, and most of the dissenters, including Roberts, had tried to portray themselves as conservative reformers rather than obstructionists. At times galvanizing and at times tedious, this debate symbolized a collective catharsis on the part of the liberal reformers. Their passionate espousal of radical reform in this most conservative institution of the British Raj, reflected the unease the liberals felt about the indefensible nature of their total ban on Indians from the officer corps. The liberals also shared a common belief with the Utilitarian predecessors: Good government and an efficient army could be achieved only with the cooperation of the Indians. Their reasons for believing this, however, differed radically from the radicals'. Before we can delve into the reasons behind their actions, it is essential to explore the role of the Indian army in the Great War, for, no matter how convincing the arguments of the liberals were, the British government would have paid little attention to this vexing issue had the war not revealed glaring inadequacies in an all-white–officered Indian army.

THE INDIAN EXPEDITIONARY FORCE IN FRANCE

At the beginning of 1914 the Indian army had about 150,000 men. As soon as the war broke out, the government of India offered Britain a corps of two infantry divisions (each of three brigades, each brigade made up of one British battalion and three Indian/Gurkha battalions) and two cavalry divisions (with three brigades, each with one British and two Indian regiments). After a brief hesitation, this offer was accepted in August 1914.[67]

The Indian corps, led by units of the Lahore and Meerut divisions, disembarked in France in October 1914. They were hurriedly equipped with short Lee Enfield .303 rifles, machine guns, and field artillery (British units) before being despatched to the front.[68] The Indian corps had been thrust pell-mell into a war the likes of which it had never seen before, and the effect on the men was devastating. Unit after unit including the vaunted marital races (Gurkhas, Sikhs, and Rajputs) broke and fled the horror of the trenches. The fact that neighboring British units did not desert the trenches like the Indians made their actions all the more troubling for the commanders.

The official British exploration at the time laid the blame on the fact that heavy officer casualties had denuded the Indian units of their leadership element. The British high command believed that Indian soldiers were in effect lost without their white officers.[69] Although the opportunity for granting commissions to Indians was ripe, the reaction from the commanders was wholly negative. Both General Sir James Willocks, commander of the Indian Expeditionary Force (IEF), and General Sir Beauchamp Duff, the commander in chief for India, remained adamantly opposed to the move: They were convinced that the Indians lacked the ability to command, especially on the western front.[70]

Historian Jeffrey Greenhut attributes the IEF's destruction in France to a traumatic form of culture shock. He explains the Indian soldiers' dependence on their white officers and their inability to take command by the fact that the British officers were more than mere leaders. "They were the interpreters of totally unfamiliar environment, of a military system so completely foreign that Indian soldiers could not function without them . . . they fulfilled a role no uneducated peasant could hope to emulate."[71]

Yet culture shock and a new military system alone fail to explain the total reliance of the Indian troops on British officers. The real answer lies in the fact that the Indian troops had been thoroughly indoctrinated into a subordinate position within the army. No Indian officer wielded command over even the lowliest British ensign. As one British observer noted in regard to native Indian officers, "Their present position of subordination to British officers in the regiment is calculated to impair any initiative or leadership they may have originally possessed."[72] Sir Harvey Anderson, the lieutenant governor of Burma, also noted in September 1915 that Indian officers in the war lacked the initiative to command because they had never been taught to do so.[73] With no Indian role models who could stand alongside their white officers, Indian Viceroy's commissioned officers (VCOs) and NCOs had little or no self-confidence to take on any leadership role after the loss of their white officers. Although it was the debacle at Kut in Mesopotamia that captured the imagination of the British public and the postwar military reformers, it was the performance or lack thereof of the IEF in France that had the most significant long-term impact in the Indian army in the interwar period.

CONCLUSION

The First World War was the catalyst for substantive military reform in India. However, in one aspect of this reform—the institutional—an internal debate within the Indian army and Whitehall had been resolved prior to the outbreak of the Great War in favor of the reformers. The experience of the war, and in particular the threat of the IEF in France, merely helped accelerate the scope and time frame for the implementation of these reforms.

What is remarkable about this entire debate is that it appears to have been generated internally. Pressure from Indian politicians seems to have been rather muted at this stage. The only major Indian figure to have advocated such reform was Dadabhai Naoroji,[74] who made an appeal on behalf of the maharajah of Cooch Behar's son for entry into a British regiment, only to be turned down by the British.[75] The annual conference of Indian residents in the U.K., convened by the London Indian Society under the presidency of Dadabhai Naoroji on 20 December 1898, passed a resolution demanding "that Indians should be allowed commissions and command the Indian army in the same manner and through the same methods as are open to Englishmen, by competition and training, and by promotion for distinguished ability and gallantry in the field."[76] Such demands appear to have been the exception rather than the rule, as most Indian politicians' main goal was to Indianize the bureaucracy. At a 1912 military conference in Calcutta, which included Lord Crewe, Lord Hardinge, and General Sir O'Moore Creagh, a collective decision was reached that "for the time being, the admission of Indians into the higher ranks of the army had become quite a secondary consideration, and that it was best to let sleeping dogs lie."[77] The government of India itself was more worried about what it perceived as possible attempts by Indian nationalists such as Gopal Krishna Goakhle and the native press to sow sedition in the other ranks of the army.[78]

The reform of the Indian Civil Service (ICS) has attracted much attention from researchers who feel that reform was the harbinger of similar reform in the army officer corps. Indeed, Secretary of State Edwin S. Montagu pointed to the progress made in the inclusion of Indians in the civil service to pressure of the War Cabinet into authorizing the grant of King's commissions to Indians. He noted that it was impossible to tell an Indian that he might control the destinies of Englishmen if he became a judge but that he could never expect to hold a position of authority even while defending the empire.[79]

However, closer examination of the evolution of the Indianization of the civil service and the army officer corps will indicate that the gap between the two was far less than first imagined. The East India Company's civil service was divided into two categories: the "covenanted" and the "uncovenanted." The covenanted comprised of men recruited by the company in England and sent to India to work their way up in the ranks from the bottom. They secured their contracts by signing a covenant with the company, hence the term *covenanted*. As the administrative services in India expanded rapidly, the company signed up a number of ad hoc administrators without a covenant; they became part of the uncovenanted service. Generally, the uncovenanted officers worked in junior positions, although a few European and Eurasian officers did hold high positions. Indians held only junior positions in the provincial cadres.

By 1804 Indians began to enter the covenanted service. In 1886 the Public Services Commission, headed by the Lieutenant Governor of the Punjab Sir Charles Aitchison, essentially segregated the covenanted and uncovenanted services into the ICS and the Provincial Civil Service respectively. The ICS cadre would be recruited from England after a competitive exam, while the Provincial Civil Service would be recruited separately in each of the Indian provinces.[80] Critics of the British have seen this move as an attempt to isolate Indians from the top positions in the ICS, for in practice few Indians could afford to make the trip to England to sit for the exams.[81] Indeed, there is some evidence to suggest that the British were increasingly apprehensive about a possible influx of Indians into the hitherto all-white ICS. In 1900 Lord Curzon warned Secretary of State for India Lord Hamilton of "the extreme danger of the system under which every year an increasing number of the government and odd higher posts that were meant, and ought to have been exclusively and specifically reserved for Europeans, are being filched away by the superiority of the native in the English examinations."[82]

Curzon's remarks in this context are most interesting, for it was Curzon himself who, over the objection of Lord Kitchener, proposed the entry of young Indians into the officer corps. Curzon declared, "I would myself fearlessly lay down the proposition that India can only be held with the aid of her sons."[83] Similarly, it was Lord George Hamilton who toiled long and hard with his legal secretary in the early months of 1898 to find a way around constitutional hurdles preventing the granting of commissions to Indians. It appears that the senior bureaucrats and viceroys were Janus-faced in their attitudes toward Indianization. While they opposed it in the ICS, they were almost obsessive in their efforts to initiate it in the Indian army. Their attitude is all the more puzzling when one takes into account the fact that pressure from Indian nationalists to Indianize the army took a distant backseat to similar reforms in the ICS. If political appeasement was the goal, then surely further concessions in the ICS would have obtained far greater mileage. In fact, by 1904 even the most moderate of Indian politicians, including Dadabhai Naoroji, were growing frustrated with the British stance on Indian recruitment to the ICS and judiciary.[84]

The British viceroys and bureaucrats who governed India in the late nineteenth and early twentieth centuries were essentially products of a Victorian liberal tradition. Their main goal was to form an equitable partnership with Indians in India. They hoped to imbue the Indians with British traits, especially in running "good government" and, by doing so, turn them into good "brown Englishmen." This was in complete opposition to the views of the earlier Utilitarian reformers such as Munro. To achieve this aim, the liberals were willing to incorporate Indians into positions of authority with one proviso—that reform was to be initiated and controlled by the British, who felt that the Indians could be overzealous in their efforts to replace the British with below-average Indian administrators and officers. The ambivalence of the reformers is in part due to the fact that most of them, like those who opposed any reforms, were influenced heavily by pseudoscientific theories of race; Social Darwinism in particular was the intellectual vogue of their time. Even the most radical pro-Indian supporters in England, like Annie Besant and Keir J. Hardie, proposed equal treatment for Indians on the grounds that they came from the same Aryan racial stock as the British.[85] Whether the liberals admitted it or not, they were all convinced of the inherent superiority of the white race. Liberals such as John Morley acknowledged that, on aesthetic grounds, he would be unwilling to "submit to be governed by a man of colour."[86] Yet liberal reformers including Morley were willing to accept the argument that the Indians could in time catch up with the West and welcomed individuals such as Dadabhai Naoroji into their midst with open arms. Where the reformers differed from the outright adherents of Darwinism, such as Roberts and Kitchener, was in their belief that "civilized" Western concepts like the rule of law, justice, and humanity could permeate slowly the subcontinent; it was a nineteenth-century liberal vision of trickle-down civilization.

Unfortunately for the British, they could not exercise total control over reform in the ICS. Political pressure both at home and in India tended to hasten most of the reforms, leading to an almost instinctive "hold the fort" mentality on behalf of senior British ICS officers and viceroys. This attitude has puzzled some researchers; S.R. Mehrotra states: "The Morley-Minto reforms [Indian Council Bill 1909] were a typical product of nineteenth-century English liberalism which believed that statesmanship was mainly a question of determining how far popular demands should be conceded, but which seldom bothered to think out the fundamentals of policy, or relate it to a well-defined larger purpose."[87] M.N. Das argues that, "The Liberal policy gradually boiled down to two aims, first to interest and inform the British public about India, and second, to please the Indians by granting reforms."[88] In the Indian army, the pressure to Indianize was comparatively weak and sporadic; consequently the government was far more willing to experiment in this "controlled environment." The army's stringent requirement for total professionalism and competence also worked to aid the process of reform. It became clear early in the Indianization process that the only effective Indian officer would be one with a King's commission and the same training and status of his British counterparts. As Colonel H.D. Watson, commander of the Imperial Service Corps, noted in 1914, no compromise was possible, "you must go whole hog, or not at all."[89] The debacle on the western front liquidated any doubts that may have persisted about granting full commissions to trained Indian officers. This also explains the War Office's curious attitude toward reform. Having fought tooth-and-nail to prevent any move to grant commissions to Indians, they capitulated when the die was cast, and insisted that all Indians go through exactly the same system at Sandhurst as the British cadets. If Indianization was unavoidable, then no effort was to be spared to ensure that the Indian officers would match the same high standards as the British officers. Half-way measures, such as the establishment of an equivalent to the Provincial Civil Service, were correctly rejected as harmful to the efficiency of the Indian army. Victorian liberalism and military professionalism had entered into a fortuitous partnership to lay the foundations for the Indianization of the Indian army officer corps.

Organizational reform would take longer to impact upon the Indian army. It continued to function as a frontier army for most of the 1920s. Yet its contribution to the war effort had changed forever its role in the perceptions of strategic planners in Whitehall and New Delhi. In the decades between the two world wars, the frontier army would transform itself, in doctrine at least, into a contemporary army and would play a pivotal role in drafting British military doctrine in the Second World War.

NOTES

1. Geoffrey Parker, *The Military Revolution: Military Innovation and the Rise of the West, 1500–1800* (Cambridge University Press, 1988), 136; Bruce P. Lenman, "The Transition to European Military Ascendency in India, 1600–1800," in John Lynn (ed.), *Tools of War: Instruments, Ideas, and Institutions of Warfare, 1445–1871* (Urbana: University of Illinois Press, 1990), 120; Randolf G.S. Cooper, "Wellington and the Marathas in 1803," *International History Review*, 11 (February 1989): 38.

2. See Pradeep P. Barua, "Military Developments in India, 1750–1850," *Journal of Military History*, vol. 58, no. 4 (October 1994).

3. Nirad C. Chaudhuri, "The Martial Races of India," *The Modern Review*, no. 48. (July 1930): 41–51; no. 48 (September 1930): 295–307; no. 49 (January 1931): 215–28; David Omissi, "Martial Races: Ethnicity and Security in Colonial India, 1858–1939," *War & Society*, vol. 9, no. 1 (May 1991): 18. In his most recent work Omissi has moved away from this position. See Omissi, *Sepoy and the Raj*, chap. 1.

4. See Pradeep P. Barua, "Inventing Race: The British and India's Martial Races," *The Historian*, vol. 58, no. 1 (Autumn 1995).

5. Hew Strachan, *From Waterloo to Balaclava: Tactics, Technology, and the British Army, 1815–1854* (Cambridge: Cambridge University Press, 1985), 26.

6. Ibid., 68.

7. Ibid., 125.

8. For a detailed study of the Indian army in the first half of the nineteenth century, see Douglas M. Peers, *Between Mars and Mammon: Colonial Armies and the Garrison State in India, 1819–1835* (New York: Tauris Academic Studies, 1995).

9. *Report of the Commissioners Appointed to Inquire into the Organization of the Indian army [Peel Commission]*, Parliamentary Papers (Commons), 1859, Cmd. 2515, v. A recommendation was also made to the effect that Indian troops not be equipped with advanced weaponry and artillery.

10. Military despatch to India No. 213, 3 August 1876, quoted in K.M.L. Saxena, *The Military System of India, 1850–1900* (New Delhi: Sterling Publishers, 1974), 182–83.

11. Brian Bond, "The Effect of the Cardwell Reforms," *Royal United Services Institute Journal* (November 1960): 229–36; Brigadier Michael Calvert, "Cardwell's Army Reforms," *Army* (April 1962): 108–17.

12. Military despatch from India No. 70, 25 March 1890, quoted in Saxena, *Military System*, 183–84.

13. Report of the special commission appointed by His Excellency the governor general in council to inquire into the organization and expenditure of the army in India [Eden Commission], Simla: Government of India, 1879, British Library/India Office Records (henceforth BL/IOR), L/MIL/17/5/1687, 5.

14. Ibid., 17,43,71.

15. The 2.75in screw gun was venerated by the Indian army, much for its portability, and was even immortalized by Kipling in a poem. See T.S. Elliot (ed.), *A Choice of Kipling's Verse* (London: Faber & Faber, 1951), 176–78.

16. See Scheme for the redistribution of the army in India, Calcutta: Government of India, 1904, BL/IOR, L/MIL/17/5/1741; Scheme for the redistribution of the army in India and the preparation of the army in India for war, India Office, 1904, BL/IOR, L/MIL/17/5/1742; Kitchener's emphasis on the northwest frontier was based largely on his concern over Russian influence and encroachment in Afghanistan. See Note by Lord Kitchener: Consideration of the effect of the Anglo-Russian Convention on the strength of the army in India, India Office, 21 October 1907, BL/IOR, L/MIL/17/5/1745. Kitchener was also no doubt aided in his quest to modernize the Indian army by an earlier War Office survey in 1902, which noted that the main issue of a war between Russia and England would be decided on the Indian border. See "The Military Resources of Russia and Probable Method of Their employment in a War between England and Russia," 22 January 1902, Public Records Office (henceforth PRO), War Office (henceforth WO) 106/48, E 3/11.

17. 77th Meeting of the army council No. 278, 21 June 1906, PRO, WO 163/11.

18. Barua, "Inventing Race." For more information on the East India Company's recruitment practices, see Seema Alavi, *The Sepoys and the Company: Tradition and Transition in Northern India, 1770–1830* (New York: Oxford University Press, 1995).

19. Quoted in government of India despatch No. 57, 3 August 1917, BL/IOR, Barrow Collection, Mss.Eur.E.420/9, 60–61.

20. Ibid.

21. The word *sepoy* refers to Indian soldiers and is derived from the Persian word *Sipah*, meaning "soldier."

22. BL/IOR, Barrow Collection, Mss.Eur.E.420/9, 61.

23. Eric Stokes, *The English Utilitarians in India* (London: Oxford University Press, 1959), 1–24.

24. Quoted in notes by Lord Curzon, Curzon Collection, BL/IOR, Mss.Eur.F.111/253: 12–22.

25. Military despatch No. 47, Mss.Eur.E.420/9, 61; viceroy's memorandum on commissions for native officers, 16 July 1900, Ibid., 23, 83.

26. Military letter from the government of India No. 47, 21 March 1885, "Native Officers Reports by Selected Officers," BL/IOR, L/MIL/17/5/1721, 1, 3.

27. Ibid., 7.

28. Ibid., 2–14; BL/IOR, Mss.Eur.F.111/253, 84.

29. Taking into account the dissenters' rationale, Lord Kimberly asked for a fresh proposal incorporating a response to these questions. Sir Donald Stewart (no longer commander in chief, but holding a seat on the India council) sent another despatch on 15 April 1886 to India via the secretary of state. BL/IOR, Mss.Eur.F.111/253, 84.

30. Lord Roberts' minute, 29 July 1886, BL/IOR, Mss.Eur.E.420/9, 62.

31. Government of India despatch No. 139, 12 August 1887, Ibid.

32. BL/IOR, Mss.Eur.F.111/253, 85.

33. Lord Roberts' minute, 27 May 1890, BL/IOR, Mss.Eur.E.420/9, 63.

34. Letters regarding commissions in British army for sons of native Indian chiefs and gentlemen, August–November 1897, BL/IOR, Mss.Eur.F.111/253, 36.

35. Ibid.

36. According to Hindu custom, travel abroad would "pollute" the high-caste Hindus like the Brahmins.

37. BL/IOR, Mss.Eur.F.111/253, 37.

38. Ibid., 38.

39. The only precedent was in 1857 in the Ionian Islands when, under British rule, an act was passed empowering persons born on the islands to receive commissions in the army. Ibid.

40. Ibid.

41. Ibid., 86–87.

42. Note for His Excellency the viceroy by Military Secretary P.J. Maitland, 26 April 1900, BL/IOR, Mss.Eur.F.111/253, 54–56.

43. Memorandum by His Excellency the viceroy upon commissions for native officers, 4 June 1900, Ibid., 87.

44. Lloyd I. Rudolph, Mohan Singh Kanota, and Susanne Hoeber Rudolph, "The Diary of Amar Singh," unpublished typescript, University of Chicago Library, DS485.R26R36, 1976, vol. 1, 445. See also Susanne Hoeber Rudolph, with Lloyd I. Rudolph and Mohan Singh Kanota (eds.), *Reversing the Gaze: Amar Singh's Diary: A Colonial Subject's Narrative of Imperial India* (Boulder: Westview Press, 2002).

45. Rudolph, Singh Kanota, and Rudolph, "Diary of Amar Singh," 468.

46. Only toward the end of their course work at Meerut/Dehra Dun did the cadets receive any instruction in tactics, topography, and fortifications. Ibid., 1073.

47. Ibid., 469.

48. Ironically, rule No. XVI g. stated that "no extravagance would be permitted," Ibid., 471, 473.

49. Ibid., 468–77.

50. Indian Army List, July-October 1906, 153–55.

51. Ibid., 79. See also fn. 30 in list.

52. Letter from General Officer Commanding Southern Army General Sir Edmund Barrow to Military Secretary Major General Sir M.H.S. Grover, March 1912, BL/IOR, Mss.Eur.E.420/9, 2.

53. Ibid., 3.

54. The first officer was given a sort of honorary reserve post. Cabinet papers and notes by Curzon, 1916–1918, BL/IOR, Mss.Eur.F.111/442, 6–7.

55. Memorandum from General Kitchener, 9 September 1908, Birdwood Collection, BL/IOR, Mss.Eur.D.686/31, 2.

56. That very year the total enrollment fell to fourteen. "Diary of Amar Singh," 471.

57. Ibid., 4–9.

58. Curzon paper on admission of Indians to the major ranks of the army, sent to Mr. Austen Chamberlain and returned, 17 July 1917, BL/IOR, Mss.Eur.F.111/442, 11–12.

59. Ibid., 12.

60. Ibid., 15.

61. Ibid., 18.

62. Ibid., 17–19.

63. Letter from WO to India Office, 5 July 1917, Ibid., 33–37.

64. Note on proposal of government of India to grant at once a large number of temporary King's commissions to Indians, 1918, Ibid., 38.

65. Extract from War Cabinet minutes No. 203, 2 August 1917, Ibid., 42.

66. Telegram No. 828 from secretary of state to viceroy, 5 April 1918, Ibid., 47.

67. See Telegram No. 112 from secretary of state for War Lord Kitchener to Field Marshal Sir John French, 27 August 1914, PRO, WO 33/173.

68. WO to general headquarters (GHQ) France, 29 August 1914, PRO, WO 33/713; War Diary Lahore division, PRO, WO, 95/3911. The IEF was totally unprepared for its new role as an imperial strategic reserve. See J.O. Rawson, "The Role of India in Imperial Defense beyond Indian Frontiers and Home Waters, 1919–1939," unpublished D.Phil. (University of Oxford 1976), 6–9, 34.

69. See views of Haig's Chief of Intelligence Brigader General John Charteris, *At GHO* (London: Cassel, 1931), 66.

70. See Jeffrey Greenhut, "The Imperial Reserve: The Indian Corps on the Western Front 1914–1915," *The Journal of Imperial and Commonwealth History*, vol. 12, no. 1 (October 1983): 66–67; and Gregory Martin, "The Influence of Racial Attitudes in British Policy towards India during the First World War," Ibid., vol. 14, no. 2 (January 1986): 1002–104.

71. Greenhut, "The Imperial Reserve," 69.

72. C.R. [?] to Lord Crewe No. 266, 25, "Commissions for Indians, Indianization, 1915–1942," Col. 430, BL/IOR, L/MIL/7/19006.

73. BL/IOR, Mss.Eur.F.111/442, 18.

74. Dadabhai Naoroji, fondly known as "the grand old man of India," was thrice president of the Indian National Congress, in 1886, 1895, and 1906. In 1893 he became the first Indian to be elected to the House of Commons, as member of Central Finsbury.

75. Lord Lansdowne to Lord George Hamilton, 20 February 1898, BL/IOR, Mss.Eur.F.111/253, 37.

76. Report of the annual conference of all Indians resident in the U.K., *India*, 30 December 1898.

77. Report on 1912 conference, BL/IOR, Mss.Eur.F.111/442, 13.

78. M.N. Das, *India Under Morley and Minto: Politics behind Revolution, Repression and Reforms* (London: George Allen & Unwin, 1964), 97, 108.

79. Secretary of state for India to War Cabinet, 8 August 1917, BL/IOR, Mss.Eur.F.111/442, 22.

80. B. Spangenberg, "The Aitchison Commission: An Introduction," in *Report of the Public Services Commission 1886–1888* (New Delhi: Concept Publishing Co., 1977).

81. Ibid.

82. Curzon to Hamilton, 23 April 1900, BL/IOR, Mss.Eur.F.111/159, 24.

83. BL/IOR, Mss.Eur.F.111/253, 87.

84. Dadabhai Naoroji, speaking before the London Indian Society on 1 June 1904, exhorted Indians "to claim unceasingly their birthright, and pledged rights of British citizenship, of self-government," *India*, 10 June 1904, 282.

85. Annie Besant, *Speeches and Writings* (Madras: G.A. Natesan, 1921), 267–68; Keir J. Hardie, *India, Impressions and Suggestions* (London: Independent Labour Party, 1909), 102.

86. Stephen E. Koss, *John Morley and the India Office, 1905–1910* (New Haven and London: Yale University Press, 1969), 125.

87. The reforms introduced by Lords Morley and Minto doubled the number of Indians in the provincial legislative council, giving them a nonofficial majority. S.R. Mehrotra, *India and the Commonwealth 1885–1929* (New York: Frederick R. Praeger, 1965), 53.

88. Das, *India Under Morley and Minto*, 69.

89. Private letter from Colonel H.D. Watson to Major Wigram, 30 March 1914, BL/IOR, Mss.Eur.F.111/442, 13.

2

The High Road to Dehra Dun: The Institutionalization of the Indian Officer Corps, 1919–1947

When the guns finally ceased thundering in 1918, sixty thousand Indian soldiers had fought and died for regiment and empire in blood-soaked battlefields from Europe to East Africa. The scale of their contribution can be judged from the fact that the Indian army earned no less than 9,200 decorations including 11 Victoria Crosses. Indeed, by November 1918 India had despatched 1,302,394 men—138,000 to France; 657,000 to Mesopotamia; 144,000 to Egypt and Palestine; and smaller contingents to Aden, East Africa, Gallipoli, and Salonika. Additionally, India supplied 170,000 animals (mainly mules and horses) and 3,700,000 tons of supplies and rations for a million men.[1] By contrast, all of the dominions together could only send 978,439 men.[2] A thankful British government recognized this sacrifice; Prime Minister David Lloyd George, supported by Austen Chamberlain and the War Cabinet, decided unanimously in favor of India's inclusion in the Imperial War Conference in March 1917.[3] Four months later, on 20 August 1917, Mr. E.S. Montagu, the liberal secretary of state for India, made a historic statement to the House of Commons. "The policy of His Majesty's Government, with which the Government of India are in complete accord, is that of the increasing association of Indians in every branch of the administration with a view to the progressive realization of responsible government in India as an integral part of the British empire."[4]

As S.R. Mehrotra points out, the declaration of 20 August 1917 "marked a definite repudiation of the concept of 'the two Empires'—the concept that there could be, under the British flag, one form of constitutional evolution for the West and another for the East, one for the White races and another for the non-white."[5] Montagu's statement represented a fundamental shift in British policy, it marked the beginning of the transition from empire to Commonwealth.

In accordance with the August 1919 statement to the Commons, the government of India moved to make representative and self-government in India more of a reality. Mr. Montagu and Viceroy Lord Chelmsford established a Central India Legislative Assembly. This move was essentially building upon the government of India's act of 1909, which had made the viceroy's legislative council and the provincial legislatures into partial representative bodies. Indeed, it is not surprising that Montagu played a chief role in this process; as under secretary for state in 1910, he had defended the Indian Councils Act as a great opportunity for Indians to vent their grievances and deemed the act an effective counter to the congress. With these latest reforms, Montagu hoped to entice "moderates" to break from the congress. The reforms were directed in part to meet the aspirations of educated Indians, loyalists, moderates, and "all those Indians who believed in the advance of self-government."[6] The new central assembly was to have 100 of its 145 members elected from a small pool of Indian voters, with the remainder being nominated by the viceroy. An upper house called the Council of State was established and consisted of sixty members, of whom a majority were nominated. The experimental nature of these bodies was evident by the fact that the British kept a number of "reserved subjects"—the armed forces, police, and judiciary—as inviolate from the legislation of these bodies.

This fact, however, did not deter the fledgling Indian parliament from expressing its views on the "banned" subjects. In the first sitting of the Legislative Assembly in early 1921, Sir Sivaswamy Aiyer tabled no less than fifteen resolutions on the Indian army.[7] Two of these resolutions called for the Indianization of the officer corps; Sir P.S. Sivaswamy Aiyer suggested that 25 percent of the king's commissions granted annually should be given to Indians.[8]

This chapter analyzes the dynamics of the postwar debate on Indianization that ultimately led to the establishment of the Indian Military Academy (IMA) at Dehra Dun. I will begin by examining the official discourse on the subject, focusing specifically on the numerous committees that investigated the issue of Indianization between 1919 and 1932. I will also analyze the reactive discourse from the Indian politicians and determine if they had any real effect upon the government's/army's Indianization policy as has been purported by researchers including Stephen P. Cohen. I will then describe the establishment of the IMA at Dehra Dun and the role played by this institution in molding the senior leadership of the post-independent Indian army. The chapter will conclude with an in-depth analysis of organizational politics, which played such an important role in determining the relationships between the Indian army and the Indian government and the Indian army and the British army. The true explanation for the prolonged opposition to an Indian Sandhurst lies not in an embedded racism in the British-controlled Indian government and army, but rather in an understanding of the inherent tensions created by intricacies of the above-described relationships.

A DECADE OF COMMITTEES

During the course of his famous speech to the Commons on Indian self-government, Montagu also announced the decision of His Majesty's government to

> remove the bar which has hitherto precluded admission of Indians to commissioned ranks in His Majesty's army and steps are being taken respecting the grant of commissions to nine Indian officers belonging to Native Indian Land Forces who have served in the field. . . . The Secretary of State and the Government of India are discussing the general conditions under which Indians should in future be eligible for commissions. In due course the Army Council will be consulted with a view to introduction of a carefully considered scheme to provide for the selection of candidates for training them in duties which will devolve upon them.[9]

The response from the Indian army was quite amazing. In 1921, Lord Rawlinson, the new commander in chief of the Indian army, convened the Military Requirements Committee (chaired by himself) to promote a radical scheme that would completely Indianize the officer corps in only thirty years! Rawlinson proposed 25 percent of the seats at Sandhurst be reserved for Indians. This was exactly what Sir Aiyer had asked for in his resolutions; Rawlinson also agreed to a 2.5 percent annual increase to accelerate the process. He proposed the opening up of engineer, supply, and artillery wings to Indians.[10] The British government, not surprisingly, vetoed this enormous first step into Indianization. The military secretary to the India Office, reiterating the traditional arguments of the prewar "dissenters," proposed instead the establishment of a separate Indian Dominion army that would exist and develop alongside the existing Indian army. As this new Dominion army evolved, it would assume the responsibilities of the Indian army, eventually replacing it.[11]

In 1922 Rawlinson convened yet another committee, this time taking caution not to involve himself in its proceedings. The committee, led by Lieutenant General John Shea, rejected the Aiyer proposal on the grounds that it would prove too complicated in practice. Alternatively, the Shea Committee proposed a three-stage plan. In the first stage (fourteen years) the British would Indianize one regiment per group of cavalry, one battalion per group of infantry, and a corresponding proportion of other services. A total of eighty-one commissions were to be granted every year. In the second stage (fourteen years), seven cavalry regiments, forty infantry battalions, three pioneer battalions, and six pack batteries would be Indianized. During the third and final stage (seven years), all recruitment of British Sandhurst officers would be halted and the remainder of the army would be Indianized. In this manner it was theoretically possible to Indianize the army within thirty-five years. An important part of the Shea Committee's report called for the immediate establishment of an Indian military college. This college was to be the sole avenue of entry by Indians to the commissioned ranks of the Indian army. The college was to have two wings, one for cadets from the Prince of Wales Royal Indian Military (PWRIM) College[12] and from colleges and universities, and one for selected holders of the viceroy's commission. Addressing Lieutenant General Alexander Stanhope Cobbe's crucial proposal for an Indian Dominion army, the Shea Committee noted that "in absence of a conscious, mature and homogenous national spirit in India the moral factor most essential to the creation of a 'Dominion' army does not exist."[13]

However, even Shea's scaled-down Indianization plan proved too ambitious for the British government to accept. Viscount Jonathan Peel, the secretary of state, felt more inclined toward a much smaller effort involving four units in the "first stage." Ultimately a consensus was reached for eight units to be Indianized. They included five battalions of infantry, one pioneer regiment, and two cavalry regiments.[14] The adoption of the eight-unit scheme was an acknowledgment of earlier worries about problems that might arise when Indians were in a position to wield command over British officers. As the joint secretary to the India Office Military Department noted in a lecture to the Imperial Defence College in October 1931, there was clear evidence that British officers were reluctant to take orders from Indians. He noted "whether right or wrong does not concern us; the fact is that it existed and had to be faced."[15] The British instituted the eight-unit scheme to ensure the continued recruitment of British officers, which was essential to the efficiency of the Indian army.

In avoiding this pitfall, the British, unfortunately, stumbled into another; the inevitable negative side effects of establishing segregated units within the army. The governments in Whitehall and Delhi basically were duplicating the negative segregation of the ICS into provincial (lower) and federal (higher) categories for Indians and British respectively. They ignored the astute advice of earlier reformers like Colonel H.D. Watson to avoid such harmful halfway measures.[16] This became apparent in June 1923, when the Commander in Chief Lieutenant General Alexander Cobbe appointed a committee headed by the Chief of General Staff General Claude W. Jacob to report on the progress made by Indianization. The Jacob Committee noted that the British perceived the eight Indianizing units as inferior and that in the four years since Indianization had been in effect, no Indian officer from Sandhurst had opted for the eight units.[17]

In fact, the report of the Jacob Committee was wholly negative. The committee reported that the results up to 1923 indicated that Indianization was not likely to succeed and that it was wise to restrict it to a small portion of the army. They noted the tendency of Indian officers to gravitate toward men of their own "class" (caste), a move which threw serious doubt on the officers' impartiality and ability to command the respect and obedience of the men. The committee also remarked on the possibility of discontent in the ranks if the viceroy's commissions were abolished.[18] The committee felt that the presence of British officers was essential to ensure the success of any Indianizing program. It advised care be taken in assigning Indians to non-Indianizing units, so as not to further perturb British parents who wondered if their sons would have a viable future in a rapidly Indianizing Indian army. Such doubts, the committee noted, had resulted in the decline in the numbers of young British officers opting for a career in the Indian army.

The Jacob Committee reserved the most damaging criticism for the Indian officer candidates themselves. The committee revealed that there was a 60 percent attrition rate in the first four years of Indianization! Of the twenty-five cadets sent to Sandhurst, ten failed the course, two died, two resigned after receiving commission, and one was deprived of his commission, thus leaving only ten successful candidates, a mere 40 percent success rate. To explain these astonishing figures the committee pointed out the lack of an Indian equivalent of the British public schools. The committee highlighted the fact that, with the exception of the PWRIM at Dehra Dun, there was no public school in India. The committee also opined that in order to obtain officer-grade material, Indian entrants to Sandhurst should enter a competitive exam similar to their British counterparts. The committee concluded with a warning against

> . . . the impatience of the Indian politician, who will not understand that the safety of India may be endangered by too great a rapidity in Indianization, and who will constantly press for speedier methods. There must be no question of yielding to his pertinacity in years to come, until such time as it is conclusively proved that Indianization will succeed.[19]

The British, although determined to stand their ground against the Indian nationalist politicians, had to concede the fact that the present system of nominating Indian cadets to Sandhurst was unsatisfactory. As moderate Indian politicians of the National Liberal Federation pointed out, at this pace it would take two hundred years before the entire Indian army was Indianized![20] In June 1925 the Indian government, following the recommendation of the Legislative Assembly, appointed a committee of ten Indians under the chairmanship of Chief of General Staff Lieutenant General Sir Andrew Skeen to investigate the requirement of an Indian equivalent to

Sandhurst. After an exhaustive investigation the report was presented to the government in November 1926.[21]

The Skeen Committee analyzed the performance of Indian cadets at Sandhurst. It noted that since 1918, 243 applicants (including sixteen Indians educated in England) had applied for eighty-five vacancies at Sandhurst reserved exclusively for Indians. Of the successful entrants, eighteen were still undergoing training, forty-four had graduated (two subsequently resigned their commissions), two died, and nineteen failed to qualify. This represented a failure rate of 30 percent, much better than the 60 percent failure rate reported by the Jacobs Committee. However, when compared to the 3 percent failure rate of British cadets, it was still quite shocking. The report explained that until quite recently the educated Indian middle classes had been barred from military service and, as a result most educated Indians were generally ignorant of the possibility of a career in the higher ranks of the army. The committee laid great stress on the fact that the weak educational system in India placed Indians at a disadvantage to British cadets from the public school system, who were physically and mentally much better prepared for Sandhurst. The committee also noted the emotional and financial burden Indian parents had to incur to send their sons to Sandhurst. In addition, the committee branded the eight-unit scheme as an invidious form of segregation that ultimately would result in the failure of Indianization.

In its recommendations to the government, the committee called for an immediate increase of ten vacancies at Sandhurst, making a total of twenty vacancies (although the government did not follow exactly the committee's recommendations). This would be followed by an increase of four per year until 1933, at which point an "Indian Sandhurst" with a capacity for 100 cadets would be established. This number would be increased by twelve every three years, while the vacancies at the "real" Sandhurst would be reduced to twenty per year. The committee expected that by 1952 half the total cadre of officers of the Indian army would be Indians. It recommended that the PWRIM at Dehra Dun be expanded and that additional similar schools be established since it was the only school in India comparable to the English public school system. The committee strongly recommended that the selection of candidates be as widely based as possible and that the candidates be selected only after passing an examination and being interviewed by a board similar to that which interviewed British candidates for Sandhurst. For reasons given above, the committee also recommended the abandonment of the eight-unit scheme. It recommended that the Indian King's commissioned officers be made eligible for posting to any unit in the Indian army, just like their British counterparts. The committee felt that the establishment of an Indian Sandhurst was unavoidable not only because of the difficulties facing Indians who were sent to Sandhurst, but also due to the fact that Sandhurst itself could not accommodate greater numbers of Indian cadets without losing its character as a British academy. The committee also insisted that the King's commission granted to cadets of the Indian Sandhurst were of the same status, authority, and precedence as the King's commission granted to cadets trained at Sandhurst.

The Indian government's reaction to the Skeen Committee's proposals were mixed. On the one hand, the government acknowledged grave defects in the system of nominating Sandhurst cadets, the high expenses to Indian parents, and the lack of adequate educational facilities in India to prepare young Indians for entry into Sandhurst. On the other hand, the government was reluctant to scrap the eight-unit scheme until the present "experiment" proved successful and there were a continuous supply of good officers. The government also came out against the proposal for an Indian military college on the grounds that such a college inaugurated prematurely in 1933 could not be comparable to Sandhurst. The government felt that, as long as Sandhurst could accommodate Indian cadets, there was no need for an Indian military college. In one respect, however, the government revealed itself further advanced in reformist thought than the Skeen Committee. The government saw Indianization as part of the eventual formation of a Dominion army: "Our aim if we can obtain sufficient officer material, is the eventual creation of a *Dominion* army, that is, an army manned and officered throughout by Indians, comprising of all arms in which Indians desire to serve and to bear commissioned rank."[22]

The reaction from some members of the "old guard" to the Skeen Committee's proposal was highly negative. Sir Michael O'Dwyer, the former lieutenant governor of the Punjab (1913–1919), writing in the *London Evening News*, compared the Indian Empire to

> a great edifice which is held together by the "steel frame" of a few thousand British officers. Remove or weaken that steel frame and the whole edifice collapses, bringing down not only India's 320 millions, but the British Empire. . . . Surely if Britain has to play the piper in British blood—it should call the tune. Let us hope that the Viceroy and the secretary of State for India will see to that in handling these amazing proposals.[23]

The opinions of O'Dwyer and others undoubtedly influenced Indian nationalist politicians and present-day scholars who have criticized the Indian government for obstructing the Skeen Committee's proposals.[24] In reality and as we have already seen, the government had committed itself to the total Indianization of the Indian army. Dissenters to Indianization were in a minority at this time, and most of them, like O'Dwyer, were either retired or in positions too powerless to have any effect on the policy. The Indian government, however, was determined to see the process through as carefully as possible with minimal degradation to the army's efficiency.

By 1927 the dust that had been raised in the furor created by the Indian

Sandhurst Committee report had begun to settle, and the dialogue on reform began to proceed more smoothly. One of the main worries had been that British officer recruitment to the Indian army would dry up if the pace of Indianization was increased. Indeed, early indications appeared to point in that direction. Between 1818 and 1923, an average of sixty British cadets annually applied for entry into the Indian Army. Soon after the publication of Lord Rawlinson's report, the numbers began to fall; in 1923 there were only forty-five applicants, in 1924 there were thirty-seven, and by 1925 there were only thirty-four. However, by 1926, as the actual effects of the schemes became apparent, the numbers rose to forty-four and continued to increase to fifty and sixty-eight for 1927 and 1928 respectively.[25]

In 1928 the British government appointed a parliamentary commission under the liberal barrister Sir John Simon to evaluate the impact of the Montagu-Chelmsford reforms. The all-British commission was rejected soundly by Indians, and its voluminous seventeen volumes) proposals made little headway with the governments in Britain and India. The Simon Commission devoted considerable attention to military reforms, with Indianization playing a major role. Sir Simon, aware of the resentment his all-British commission generated among the Indians, involved a number of Indian notables, including Sir Zulfikar Ali Khan and Sir Hari Singh Gour, to assist him in his inquiries into the Indian military. The minutes of the meeting between the Indian nonofficial members of the commission and senior army and government officials provides insight into the vast gap in understanding that divided the British and Indians over the Indianization issue (see information cited in n.25 above).

In the course of the commission's inquiry into the workings of the Indian army, Sir Hari Singh Gour stated that "Indians think that the Indian army can be Indianized in one generation, in twenty-five years."[26] Sir Gour also felt that the "scrupulous" selection process left out many candidates who might prove to be successful. At this remark Major General Walter M. St. Kirke accused Sir Gour of advocating quantity over quality. The interview with General Kirke was one of the few opportunities Indians had to put their views of Indianization before those in the army and the civil service who were connected directly with the reforms. To nationalists such as Sir Gour, Indianization was but one of many steps necessary for the British to take in order to enable India to achieve self-government. They perceived the British as slowing down the entire process by foot-dragging and they even doubted that the British were sincere in their efforts. To the British executors of the reform schemes, including General Kirke, Indianization was the crucial element in India's advance toward dominion status. They were determined to see that the process resulted in a professional and competent cadre of Indian officers capable of taking over the reigns of command from the British. The "radical" demands of Indian politicians like Sir Aiyer and Sir Gour only enhanced their determination to keep the Indians at arm's length from the entire process, and this in turn fueled the Indian nationalists' suspicions about British reluctance to Indianize the army.

By 1930, at the same time the Round Table Conferences were about to begin, the government of India conceded that the conditions were ideal for the establishment of an Indian military college. At one of the conferences a subcommittee on defense passed a resolution demanding that "in order to avoid delay the Government of India be instructed to set up a committee of experts, both British and Indian (including representatives of the Indian States) to work out the details of such a college."[27] The Indian government complied, and a committee was duly established under the chairmanship of the Commander in Chief General Sir Philip Chetwoode.

The committee's report reinforced the many positive aspects of Indianization that were becoming increasingly apparent. It noted, for instance, the marked improvement in Indian schools, which were moving in the direction proposed by the Skeen Committee (public school orientation). The committee also noted that "the material success achieved by Dehra Dun College (PWRIM) has been so great that we consider it should be gradually expanded up to a total capacity of two hundred and fifty to three hundred cadets."[28] The committee urged that the PWRIM be enlarged as soon as possible to act as a feeder to the Indian Military Academy (IMA). The success of the PWRIM is not surprising as the "college was designed to provide the necessary preliminary training for entry to the RMC [Royal Military College], Sandhurst, RMA [Royal Military Academy], Woolwich and the RAF [Royal Air Force] College, Cranwell."[29] The PWRIM came under the direct control of the commander in chief for India, thus ensuring it high standards and adequate funds to provide the best trained candidates for Sandhurst. Furthermore, it was set up specifically to deliver a public school education on English lines for unmarried Indian and Anglo-Indian youths.[30] The PWRIM also provided excellent experience in establishing an integrated military school representative of all the diverse ethnic and religious groups in India. For example, in the school, "special care was taken that no food is served in the mess which could in any way offend the religious susceptibilities of any student."[31] It would take subtle yet vital touches like these to make the IMA more of a home to Indian officer cadets than the RMC, Sandhurst, had been.

The committee determined a course three years in length for the Indian Military Academy. Applicants between eighteen and twenty years old could enter the college. Most of the sixty vacancies were to be allotted by open competition in the form of an entrance exam. Officers graduating from this college were equal in every way to British officers entering the Indian army from British colleges. The generally positive note of the Chetwoode Committee is surprising given the fact that Chetwoode in his private correspondence expressed his dislike for a separate, Indian Sandhurst. He also indicated that he had little confidence in Indian-officered units and felt that the eight units should not be considered part of the army.[32]

In a conciliatory step toward Indian nationalist politicians, the Chetwoode Committee included in its nonofficial ranks Sir Aiyer, the most virulent critic of the governments' Indianization policy. It was no surprise, then, that the committee's recommendations failed to gain Sir Aiyer's approval; he and G.R.R. Rajwade, another nonofficial Indian member of the committee, filed a separate minute. The dissenting report (which appears primarily to have been the work of Sir Aiyer) was primarily an outburst of pent-up frustration with perceived British stonewalling on Indianization, reviewing as it did the entire history of the acrimonious debate from the perspective of the sidelined Indian politicians. Unbeknownst to Sir Aiyer, many of the points of debate he sought to raise with his minute of dissent had been resolved already by the secretive official debate on the subject. Inclusion in the Chetwoode Committee, albeit in a nonofficial capacity, provided the indefatigable Indian legislator a rare attempt to join in the official discourse on the Indianization of the Indian army, and he was determined to make his case.[33]

THE INDIAN MILITARY ACADEMY

The Chetwoode Committee had recommended three possible sites for the location of the IMA: Satara, Mhow, and Dehra Dun. After some deliberations, the committee chose Dehra Dun. It was already the location of the highly successful PWRIM; furthermore, the army could avail of the ready-made facilities of the empty Railway Staff College, which had been completed in 1930 but had closed almost immediately due to the financial crisis imposed by the Great Depression. The facilities of the Railway Staff College and its surrounding 155.3 acres of land were acquired for Rs. 21, 17, 597 on 1 April 1932. The former Railway Staff College proved to be an excellent choice for the Indian Military Committee. Chetwoode Hall (which is still the heart of the academy today) was formerly the Railway Staff College's Dormer Hall, an imposing and unique structure sunk several floors below ground level; it was used to demonstrate model train movements to the railway's students.[34]

The infant academy soon became the focus of gifts from well-wishers far and wide. The most impressive gift is probably the champion company silver cup trophy from Sandhurst that was presented by the Chief of Imperial General Staff Sir Montgomery-Massingbird at Sandhurst in December 1933.[35] Such gifts helped build the corporate identity of the new institution; indeed, the unique rituals and traditions that characterize such institutions the world over were well in the making at the IMA soon after it was opened.

The IMA sought to emulate Sandhurst in all ways except one—the duration of its course. The Chetwoode Committee had recommended a three-year course for the IMA instead of the eighteen-month course in place at Sandhurst. The army settled for a two and a half–year course. This was in recognition of the fact that academic preparation would be needed at the IMA itself to make up for the deficiencies of the Indian school system. In all other respects, the IMA followed Sandhurst; the entrance exams held on the third Monday of October, for instance, were conducted by India's Federal Public Service Commission, which was similar to the system in England. The format of the exam also closely mirrored that of the Sandhurst entrance exam. The exam was divided into four parts, the most important of which was the Interview and Record Test. While the IMA curriculum reflected greater academic emphasis than did that of Sandhurst, the annual exam system was very similar. One exam was held at the end of the term; the entire course was comprised of five terms over a two and a half–year period. It was comprised of two main sections: General Military Education and Detailed Military Education. As at Sandhurst, the company commander's grades and remarks on each cadet were recorded at the end of each term and reviewed by the commandant.

The IMA was open to competition for unmarried candidates who were British subjects of Indian domicile, or subjects of a princely state in India. Applications usually were routed through the local collector, the deputy commissioner, or the local police officer. Students from the PWRIM had to send their applications via their principal, indicating the special status this school enjoyed over its civilian counterparts in India. A total of thirty vacancies would be opened every half-year, fifteen by open competition and fifteen to Indian army cadets.[36]

Between October 1932 and May 1941, there were sixteen regular or prewar courses. Of the 693 cadets who were admitted, 535 were commissioned, giving a success rate of 85.72 percent, a remarkably high number when compared to the Indian Sandhurst cadets. The first five of the sixteen courses have been recorded in the annals of the IMA:

1. Pioneers—1 October 1932 to 22 December 1934
2. Immortals—1 March 1933 to 4 June 1935
3. Invincibles—1 October 1933 to 21 December 1935
4. Stalwarts—1 February 1934 to 3 June 1936
5. Bahadurs ("Braves")—23 August 1934 to 29 December 1936

These five courses, and the Pioneers in particular, represent the elite of the Indian officer corps in preindependent India. Not only did they have to set an example for future generations, but also they were the products of a rigorous process of selection and a comprehensive one and a half– to two–year training course. The Indian officers coming out of the OTC during the

Second World War received only a fraction of the attention and care lavished upon the prewar cadets by their British mentors.

The onset of the Second World War drastically changed the nature of the training at the IMA. Between February 1940 and January 1946 there were no less than forty-nine "war courses" at the academy. They included eight courses, taught between October 1941 and October 1943, for British cadets (fresh from schools in Britain).[37] The war courses were run for Indians and Europeans residing in India. The general duration of these courses was six months. In all, no less than, 3,887 cadets (Indian and British) were commissioned during this period. Out of a total of 4,744 cadets entering the war courses, 3,013 were commissioned, reflecting a relatively low attrition of 14.31 percent.[38] In addition to Dehra Dun, three additional accelerated OTCs opened up during the war—at Mhow, Bangalore, and Belgaum. The latter originally was reserved exclusively for British cadets but did train four to five mixed batches of British/Indian cadets toward the end of the war.[39]

The IMA proved invaluable to the British war effort in the Southern Hemisphere. Without the academy's invaluable work in churning out emergency commissioned officers (ECOs), it is doubtful that the Indian army could have maintained the massive formations it had on the Burma front. That the academy was well up to this task is proven by the fact that no less than 727 British cadets were sent directly from England to Dehra Dun to receive their emergency commissions.[40] In reality, any significant doubts that the British might have had about the viability of the IMA had been dissipated by the excellent crop of officers that emerged from the five prewar courses. As the concluding chapters of this book will show, it was on the shoulders of that group of Indian officers that the burden of command would fall in the postindependence period.

ORGANIZATIONAL POLITICS

In the previous chapter I analyzed the motivations of generations of liberal British reformers in promoting Indianization. It was evident that intellectual background played a major role in determining their ambivalent approach to reform. To a degree this is also true for the British reformers of the interwar period. Yet, there remains a serious gap in our understanding of the dynamics of reform during this period. Despite the fact that the British governments in India and England had committed themselves to the introduction of Indian commissioned officers, by the close of the First World War constant roadblocks were thrown up at every stage of the reform process by senior officials both in England and in India. The continued reluctance of the British War Office to reform may come as no great surprise, but the opposition of senior officials within the Indian army and the civil service's military bureaucracy is something of a mystery. A partial explanation can be found in the fact that greatly increased pressure from the Indian nationalist politicians had made the British more cautious. Not only had Indian nationalist politicians, including Sir Aiyer, become more vocal about Indianization of the officer corps, but also they could voice their grievances in the new, highly visible legislative houses created by the Montagu-Chelmsford reforms.

The Indian legislators, however, had absolutely no control over the army. The military continued to be the sole responsibility of the viceroy and his handpicked council. At no time could the Indian politicians have dictated to the army, even on the minutest aspect of military administration, let alone forced it to accelerate the pace of Indianization. Although senior officers publicly expressed great concern over the pressure being applied by the Indian politicians, their internal correspondence shows a very casual disdain of the efforts of the Indian legislators. Take, for example, a private letter to Sir Cobbe, the headmaster of PWRIM, from Sir Philip Chetwoode, in which he noted that "a lot of nonsense was talked by Moonje, Gidney, etc., etc., but we got everything we wanted out of them without using the official majority at all."[41] Chetwoode and his fellow officers were secure in the conviction that the Indian nationalist politicians had no power to interfere with the Indianization process. The British press' reaction to Indianization also was generally neutral, if not favorable. The India Office information officer pointed out that, with the exception of "peculiar . . . *Daily Mail* propaganda, . . . [n]o similar report has appeared in any [other] newspaper."[42] The reaction of the British press seemed to indicate a sense of guarded optimism among the British public that Indianization of the officer corps was not necessarily a hindrance to the career of British officers in the Indian army. Perhaps more important was the fact that, from 1924 onward, the performance of Indian cadets was showing remarkable improvement. Table 2 shows the annual number of Indian cadets admitted to the RMC, Sandhurst, since 1918, and the numbers granted King's commissions after successfully completing a course there. Why then did these officers attempt to slow, if not stop, the pace of reform? The answer to this question lies not in the nascent Indian nationalist politics of the period, but within the British and Indian military establishments.

Organizations react instinctively against any external force that is seen to impinge upon their independence and authority. Nowhere is this reflex action more apparent than in military organizations. Specialized knowledge of military administration and functions are often the sole preserve of the military itself. This exclusive knowledge gives the military a considerable degree of autonomy from civilian authority, and, as Max Weber points out, the military bureaucracy will go to great lengths to keep this knowledge to themselves.[43] This is precisely what seems to have happened in regard to the Indian army during the interwar period. In the previous chapter we learned that it was the senior officers of the Indian army who

Table 2
Annual Number of Indian Cadets Admitted to the RMC, Sandhurst, 1918–1931[44]

YEAR	NO OF VACANCIES	NO ADMITTED	NO COMMISSIONED
1918 (half year)	5 Sandhurst	5	-
1919	10 Sandhurst	10	-
1920	10 Sandhurst	10	1
1921	10 Sandhurst	9	6
1922	10 Sandhurst	8	3
1923	10 Sandhurst	12	6
1924	10 Sandhurst	12	10
1925	10 Sandhurst	10	11
1926	10 Sandhurst	11	7
1927	10 Sandhurst	15	6
1928 (half year)	5 Sandhurst	3	14
1928 (half year)	10 Sandhurst 3 Woolwich 3 Cranwell	3 Sandhurst	-
1929	24 Sandhurst 6 Woolwich 6 Cranwell	9 Sandhurst	11 Sandhurst
1930	24 Sandhurst 6 Woolwich 6 Cranwell	22 Sandhurst 2 Woolwich 6 Cranwell	3 Sandhurst
1931	24 Sandhurst 3 Woolwich 1 Cranwell	23 Sandhurst 4 Woolwich 1 Cranwell	20 Sandhurst

acquiesced to—indeed, assisted in—the efforts to secure commissions for Indians. Their participation in this reform was eased by the fact that this decision was primarily political in nature, with no military rationale to oppose it. In fact, the experience of the First World War had revealed crucial weaknesses in an all-white–officered Indian army (see above). During the interwar period, however, the implementation of the Indianization policy became an internal matter for the army, at least as far as the military bureaucracy was concerned. Senior officers—including Field Marshal Sir Claude W. Jacob, the military secretary at the India Office in London, and Deputy Chief of General Staff General Sir Walter M. Kirke—resented what they perceived as dangerous interference by the British civil servants and politicians to hasten the pace of Indianization. General Kirke characterized this haste as being "purely political."[45]

Interservice rivalries also promoted organizational secrecy and reticence toward reform. This was the primary cause of the British military's reluctance to back the reforms wholeheartedly. The British Air Ministry, for instance, was reluctant to admit Indian cadets to the Royal Air Force (RAF) College at Cranwell, for it feared that this might be the first step toward the establishment of an Indian army royal flying corps, independent of the RAF.[46] This interservice rivalry was indicative of a far deeper and profound division between the British and Indian armies. The post-1919 Indian army was, for all intents and purposes, completely independent from the control of the British home army, a reality that many senior British army officers refused to acknowledge.

ADDISCOMBE TO DEHRA DUN

Ironically, the establishment of the IMA had turned back the clock to the pre-1857 period when the East India Company's armies were independent of the British army. This independence was largely due to the fact that the East India Company (EIC) trained most of its cadets at its own military academy in Addiscombe. A brief survey of the history of this academy will help us understand the institutional reluctance the British army had toward an Indian Sandhurst. In the first decade of the nineteenth century the EIC military establishment found itself in an awkward situation. Its ever-expanding armies had just vanquished the armies of the Maratha Chieftain Sindhia, but the EIC was unable to obtain enough officers to command its growing forces. Since 1798 the EIC had made do with an arrangement with the Royal Military Academy (RMA) at Woolwich to train forty artillery and engineer cadets at a time. The arrangement was only partially satisfactory for the company, for its cadets took second place to British army requirements. As the EIC's requirements for additional officers grew, it became obvious that the limited openings in Woolwich were inadequate. The company's problems were exacerbated when the master general of the Board of Ordnance prohibited Woolwich professors from tutoring EIC candidates for entry into the academy.[47]

The EIC's problems actually predated those faced by the Indian government in the interwar period when it sought to increase the pace of Indianization. Its solution to these problems was also remarkably similar to those adopted by the Indian government in the interwar period; in 1809 the directors of the company authorized the establishment of a military seminary to train its cadets. That year, the company acquired the house and premises at Addiscombe Place near Croydon, formerly the residence of the late earl of Liverpool, comprising a mansion and 5.7 acres of land.[48] The

Addiscombe Seminary proved such a success that by 1813 the company reserved all officer appointments in its artillery and engineers to Addiscombe students, and in 1816 the seminary opened its gates to infantry and cavalry officers of the company.[49] Addiscombe now combined the functions of both Woolwich and Sandhurst, the latter having been opened in 1813 to train cavalry and infantry officers for the British army.

Given the great number of ground forces maintained by the EIC in India it was entirely possible that, in time, the Addiscombe military might have surpassed the Woolwich and Sandhurst academies in the number and quality of cadets it produced. This was not, however, to be the case, for following the mutiny of 1857, the company's armies were taken over by the crown, and the decision was made to shut down the Addiscombe Seminary. The official reason was that the existing facilities at Sandhurst and Woolwich were adequate for future needs, but there can be little doubt that the British army, and Sandhurst in particular, were glad to see the demise of this highly successful rival.

The potential rivalry that a sister military academy might represent may help explain the institutional opposition of the British army toward an Indian military academy. Such an academy, eventually would, and did, stop any involvement Sandhurst might have with the training of officers of the Indian army. This in turn would diminish the influence of the War Office in the Indian army, which, again, is precisely what happened. The British army's guarded opposition to the IMA suggests that it, unlike the British government, was unable or unwilling to recognize the fact that the Indian army was inexorably headed toward becoming a Dominion army. The attempts by the British army to maintain a facade of control over its Indian protégé thus formed the final obstacle on the high road to Dehra Dun. Nevertheless, for reasons discussed above, the decision to establish the IMA became a reality in 1931, and, once the die was cast, the British army, including Sandhurst, spared no effort to help the IMA get off to a good start.

How did educated Indian youths react to the new opportunities presented to them by the opening up of the RMC, Sandhurst, and later the IMA? What were the influences that helped mold the character of these future commanders of the postindependent Indian army? These are important questions that must be answered, for no matter what was sanctioned at the official level, the success or failure of the entire Indianization plans ultimately lay in the hands of these young men.

NOTES

1. *Statistics of the British Military Effort in the Great War* (London: His Majesty's Stationary Office [henceforth HMSO], 1922), 68–9; See also *India's Contribution to the Great War* (Calcutta: Government of India, 1923).

2. See PRO, Cabinet Office (henceforth CAB) 24/70, GT 6341; and "Statistical Abstract of Information Regarding the Armies at Home and Abroad, 1914–20," PRO, WO 161/82.

3. Sir Charles Petrie, *The Life and Letters of the Right Honourable Sir Austen Chamberlain* (London: Cassell, 1940), vol. 2, 73–74.

4. Government of India, Home Department, Political notification No. 2111, BL/IOR, L/MIL/7/19006, 110.

5. Mehrotra, *India and the Commonwealth*, 106.

6. P.G. Robb, *The Government of India and Reform: Policies towards Politics and the Constitution 1916–1921*, (London: Oxford University Press, 1976), 262.

7. These resolutions were primarily in reaction to the Esher Committee report in 1920, which inquired into the administration and organization of the army.

8. See K.A. Nilkanta Sastri (ed.), *A Great Liberal: Speeches and Writings of Sir P.S. Sivaswamy Aiyer* (Bombay: Allied Publishers, 1965), 327–42; See also *India: Legislative Assembly Debates*, vol. 1, part 2 (1921), 1753.

9. Telegram from secretary of state to Army Department, Simla, 20 August 1917, BL/IOR, L/MIL/7/19006, 110.

10. Proceedings of the committee appointed by the government of governor-general in council to examine the military requirements of India [Military Requirements Committee], Simla: Government of India, 1921, 2 vols., BL/IOR, L/MIL/17/5/1773.

11. Indianization of the Indian army, Lieutenant General Alexander Stanhope Cobbe, India Office Military Department, 14 September 1921, BL/IOR, L/MIL/17/5/1774.

12. The PWRIM was established by Lord Rawlinson and formerly inaugurated by the Prince of Wales on 13 March 1922. Its purpose was to train Indians for entry into Sandhurst.

13. Indianization of the Indian army; Report of a committee appointed by His Excellency the commander in chief for India, Delhi: Government of India, 1922, BL/IOR, L/MIL/17/5/1778, 1–12.

14. Papers of Stuart Kelson Brown 1920–1931, Indianization 1924–1925, BL/IOR, L/MIL/5/844, 31.

15. Mr. S.K. Brown, a longtime proponent of Indianization, served as joint secretary to the Military Department from September 1924 to 1934. See his lecture on Indianization given to Imperial Defence College, 15 October 1931, BL/IOR, L/MIL/5/857.

16. See chap. 1 of this volume.

17. Progress in the Indianization of the Indian army: Report of a committee appointed by His Excellency the commander in chief for India [Secret], Simla: Government of India, June 1923, BL/IOR, L/MIL/17/5/1779, 4.

18. The VCO comprised of three Indian ranks above the noncommissioned ranks; it included the *jemadar* (equivalent of a King's commissioned second lieutenant), the *subedar* (equivalent of a King's commissioned lieutenant), and the *subedar-major* (equivalent of a King's commissioned major). These ranks provided a link between the British King's commissioned officer (KCO) fresh from Sandhurst and the sepoy, "whose language, customs, and outlook were utterly Indian." The VCO ranks "also provided an outlet for ambitious and able Indian sepoys, although they were not promoted beyond the regimental level." See Cohen, *Indian Army*,

43. With the advent of the King's commissioned Indian officers (KCIO), it was felt that the VCO ranks were redundant and should be abolished.

19. Ibid.

20. Mehrotra, *India and the Commonwealth*, 172.

21. *Report of the Indian Sandhurst Committee, 14 November 1926* [Skeen Committee], (London: HMSO, 1927).

22. Despatch to His Majesty's secretary of state for India No. 38, 13 October 1927, Birkenhead Collection, BL/IOR, Mss.Eur.D.703/38, 4; Recommendation of the government of India, Home Department, Political Notification No. 2111, BL/IOR, L/MIL/7/19006; Report of the Indian Sandhurst Committee, BL/IOR, L/MIL/17/5/1787. Lord Irwin felt that the Indian army, like the country, must eventually attain Dominion status and the eight units would form the nucleus of such an army. Lord Irwin to Sir William Marius, governor of United Provinces, 18 April 1927, Irwin Collection, Mss.Eur.C.152/21.

23. *London Evening News*, 7 April 1927, "The Defence of India: 'Indianization' and the Future," Sir Michael O'Dwyer, S.K. Brown Collection, BL/IOR, Mss.Eur.D.712/14.

24. These scholars include Cohen, Mehrotra, and Jacobsen.

25. Memorandum by the WO on certain questions asked by the chairman of the Indian Statutory Commission [Simon Commission], 20 June 1929, Simon Collection, BL/IOR, Mss.Eur.F.77/54, 25.

26. Interview (in camera) with Major General W.M. St. George Kirke, deputy chief of general staff, and Mr. Mackworth Young, secretary to the Army Department, Kirke Collection, BL/IOR, Mss.Eur.E.396/18, 131.

27. *Report of the Indian Military College Committee, 15 July 1931*, (London: HMSO, 1931), 1.

28. Ibid., 18.

29. Regulations for the PWRIM College, Dehra Dun (1934), Delhi: Government of India Press, 1938, BL/IOR, L/MIL/17/5/2285, 1.

30. Ibid., 2.

31. Ibid., 7.

32. See Chetwoode's notes on Indianization for Major General S.F. Muspratt, Military Department, India Office, 26 September 1932, Templewood Papers, Hoare Collection, Eur.Mss.E.240/57, a.

33. The only significant opposition Sir Aiyer had to the committee's plans was toward its restriction of the number of vacancies at the college that would be available to open competition. See minute by Sir P.S. Sivaswamy Aiyer and Major General Honorary Raja Ganpat Rao Raghunath Rao Rajwade, 2 July 1931, BL/IOR, L/MIL/17/5/2285, 75–108.

34. B.P.N. Sinha and Sunil Chandra, *Valour and Wisdom: Genesis and Growth of the Indian Military Academy* (New Delhi: Oxford and IBH Publishing, 1992), 95–96, 130.

35. Ibid., 133.

36. Regulations respecting admission to the Indian Military Academy in Dehra Dun and for the first appointments to His Majesty's land forces, 1931, Manager of Publications, Delhi: Government of India Press, New Delhi, 1937, BL/IOR, L/MIL/17/5/2284, 1–2.

37. General Gul Hassan Khan (Pakistan army), who joined the IMA in January

1941, recalls that during his first term at the academy, the course proceeded at a leisurely pace, seemingly unaffected by the war. It was only when he returned from a two-month break after the first term that he and the other cadets of his course were given a dose of concentrated training and passed out at the end of the year. Gul Hassan Khan, *Memoirs* (Karachi, Oxford: Oxford University Press, 1993), 9–10.

38. Sinha and Chandra, *Valour and Wisdom*, 155–59.

39. Lieutenant General S.K. Sinha, *A Soldier Recalls* (New Delhi: Lancer International, 1992), 42.

40. Ibid., 158, 133.

41. Personal and private letter from Sir Chetwoode to Sir Cobbe, Simla, 21 August 1931, BL/IOR, L/MIL/5/885, 97.

42. Ibid., 96–105.

43. H.H. Gerth and C. Wright Mills (eds.), *From Max Weber: Essays on Sociology* (New York: Oxford University Press, 1946), 233–35.

44. Of the 162 Indian cadets admitted to Sandhurst, 98 were commissioned, 28 resigned or were removed for various reasons, 2 died, and 34 were still under instruction. See BL/IOR, Mss.Eur.E.396/18, 15; and BL/IOR, L/MIL/5/857.

45. Copies of important papers, Deputy Chief of General Staff (DCGS) India, 1929, Kirke letter BL/IOR, Mss.Eur.E.396/13; against Indianization of armored car companies, September 1928. In a letter regarding the Indian Sandhurst Committee report from Jacobs to Kirke, 26 May 1927, Jacobs declares his intention to "take both my gloves off and . . . fight that report to the finish," Ibid.

46. Admission of Indians to Cranwell, Air Ministry letter, 9 January 1929, BL/IOR, L/MIL/5/849.

47. A diary of Addiscombe, BL/IOR, L/MIL/9/357, 1.

48. John B. Gent (ed.), *Croydon Old and New* (South Croydon, Surrey: Southern Publishing, Brighton, 1975), 7, 4.

49. Military Seminary Committee report, 6 July 1814, BL/IOR, L/MIL/1/10/39.

3

An Officer and a Gentleman: The Socialization of the Indian Officer Cadet, 1919–1945

In 1925 Mr. S.K. Brown, the joint secretary to the Military Department, India, remarked that the "future of Indianization in the army lies in the hands of the Indian officers themselves."[1] Indeed, no analysis of the modernization program can be complete without a direct examination of the Indian officers' role in ensuring the success or failure of the Indianization effort. In the previous chapter, I revealed that one of the ultimate aims of the British was the creation of a professional national army so that India could take on the status of a self-governing dominion within the empire. Contrary to popular belief, Indianization was never meant to be a half-hearted attempt to mollify Indian nationalist politicians. The evidence suggests that Indianization was not a matter of political expediency to be achieved at any cost. Military efficiency remained a priority in this reform, and, had it become obvious over a period of time that the Indian officers were not up to the task, it is quite likely that the entire reform process would have failed.

Had the Indian officers proved inept, the British could have exercised two options: They could have scrapped the program altogether, or if this was not politically viable (as seems the more likely), they could have rushed through the Indianization process regardless of the cost to military efficiency. In either situation India would have ended up with a "headless" army after independence, the all-too-common legacy of most newly independent colonies. So, in the final analysis, the Indian officers alone would dictate the outcome of the ambitious Indianization program. This chapter analyzes the first phase of the Indianization process, the training of the Indian officer cadets.

THE DIRECT COMMISSIONED OFFICERS

The first Indians to obtain commissions in the Indian army were officers of the NILF, (*Native Indian Land Forces*) and formerly of the ICC, who had seen service in France.[2] This announcement was made in a speech to the House of Commons on Indian self-government by Secretary of State for India Montagu.[3] These nine Indian officers were the first to face the consequences of the new Indianization policy. One of these officers was Kanwar Amar Singh.[4] After being commissioned into the NILF on 4 July 1905, he served as an extra ADC to various British generals, became a NILF captain on 4 July 1914, and received his King's commission at age 39 in 1917. After receiving his King's commission, Amar Singh served briefly on the staff of General Knight in Bombay before joining the 16th Cavalry (Gardner's Horse) in June 1918. Between September 1920 and March 1921 he reached the high point of his career as acting major in temporary command of the regiment. He ended his career with this regiment in Waziristan in 1923. Amar Singh's departure from the regiment was not a happy one; his diary indicates it came about as a result of a negative annual confidential report from his superior Colonel Mears. Indeed, much of the diary is replete with examples of tension with British officers—subordinates and superiors. The tension actually seems to have escalated after Amar Singh received a King's commission. The most galling incident took place on St. Patrick's Day in October 1919, when a British subordinate, Lieutenant Wilks, blatantly disobeyed Amar Singh's orders, leading to a very heated exchange.

Scholars, including DeWitt C. Ellinwood have identified the ICC and these nine King's commissioned Indian officers (KCIOs) in particular as the "first chapter in [the] Indianization of the Indian Army."[5] So it is not surprising that the entire Indianization program subsequently has been portrayed in a negative light. According to Lloyd I. Rudolph (one of the editors of Amar Singh's diary), the army's reaction toward the first nine Indian KCIOs represented a "backlash within the Indian army against the politicians' notions that Indian officers could, by a stroke of the pen, be made equal to British officers. . . . If liberal policy could not be blocked politically it could be resisted through bureaucratic sabotage."[6]

It is misleading, however, to identify the ICC or the nine KCIOs as the first step toward Indianization. The granting of the King's commission to these officers appears to have been a purely political move. The measure was a limited one and in no way was it connected to the mainstream effort to create an Indian officer corps. As for the experiences of Amar Singh, there can be no doubt that he and the other eight ICC KCIOs were subject to varied forms of racial prejudice. But their main problem appears to have been the awkwardness of their official position, as highlighted by Amar Singh's experiences. The King's commission had given him the right to command field formations, which he did, albeit briefly. Unfortunately, neither Amar Singh nor his cadet corps colleagues had passed through Sandhurst to obtain their commissions. So it was not surprising that British officers, even subordinates such as Lieutenant Wilks, resented the authority and rank bestowed upon Amar Singh. In his case the problem was exacerbated by the fact that he had served as an ADC throughout the war and had seen no action. Therefore it was the lack of professional training, and not "bureaucratic sabotage," that ended his career. He and his fellow cadet corps officers were the unfortunate pawns of a political statement, and, as such, his experiences cannot be considered the norm by which the Indian army's reaction to Indianization can be measured.

Take, for example, the career of Major General A.A. Rudra. Like Amar Singh and the eight other cadet corps officers, he, too, served in the Great War and was commissioned in 1918. Yet, unlike these officers, Rudra went on to serve with distinction, ending his career in the independent Indian army with the rank of major general. What was it that differentiated Rudra from the cadet corps KCIOs? To begin with, Rudra joined the British army and not the Indian army. He was studying in Cambridge when the war broke out and joined the Universities and Public Schools Brigade. He left with the brigade for France in November 1915 and took part in the battle of Mons. In April 1916 his unit (16th Middlesex) joined the 29th Gallipoli Division. Since Rudra did not qualify for a commission, he, along with others, joined the 2nd Battalion of Royal Fusiliers in the 29th Division and took part in the Somme bloodbath. In 1918 Rudra's name finally went up for commission. He and another Indian, K.A.D. Naoroji—grandson of the grand old Indian nationalist politician Dadabhai Naoroji—were selected for and sent to an OTC at Berkenstead, the Inns of Court, where they joined the 17th OTC Battalion. Just before their training was due to complete, in November 1918, the armistice was declared.

Soon afterwards, Rudra and Naoroji were sent to General Sir Herbert Cox, military secretary at the India Office. Cox was greatly impressed with their war experience, his opinion no doubt aided by the happy coincidence that he had served as commander of the 29th Division at Gallipoli. Although Cox tried to obtain commissions for Rudra and Naoroji, the War Office refused, saying that the two must go to Sandhurst first. Both Rudra and Naoroji already had completed most of the OTC at Berkenstead and therefore refused, requesting instead to be discharged. Fortunately, the War Office relented, and—along with the first fifty Indian officers—the two sailed to India to join the Indian army. This group included K.M. Cariappa, the first Indian commander in chief and the last officer to be commissioned with this group.

The key to Rudra's success appears to have been his brief stint in the OTC in England. Being a veteran of the Great War with tremendous experience in some of the bloodiest battlefields of the western front no doubt strengthened his case. As far as the War Office and the Indian army were concerned, Rudra was a genuine candidate for a King's commission. Unlike the ICC officers, Rudra was not tainted by having belonged to what essentially amounted to a princely boy's club. The fact that Rudra did not come from royal Indian stock obviously did not hamper his case. Unlike Amar Singh, Rudra "earned" his commission in much the same way his British colleagues had done, and not via political machinations. This no doubt made pre-Sandhurst KCIOs like Rudra far more acceptable to their British subordinates, colleagues, and superiors in the Indian Army.[7]

There were, of course, exceptions to this rule, the most notable being Cariappa. In 1920 he was one of only six out of sixty military trainees at Daly College, Indore, to qualify for a commission. A cadet school had been opened at Daly college in October 1918, with accommodations for fifty cadets. The plan was to train cadets for the Indian army. The Indore cadet school had been opened as a temporary measure to meet the exigencies of the war. The very same year, ten vacancies per year were allotted to Indians at the RMC, Sandhurst, and the cadet school was closed within a year. In all, forty-nine cadets were admitted to the Dally/Indore cadet school (including Rudra and Cariappa) and thirty-nine were granted commissions. After the Dally cadet program was shut down, Sandhurst became the only avenue for Indians to obtain a commission in the army for more than a decade.[8]

There is little doubt that Cariappa was exceptionally talented. Despite the fact that he lacked "via Sandhurst" credentials, he was the first Indian officer to graduate from Staff College, Quetta; the first Indian to hold a Grade 2 (from Staff College) appointment; the first Indian to command a battalion; and the first Indian to be appointed an army commander.[9] Cariappa, however, is the lone star among direct commissioned officers of the pre-Sandhurst and pre–IMA group. The vast bulk of these officers, about fifty in number (see data from Rudra above), came nowhere near matching this *Kodava* (inhabitant of Coorg).

The most important contribution to the Indian officer corps, especially to that all-important group that formed the core high-command element of the Indian army from the late 1950s to the late 1970s, came from the graduating classes of Sandhurst and the prewar IMA courses in the 1920s and the 1930s. A detailed study of their careers in these formative years is essential in order to obtain an understanding of the mindset of the postindependent Indian army officer corps. The following section examines the contrasting experiences of the Indian officer cadets at Sandhurst and the IMA Dehra Dun.

BOYS IN THE SQUARE

For much of the 1920s Indian candidates for Sandhurst were selected to sit for army entrance exams. Thus there was no open competition to enter this first entry phase. Some months before the exam, the government of India informed local governments and administrators of the date fixed for the examination and provided a press release stating the same. Applicants usually were asked to forward their names in the first instance to the deputy commissioners of their districts, who in turn would forward applications to the deputy commissioner, who in his turn would forward them to the local government. At any stage either of the three officials could reject an applicant. In some instances education authorities like the PWRIM were permitted to send names directly to the local government.[10]

According to paragraph 4 of the "Provisional Regulations respecting Admission of Indian Gentlemen to the R.M.C., Sandhurst, England, 1925," "The general rule in selecting candidates should be that selections should be made from the communities which furnish recruits, in proportion to the numbers in which they can furnish such recruits. Regard should also be had to the claims to consideration of candidates from the educated middle classes."[11] The appropriate authorities were specifically instructed to select candidates generally from the communities furnishing recruits for the army. This emphasis on the selection of candidates from the so-called martial races was the reason behind opting for a "selection" process rather than a system of open competitive exams and would form the cornerstone of the recruiting policy for the next five years.

Candidates who filtered through to the local government level or were selected by the principal of the PWRIM were called in for an interview by the Provincial Selection Board, presided over by the governor. After this hurdle, the candidate's name was sent to the government of India and he was permitted to sit for a competitive entrance exam. This exam was comprised of a written test, a medical test, and an oral examination. It was administered by two senior military officers and an educational officer. Finally, the viceroy himself participated in the process and selected candidates whose names were recommended to the secretary of state for India for admission into Sandhurst.[12]

This daunting road to the gates of Sandhurst reflects the desire of the army and the government of India not only to secure the best possible candidates, but also to find the "right type" of Indian cadet. This requirement envisioned an ideal Indian candidate of martial race stock, good breeding, and other imperceptible social skills. Perhaps no candidate more so than Koodendera Subayya Thimayya exemplified this ideal candidate. Like Cariappa, Thimayya too hailed from Coorg—a bonafide, if somewhat obscure, martial district. The son of a wealthy coffee planter, Thimayya (or Timmy, as his friends knew him) attended school at St. Joseph's College in Conoor. He and his brother were the first Indians to attend the school. They spent six years in a harsh boarding school environment run by Irish brothers, just the sort of upbringing that would garner the welcome attention of the Sandhurst recruiters. Nevertheless, after a particularly brutal punishment that resulted in lacerated knees from having to crawl on broken glass, Thimayya and his brother finished their schooling at the more contemporary Bishop Cotton's School in Bangalore. Here, too, the two brothers were pioneering trailblazers for other Indians.

When Thimayya finished schooling in 1922, the PWRIM was being opened, and he was perceived to be right type for the college. According to his biographer, "his english was perfect and english manners were second nature to him. He was five feet nine, physically hard, and a good athlete."[13] Thimayya became one of thirty-two cadets in the first class at the PWRIM. The majority of the cadets in Thimayya's batch, unlike him, were connected to the military. Apparently, the PWRIM at this early stage was following the government's dictum of selecting candidates with a martial background. It also could have been that the PWRIM provided the only opportunity for sons of the VCOs and the other ranks of the Indian army to give their sons the required education for entry into Sandhurst. Whatever the case, it was apparent that educational ability was not the primary criterion for entry into the PWRIM. Thimayya's grades had been too low for entry into Oxford or Cambridge, but not for the PWRIM. At Bishop Cotton's School, Thimayya had passed with a mediocre academic record, but at the PWRIM, he found himself at the top in scholastic ability.

After his eighteen months at Dehra Dun, Thimayya went to Simla to sit for the Army Entrance Exam. The entire process was quite daunting. A British officer was assigned to small groups of candidates to observe them minutely and report on their personality and "deportment." Any slipup would result in termination of the exam for the unfortunate candidate. Thimayya got through the written and oral exams quite easily even though he was unable to speak a word of Urdu in the oral language test. He was then interviewed by the Chief of General Staff General Sir Claude W. Jacob, who, fortunately for Thimayya, recalled seeing him play excellent cricket at the PWRIM, and the interview came to a successful conclusion. The next all-important step was the final interview with the viceroy himself. At the viceroy's request, Thimayya launched into a lecture on his native Coorg and its coffee-based economy. The viceroy stopped him in mid-speech with a question: "What games do you play?" Thimayya replied, "Hockey, cricket, football, tennis, and squash." He was on his way to Sandhurst.[14]

Thimayya's progress through the entrance exams and the all-important interviews appears to have been quite smooth and even cursory. His Westernized social graces, excellent communication skills, and scholastic ability appear to have carried him through. The fact that he was a highly successful graduate from the PWRIM greatly helped his cause.

A casual glance at the list of sixty-seven cadets admitted to Sandhurst between January 1919 and September 1924 indicates that the government of India was adhering strictly to its "right type" of Indian cadet. The vast majority of the entrants came from the Punjab; they included Sikhs, Punjabi Hindus, and Muslims.[15] It is also interesting to note that Anglo-Indians, who were so greatly overrepresented in the exclusive Indian boarding schools such as Doon and Bishop Cotton's, were conspicuous by their absence. Only one—Herbert Arthur Francis—seems to have entered in September 1924. Francis, however, was removed in 1926 for falling below the "lowest standard" and for possessing an "unpopular personality."[16]

It was this initial group of Sandhurst cadets that provided the bulk of the dismal reports that the Jacob and Skeen Committees made to the government of India. A significant number of these early cadets appear to have been the sons of ex-Indian commissioned officers or other ranks of the army, and they quite simply lacked the necessary education and mental adaptability to get through Sandhurst. A rare exception was Agha Mohammed Ayub Khan, son of *Risaldar*-Major Mir Dad Khan Bahadur. Nevertheless, by the mid-1920s the Indian government was beginning to widen its recruiting base for Sandhurst cadets, and the educated middle class was the main beneficiary.

One less-than-ideal "type" of candidate was Jayanto Nath Chaudhuri (yet another future army chief), the son of a most "nonmartial" Bengali barrister in Calcutta. Chaudhuri, however, was somewhat fortunate in that he sent in his application while studying in England. He was called in by the India Office in London and interviewed by a "small, bald, bright-eyed Field Marshal." During the interview Chaudhuri "admitted to a comparatively undistinguished academic record and not much skill at sports," but he was accepted nonetheless![17]

By 1927, however, entry into Sandhurst by interview selection had stopped. Henceforth all candidates sat for the same entrance exam for Sandhurst, Cranwell, and Woolwich as did the British candidates. In Exam 1, there were four sections:

1. English, 100 pts
2. General Knowledge, 100 pts
3. Interview and Record Test, 400 pts
4. One of the following: Modern Language, including oriental; General History; Elementary Maths; Everyday Science, 100 pts

Exam 2 also offered choices. The candidate could select one topic from Languages, Maths, Science, and other subjects for three hundred points.

To secure entry into Sandhurst a candidate had to earn a minimum of 35 percent in the Interview and Record Test. To get into the RMA, Woolwich, a candidate required a minimum of 40 percent in lower maths and physics or chemistry. The interview test with three hundred points was the most important part of the exam. The format, indeed, was quite similar to the Army Entrance Exam, the only difference being that the Indian candidates went through exactly the same examination process as their British counterparts, with their papers being set and graded by civil service commissioners in England.[18]

Those Indians who were fortunate and capable enough to survive the intense two-year Sandhurst course were subjected to a remarkable process of indoctrination. The Indian cadets not only were transformed into army officers, but also were given a good dose of elitist British socialization. Even highly Anglicized cadets like Thimayya and Chaudhuri were jolted by the culture shock of Sandhurst. The first shock the Indians had to endure was the ten-week introductory course to which all Sandhurst cadets were subjected. During this period the cadets spent most of their free time drilling on the square and thus were collectively referred to as "Boys on the Square." Their uniform for this ten-week period was a coarse fatigue suit of brown denim that nevertheless had to show gleaming buttons and razor-sharp creases! In case the new cadets forgot their lowly status, they were subject to constant abuse, first from the sergeant major and then from the senior cadets. Once through this harrowing ten-week period, the cadets lost their uniforms and gained a degree of respectability. They also settled down to absorb the more serious aspects of learning to become an officer and a gentleman. The on-the-square period was a particularly good time for weeding out non-Western cadets of an aristocratic upbringing who were unwilling to subject themselves to iron discipline and ritualized abuse. Chaudhuri recalls a "Mister Ali" of Egyptian noble stock who, enraged at the treatment he was receiving, stalked off the square at Sandhurst.[19] To most successful Indian cadets the ten-week initiation and the subsequent military education they received was not a time of bitterness. Indeed, they remember it with a degree of awe and respect for their teachers, the raucous sergeant majors in particular. These incredibly loud and abusive soldiers who insisted on being called "staff" and not "sir" appeared to have a good idea of the problems Indian cadets faced. S.D. Verma, who joined Sandhurst in 1927, remembers feeling particularly dejected during his first term when he, the only Indian in his squad, was the least coordinated during drill. His flagging morale received a tremendous boost when the sergeant instructor, noting his depression, approached him and told him that he was learning drill the right way, from the bottom up, while the "johnnies" who thought they knew everything would have to discard a lot of their misconceptions about drill.[20]

"COLOURED MEN AND WHITE WOMEN"

Unfortunately, nearly none of the Indian alumni of Sandhurst recalled their stay in England with fondness from a social standpoint. For most of them, the very first contact they had with the British after stepping off the boat was a very cold, formal affair. The Indian government and the India Office had arranged for every small group of Indians at Sandhurst to have an official guardian, usually a retired ex-Indian army officer. The role of these guardians was more negative than positive. Instead of offering constant support and encouragement to the Indian cadets, they were there primarily to ensure that they did not get into trouble. Thimayya took an instant dislike to his guardian, Colonel Sturgess, upon their first meeting. He recalls Sturgess as being more concerned about the cadets' ability to handle their finances and their morals than about the obvious emotional and cultural dislocation they were enduring.[21] The attitude of the official guardians often led to considerable friction between them and the parents of their charges. A glimpse into this tense relationship is available in the exchange of letters between a Colonel Stooks (Verma's guardian), the guardian of cadet Rustom Manekji Bilimoria, and Mr. Bilimoria, the cadet's father. Instead of offering the faltering Rustom Manekji Bilimoria support and encouragement, Stooks immediately asked Mr. Bilimoria for permission to remove his son from the college. The ensuing exchange of angry letters finally resulted in Stooks' stepping down as guardian to cadet Bilimoria.[22] Stooks indeed generally seems to have been disliked by most of the Indian cadets in his charge. In confidential talks with subcommittee members of the Indian Sandhurst Committee, at least three Indian cadets complained that Colonel Stooks, in addition to showing no sympathy for the cadets, never acknowledged their greetings, never shook their hands, and even made one of them wait in the rain for half an hour for a meeting.[23] Only cadets like Chaudhuri who were fortunate enough to have British family or friends nominated as their guardians in England, managed to experience warm British hospitality.[24] Most Indian cadets were stuck with their official guardians and had only one another to rely upon for emotional support and social activities.

Under these circumstances it is not surprising that most Indian cadets formed tight-knit groups. For many of them, this was the first experience they had as foreigners, and a sudden awareness of being "Indian" came to the fore. By the time Chaudhuri entered Sandhurst in 1926, a tradition had developed whereby senior cadets would watch over one another and the new Indian cadets outside of Sandhurst. Indian cadets apparently had to maintain certain standards. Servants, for instance, had to be tipped an astronomical five shillings weekly instead of the normal half-crown.[25] If an Indian gentleman cadet (GC) went to the movies, he was always expected to buy the most expensive balcony seats. Snobbish and silly at first glance, these "rules" of behavior appear to have been an attempt to carve a niche of respectability amidst a sea of subtle racial ostracism. The fact that many of the earlier batches of Indian cadets came from very wealthy, princely families also may have contributed to this tradition.

Of greater interest, perhaps, is the tradition whereby Indian cadets generally avoided the Sandhurst end-of-term dance. Chaudhuri feels that this custom had something to do with the taboo of "coloured men and white women."[26] In addition to his other duties, Chaudhuri's official guardian, also a retired Indian army colonel, "was also responsible for seeing that none of them [Indian cadets] took home a European wife."[27] Indeed, nowhere was the British hostility toward Indians on a social level more apparent than in their attempts to keep the Indian cadets away from white women. Years later, Thimayya would recall the affront he and other Indian cadets felt when their official guardian, Colonel Sturgess, treated them as if they were all degenerates waiting only to be unleashed so that they could fall upon the unprotected womanhood of Britain.[28] When Thimayya began to correspond with an English girl he had met at a community charity dance near Reading, Colonel Sturgess began to intercept and read the letters from the girl addressed to Thimayya. In fact, Thimayya's volatile relationship with Sturgess came to an end over a fracas that developed between the two after Thimayya danced with a European girl while on a vacation in Switzerland.[29] The highly unpopular Colonel Stooks also was accused by at least one Indian cadet of banning Indian cadets from the dance floor.[30]

There can be little doubt that the relentless efforts by the British to separate the Indian GCs from white girls is evidence of racial prejudice and stereotyping on the part of the British. Somewhat more ambiguous was the attitude of the Sandhurst authorities toward Indian cadets in regard to the college's sports activities. Indian cadets, no matter how much they excelled in a sport, could not participate in interbattalion matches or prestigious matchups with other colleges. One senior Sikh cadet, Sant Singh, was an outstanding hockey player, described by the local press as "that dexterous red-bearded Indian . . . the most brilliant player we have seen in years." However, at the time of picking players for the prestigious matches against Oxford and Cambridge, Sant Singh's name was dropped. In fact, he never was chosen to represent the college for any major game.[31] S.P.P. Thorat, who was an excellent marksman, was not allowed to take part in the rifle championship, despite his putting his name down to compete.[32] When another Indian dared to query as to why he was being dropped from a team, he was told that "these minor sports had a social aspect."[33] The real reason for their exclusion was never explained to the Indian cadets (see below), and these actions served only to convince the Indian cadets that they were victims of blatant racism.

Another form of discrimination practiced in Sandhurst against the Indians was in the appointment of cadet corporals, sergeants, and under officers. Only cadet Ayub Khan got promoted to the rank of honorary (not actual) cadet corporal.[34] These ranks, especially that of cadet under officer, carried great responsibility and authority, correspondingly conferring great respect on the deserving cadet. According to Chaudhuri, "As the average British cadet went through his three terms at the R.M.C., all but a few real incompetents got promoted. . . . This same convention regarding promotion unfortunately did not apply to foreigners."[35]

Thimayya held the opinion that the discrimination against the Indians in sports was partly "political" and partly "snobbery." He noted that, in the past, Indians had earned "blues" in sports and rank in the cadet corps. However, with the arrival of Gandhi and the Congress Party, the British began to fear the prospect of Indian officers leading an uprising against them. So they sought to discourage the Indians as much as possible.[36] Thimayya does not offer any evidence of this to his biographer, and it is doubtful if this was a primary motivation. Whatever the reason (see below), it only served to alienate the Indian cadets even further and make them feel like outsiders and "colonials."

This discrimination against the Indians does not seem to have been transferred into their military education at Sandhurst. Although some evaluating officers frequently referred to "the right type of Indian cadet" in their reports, there is no evidence to suggest that they were anything but professional and impartial in their judgments. In 1926, the subcommittee of the Indian Sandhurst Committee questioned the Sandhurst authorities about the performance of Indian cadets in comparison with their British comrades. The latter, including the commandant General Corkran, felt that while Indian cadets compared quite well with the British cadets in general education and conduct, they lagged behind in leadership ability. They attributed this to "the natural diffidence of Indians when as boys they are among a class of a different race."[37] However, the authorities were certain that this characteristic would wear off with time. This appears to be borne out in the case of at least one Indian cadet. Thorat, who joined Sandhurst in 1925, recalls, "In the beginning I suffered from a sense of inferiority complex vis-à-vis the British cadets. Never having mixed with Europeans in my school and college days in India, I was diffident about my ability to compete with them. Gradually I overcame this failing."[38] General Corkran also added that the same criticism probably could be made of a handful of "British boys if you put them in a[n] Indian Sandhurst."[39] Corkran and his staff vehemently rejected any suggestion that the staff of the college were less sympathetic to Indian cadets. When asked if Indian cadets got along well with their British colleagues, the answer was "yes" provided they entered into the "spirit of the R.M.C."[40] Individual company commanders at Sandhurst who were interviewed by the subcommittee also declared Indian cadets to be on par with the average British cadets. Some of them (Thimayya's name is mentioned) were considered to be "very good."[41] A review of the confidential reports of the Indian cadets who failed to get commissions shows that the most commonly cited weaknesses were lack of leadership ability, initiative, self-confidence, academic ability, and communication skills.[42]

It is possible that the Sandhurst staff was trying to paint an encouraging picture for the Indian subcommittee members (M.A. Jinnah, Phiroze Sethna, and Zorawar Singh). Nonetheless, the evidence suggests that on a professional level the British appear to have been quite fair in their dealings with the Indian cadets. Thimayya, Chaudhuri, and other successful Indian graduates of Sandhurst have attested to this in their memoirs.

A TOUCH OF CLASS?

The ambiguous nature of the discrimination of the Indians at Sandhurst can be attributed to the fact that it was, to a large extent, class-based and not solely racial. Up until the mid-1850s, recruitment to the British officer corps was essentially the sole preserve of the aristocracy and the landed gentry. This was ensured by the extremely low pay and the system of purchasing a commission via nomination by either the commander in chief, Sandhurst, or the master general of the Board of Ordnance, Woolwich. When the system of nomination and purchase were abolished and competitive exams introduced, the aristocratic stranglehold on the system was loosened. However, the army was more than a little relieved to discover that almost all the entrants came from "good homes."[43] By happy coincidence, or as a result thereof, the army found itself drawing most of its new officer candidates from the rapidly expanding British public school system. The public schools provided the necessary socialization for the sons of the affluent British professional class to stand alongside the traditional aristocracy. A few elite British schools (approximately twenty-three in number)—including Rugby, Eton, Harrow, and St. Paul's—supplied the majority of the officer cadets to Sandhurst and Woolwich right up to the Second World War. According to Maurice G. Garnier, in 1947, 65 percent of all Sandhurst entrants originated from a public school and no less than 88 percent of them became cadet leaders. Even as late as 1957, 53 percent of all cadets came from public schools and 67 percent were cadet leaders. However, the number of elite public school cadets had dropped dramatically, so that by 1957 only 28 percent came from the elite schools, but a relatively high 44 percent were cadet leaders. By 1957, 23 percent of the cadets came from the elite public schools and only 29 percent were cadet leaders.[44] An examination of the data on senior British army officers from the rank of lieutenant general upward, shows that from 1870–1959, an overwhelming 90 percent came from the propertied and "newly" elite professional classes. About 40 percent came from the old ruling class, mainly landowning. Merely 3 percent of all senior officers came from a middle-class background. None came from a working-class background.[45] According to C.B. Otley, "The great majority of [senior] officers studied had undergone a privileged minority education, an education lying wholly outside what might be called the 'state' sector. A handful of great boarding schools produced a legion of army generals."[46]

The public schools, Sandhurst, and Woolwich were part of the socialization effort to bring first professional and later even middle-class cadets up to the same level as the aristocracy. Research from the late 1960s and early 1970s of middle-class British officer cadets reveals that the staff of Sandhurst felt that, ideologically, little had changed and that the socialization of the middle-class entrants was well under way.[47]

It is within this context that we must evaluate the attitudes of the British staff and cadets toward the Indian cadets. The Indian cadets who went to Sandhurst came from a markedly different social and educational background than that of their British colleagues. To begin the Indian officer corps did not evolve out of an old aristocratic tradition as did its British counterpart. It originated, instead, from a largely professional background—lawyers, government officials, doctors, and so on. As a result of the nature of the colonial Indian army, the traditional Indian elites, the princely class, and the great *zamindars* (landlords) never had a great interest in the army. Barred from service as officers, few were desirous of serving with the rank and file. The ICC and the honorary commissions granted to Indian princes were political moves by the British government to placate the Indian elites, to offer them an honorable avenue to serve in the army. When King's commissions were finally granted to Indians, most British officers and civil servants hoped to create British Indians.

The deliberate adoption of a process of nominating Indian cadets to Sandhurst was merely a throwback to the British system in the pre-1850s era. The entire process was fine-tuned to ensure that the "right type" of Indian cadets were sent to Sandhurst. As in Britain, qualifications for the officer corps were not decided by educational merit alone, but by social affiliation. On this basis, the traditional elites were far more desirable than the educated Indian middle class, which was perceived by the British to be ideologically and politically unreliable. Senior British officers like General Sir Edmund Barrow made it clear that they were in favor of granting commissions to Indians of royal lineage. In 1912, Barrow called for the granting of field appointments to two such officers—Lieutenant Agha Casim Shah, ADC to the general officer commanding the 6th Poona Division, and Lieutenant Kanwar Amar Singh, ADC to the general officer commanding the 5th Mhow Division—saying, "I consider both of them fit to take their place among British officers of an Indian cavalry regiment, whether in an educational, a professional or a social sense.[48] The real emphasis here was social, for neither of the Indians had any professional military education to qualify them for a commission in the field (see above). Both, however, had impeccable social connections; Lieutenant Casim Shah was the nephew of His Highness Agha Khan and Lieutenant Amar Singh came from the old Rajput royal families of Jaipur and Jodhpur.

Unfortunately for the British, the socially acceptable Indian candidate was not necessarily the best qualified, and so their attempt at social engineering failed. There are two primary reasons for this. First, many of the elite Indian youths selected lacked the educational and mental abilities to get them through Sandhurst. Second, it was the rapidly growing Indian middle class in the interwar period that proved to be the more aggressive and well educated. As the Indian education system expanded and matured in the 1920s and 1930s, the young men from the Indian professional, business, and planter classes began to monopolize it. The second most-favored group after the old aristocracy were the sons of Indian soldiers from the ranks. It was the poor performance of many of these cadets who made up the initial batches of Sandhurst cadets that ultimately opened the way for the Indian middle class.

If Indian cadets felt less than welcome on a social level in Sandhurst, they were in all probability confronting a class barrier alongside a subtle racial one. The British instructor officer who informed a Indian cadet that he was being kept out of a Sandhurst sports team to maintain social standards of behavior was most probably telling the truth and not covering up a blatant act of racism.[49] The overwhelmingly class-based discrimination practiced in Sandhurst was evident by the fact that Indian cadets were not the only ones to feel the sting of British social elitism. Those rare British cadets who did not come from an "acceptable" social background were shunned ruthlessly by their upper-class colleagues. Thimayya recalled the case of one such cadet by the name of Dalrymple, who, despite winning the coveted Sword of Honour when he graduated from Sandhurst, was extremely unpopular among the socially elite cadets who rarely spoke to him.[50] Chaudhuri, too, noted that "among the British cadets, there seemed to exist a pattern of groups based on schools, common interests and old family friendships. It was a sort of caste system."[51] In the case of the Indian cadets at Sandhurst, not only were they considered socially inferior to the upper-class British, but also they were perceived as inferior "natives." This last perception condemned even the most aristocratic Indian cadets to some form of discrimination at Sandhurst. M.R.A. Baig, the scion of an old aristocratic Indian family (which claimed descent from a Turkish sultan, no less) and one of the few Indians to attend one of the twenty-three elite British public schools (Clifton), recalled with some bewilderment when "I entered Sandhurst in January 1923, and for the first time in my life encountered racial prejudice. Our position there was much the same as that of the Jewish boys at Clifton. We did not belong and were made to feel it."[52] Baig, who had spent thirteen years in England (1910–1923) prior to entering Sandhurst, considered himself to be "a young Englishman in everything except race, religion and color. To be suddenly treated like this by those who up to now had treated me as one of themselves gave me a wound from which I never recovered.[53]

The discrimination meted out to Indians at Sandhurst, therefore, arose from several different sources. The first and the most easily identifiable was racism itself. It, however, was accentuated and probably caused by an existing and entrenched class system in Sandhurst. The official guardians of the Indian cadets, the ex-Indian army colonels, were actually enforcing a class-cum-racial exclusiveness system not too different from the one practiced by the upper-class British cadets. Another form of discrimination was institutional, with Indians being excluded from high-visibility positions as cadet leaders and sports team members. In all probability the authorities in Sandhurst were trying to preserve the British identity of the college. They also might have been concerned about the possibility of a negative reaction from the parents of current and future British cadets if they were to see too many Indians in high-visibility and/or high-ranking positions, either on the sports teams or in the corps.

AN IMPOSSIBLE SITUATION

Although England itself was far more welcoming to the Indian cadets than was Sandhurst, it remained an unfamiliar place for most of them. Cultural differences often resulted in acute homesickness. Food, probably more than anything else, made the Indians—Hindu, Muslims, and Sikhs alike—yearn for home. This problem was not one of religious sensibilities; the Sandhurst mess avoided this potential problem by serving Indian cadets mutton and eggs. Furthermore, many Anglicized Hindus, like Chaudhuri and Thimayya, had long since broken all dietary taboos while attending exclusive boarding schools back in India. Food in England was a problem because it was extremely bland to the Indian palate—it lacked spice! Chaudhuri and his fellow Indian cadets were sustained by weekend trips to Shafi's on Gerard Street, one of only four Indian restaurants in London in 1926.[54]

Despite the fact that the success rate for Indian cadets at Sandhurst had greatly increased since the mid-1920s, the number of qualified applicants for the ten Sandhurst positions had not shown a great increase. This in turn fueled a growing fall in public confidence in India about the entire scheme. The Indian Sandhurst Committee pulled no punches in its report. Beginning with the initial application process, the committee regarded it as "seriously objectionable that the channel of application should be so rigidly official and that the intending candidate should have so many official stages to traverse."[55] Regarding the actual process of sending cadets to Sandhurst, the committee acknowledged two permanent deterrents. First was the sheer cost of the whole endeavour to Indian parents. The committee noted that the cost of an eighteen-month course at Sandhurst to an Indian parent was Rs 11,000.[56] If the pretraining costs at the PWRIM, Dehra Dun, were added, this would add another Rs. 10,000 (serving or retired members of the Indian Army could pay substantially smaller amounts of Rs. 7,000 and Rs. 5,000 respectively). According to the report, "It has been represented to us and we believe it to be true, that expenditure on this scale is altogether beyond the capacity of the average Indian parent belonging to the middle classes."[57] Second, the average Indian parents were reluctant to send their sons to distant foreign lands. The main report and the secret subcommittee report both noted that the emotional trauma of separation was "repugnant" to most parents and depressing to many cadets:

> Noting the lack of educational and mental preparedness of Indian cadets sent to Sandhurst, the committee pointed out, . . . it cannot be expected that the educational authorities will interest themselves in the special preparation of boys for the army or will introduce the changes which are certainly necessary in the educational system in the country, so long as the prizes to be gained are limited to ten vacancies in Sandhurst per annum for all of India.[58]

In the final analysis, it was the necessarily limited spaces available at Sandhurst to Indian cadets that doomed that route to Indianization to failure. Although the report made no mention of it, there can be little doubt that a mere ten seats would not encourage many parents to urge their sons to go through the arduous application process. Even when the success rate of Indian cadets at Sandhurst went up, the institution could only absorb a limited number of Indian cadets. The problem was not the lack of space: The facilities could have been expanded. But, as the report acknowledged, "in every educational institution there comes a time when the authorities responsible for its efficiency must set a limit to further acceptance of foreign students lest the character of the institution may be changed."[59] The British government had indicated to the Indian subcommittee that Sandhurst would be willing to accept a maximum of 5 percent of the establishment of Sandhurst (thirty) and Woolwich (twelve) as being reserved for Indian cadets.[60] Thus, the need to preserve institutional identity, and not the inadequacy of Indian cadets to perform in a foreign environment, resulted in a positive report for the establishment of an IMA.

A HOME AT LAST

Indeed, as the report had suggested, the IMA at Dehra Dun proved to be a vastly more friendly environment for Indian officer cadets. No longer would Indian cadets be looked upon as visiting "natives." This was an academy built specifically to cater to Indian needs and Indian cadets. The early batches of Indian cadets in the 1930s must have had a special bond with the college, for, like them, it was at an early stage of growth. All year round the cadets were surrounded by hectic building activity, as the "Sandhurst of the East" began to take shape. Although the staff of the IMA was predominantly English (exclusively until 1939), relations with the Indian cadets were markedly warmer. The precedent was set by the first commandant, Brigadier Peter Collins (Gurkha Regiment), who worked very closely with the Indian cadets. The bonds of affection that tied Collins to the

Indians can be gauged from the fact that they endearingly referred to Mrs. Collins as their "mommandant."[61] Mrs. Collins responded with typical affection, presenting eight colored glass bowls to adorn the mess tables that were still bare.[62]

At the IMA the Indian cadets could participate freely in all sporting and social events. The authorities at Sandhurst, probably touched by a twinge of conscience, made a gift of a magnificent champions silver cup trophy to the IMA. All of these activities helped build up the *esprit de corps* among the Indian cadets. Even though the Indian cadets at Sandhurst were proud of their links with the institution, their sense of belonging to an elite group was hamstrung by their exclusion from such crucial bonding activities. Finally the IMA cadets had definite and identifiable goals of excellence for which to apply. All could compete for senior cadet appointments as lance corporals, sergeants, and underofficers. Cadets were also eligible to compete for that greatest of prizes, the Sword of Honour. Cadet Smith Dun won the very first IMA Sword of Honour in 1934.[63] Mess arrangements were a significant improvement over Sandhurst. Not only was the catering attuned to religious sensibilities, but also the preparation of the food allowed for the more pungent and savory proclivities of the Indian palate. In terms of cost, too, the IMA was a great improvement over Sandhurst. The fee was set as Rs. 800 for each of the first two terms and Rs. 750 per term thereafter. The total sum for the entire course was Rs. 3,850, a far more sustainable sum for an Indian middle-class family of some means.[64]

In 1938, a government committee reviewing the performance of the IMA cadets was relieved to learn that it was an unqualified success.[65] Three witnesses—Lieutenant Colonel Crawford, Major General R.D. Inskip, and Lieutenant Colonel E.E. Watson—were of the opinion that "the young officers from the Indian Military Academy were considered . . . to be better trained than the average product of Sandhurst. Their tactical training was thorough and of a very high order and as platoon commanders they were considered superior to the old Viceroy Commissioned Officers."[66]

The Indian government, having learned its lesson from past attempts to maintain a system of selection for Sandhurst cadets based purely on nomination, had decided to obtain candidates for the IMA via a competitive exam system. The three-part exam covered general knowledge, languages, maths and sciences, history, and geography.[67] The primary emphasis, however, continued to be placed on the Interview and Record Test, which accounted for a total of five hundred out of two thousand or 2,150 points.[68] It was quite possible for a cadet to pass or fail the entrance exam based purely upon his performance in the interview test. Take, for example, the case of Lieutenant General Gul Hassan Khan (Pakistan army):

> In March 1940, I appeared for the competitive entrance examination to the Indian Military Academy. . . . I managed to fail, not because of ignorance in academic

subjects but because I was late for my interview, which carried five hundred marks. The Board did not take kindly to it . . . [T]he crux of the examination, provided one was an average student, was to hope for good marks in the interview. Six months later I appeared again and on this occasion I made certain I was not late. I passed, being seventh out of the fifteen who were not normally selected.[69]

Successful candidates like Jagjit Singh Aurora and Mohammed Attiqur Rahman usually obtained more than four hundred marks in this test (460/500 and 500/500 respectively). Aurora's total score was a very low 1,087 out of 2,150, and his rank was dead last out of a total of forty-one candidates who passed the exam in October 1935. There is little doubt that Aurora would not have passed the exams without having scored high marks with the interview board.[70] As in the PWRIM, the emphasis at the IMA was on character rather than academic accomplishment. Whatever the interviewing formula used, it seems to have worked. A cursory glance at the postindependence Indian/Pakistani officers who made senior rank indicates that a substantial portion of the most successful ones did exceptionally well in the interview test (see Table 3).

In 1943, as a result of the devastating losses suffered by the Indian/British armies in 1941 and 1942, the lengthy entrance exam process was given up in favor of a faster selection process. Groups of eight candidates were kept under a group testing officer. They were put through a battery of psychological tests, individual and group obstacle tests, group discussions, and then a final interview. According to Lieutenant General S.K. Sinha, during the height of the war (1942–1943), selection standards for officers had been relaxed greatly and just about anyone who applied was accepted. However, by 1944 as the allies were on the threshold of victory, the authorities became much more circumspect in their selection. Sinha recalls that in his batch of sixty applicants, only twelve were selected.[71] The accelerated OTCs at Mhow, Bangalore, and Belgaum probably were opened at the same time the new wartime selection system was introduced at the IMA. Although there were three other officer training programs during the war, all prospective candidates had to enter via the Dehra Dun selection process.

The IMA was able to produce an average of twenty-eight officers each half-year. They were commissioned as second lieutenants on the special list, Indian land forces for a one-year period. Generally, not more than two Indian commissioned officers (ICOs) were attached to one British unit. After an interval of four months, they were asked to state a unit of their preference; care was taken to ensure that they were posted to Indian units as often as possible.[72]

Even before the IMA was in operation, in 1931 the decision was made to expand the eight units to the equivalent of a war division, along with its artillery, armored car, and other support units. More crucial, Indian officers hitherto restricted to staff duties were henceforth allowed to do

Table 3
List of Candidates Securing 400 Plus in the Interview Test, March 1933 to April 1939[73]

MARCH 1933 Joginder Singh Dhillon 450/500
OCTOBER 1933 Mohinder Singh Pathania
OCTOBER 1934 Gopal Gurunath Bewoor 425/500 Jemi H.F. Manekshaw 405/500
OCTOBER 1935 Agha Mohammed Ayub Khan 490/500 Jagjit Singh Aurora 460/500
MARCH-APRIL 1935 Niranjan Prasad 450/500 Sukhwant Singh 400/500 Krishna Lal Thapan 405/500
MARCH-APRIL 1936 Gurbax Singh 490/500
MARCH-APRIL 1937 Mohammed Attiqur Rahman 500/500 Mirza Sikander Ali Baig 460/500
OCTOBER 1937 Sartaj Singh 465/500 Dharti Kumar Palit 465/500
APRIL 1939 Mohammed Asghar Khan 460/500 Sahebzada Yakub Khan 500/500

staff work and cooperate with other units, thus qualifying them for higher command positions.[74] The expansion of the eight-unit scheme to a full division was official acknowledgement of the fact that the first phase of Indianization was working. As the IMA swung into high gear, more and more Indian officers began to join the army, and by 1938 the division had a cavalry brigade attached to it. In April of that year, the Indian Air Force (IAF), too, literally got off the ground with two flights operating from Peshawar and Drigh Road.[75]

The instructors at Sandhurst and the IMA had done their jobs; once again the burden fell upon the somewhat steadier shoulders of the starry-eyed, green Indian second lieutenants to prove to the British and indeed their own countrymen in the ranks that they were fit to command. The experiences of these officers in the formative stages of their army careers amidst an all-white elitist organization must be examined in order to understand the character of the independent Indian army.

NOTES

1. S.K. Brown to governor general of India in council, 1925, BL/IOR, L/MIL/5/844, 30.
2. They included seven captains and two lieutenants, BL/IOR, Mss.Eur.F.111/442, 22–24.
3. "Steps are being taken respecting the grant of commissions to nine Indian officers belonging to the Native Indian Land Forces who have served in the Field," Telegram from secretary of state to Army Department, Simla, 20 August 1917, BL/IOR, L/MIL/7/19006, 110.
4. I have referred to Kanwar Amar Singh's diary extensively in the first chapter. See also Lloyd I. Rudolph, "Self as Other: Amar Singh's Diary as Reflexive 'Native' Ethnography," *Modern Asian Studies*, vol. 31, no. 1 (1997): 143–75.
5. DeWitt C. Ellinwood, "The Special Experiences of Amar Singh," paper presented at Conference on South Asia, November 1994, University of Wisconsin at Madison, 8.
6. Lloyd I. Rudolf, "A Soldier of the Raj? Amar Singh's Military Career," paper presented at Conference on South Asia, November 1994, University of Wisconsin at Madison, 21.
7. Rudra's experiences are detailed in a letter he wrote to Jack Gibson, former headmaster of the Doon School, 9 March 1989, BL/IOR, Mss.Eur.C.478.
8. *Report of the Indian Sandhurst Committee*, 5–7.
9. I.M. Muthanna, *General Cariappa* (Mysore: Usha Press, 1964), 27.
10. The PWRIM was established in March 1922 specifically to prepare cadets for entry into Sandhurst.
11. *Report of the Indian Sandhurst Committee*, 8 (note).
12. Ibid., 9.
13. Humphrey Evans, *Thimayya of India: A Soldier's Life* (New York: Harcourt, Brace, 1960), 40.
14. Thimayya entered Sandhurst in September 1924, Ibid., 56. An interview with the viceroy was an awe-inspiring moment for the young officer cadets. General S.P.P. Thorat was so overwhelmed by the situation that he addressed the viceroy as "Your Majesty," which drew a smile from the usually impassive face of Lord Reading. Lieutenant General S.P.P. Thorat, *From Reveille to Retreat* (New Delhi: Allied Publishers, 1986), 4.
15. See list of Indian cadets at RMC, Sandhurst, BL/IOR, L/MIL/9/319, 97–102.
16. Confidential reports on Indian cadets sent to Sandhurst under the Indianization policy, BL/IOR, L/MIL/9/319, 29.
17. "Muchu" Chaudhuri, "Sandhurst Revisited," *Blackwood's Magazine*, vol. 306, no. 1847 (September 1969), 194.
18. Provisional regulations respecting admission of Indian gentlemen to the Royal Military Academy Woolwich, the Royal Military College Sandhurst, and

Cranwell, Calcutta: Government of India, Central Publication Branch, 1928, BL/IOR, L/MIL/17/5/2290, 3–8.

19. Chaudhuri, "Sandhurst Revisited," 198.

20. S.D. Verma, *To Serve with Honour: My Memoirs* (Kasauli, India: Author, 1988), 6.

21. Evans, *Thimayya of India*, 59–60. General S.D. Verma's official guardian, a Colonel Stooks, lived in Yately, some three miles from Sandhurst, and, on the first Sunday of every month, Verma and the other Indian cadets under Stooks' charge had to bicycle over to receive their monthly pocket money of three pounds. Verma notes, "It was our money, but we had no direct control over it." Verma, *To Serve with Honour*, 9.

22. The unfortunate cadet Rustom Manekji Billimoria, a Parsee, was finally removed from Sandhurst after being described as "distinctly below average" in the official report. Letters, October to December 1928, BL/IOR, S.K. Brown Collection, Mss.Eur.D.808/1, 68–77.

23. *Indian Sandhurst Committee: Report of the Sub-Committee which visited various military education institutions in England and other countries* (Simla: Government of India Press, 1926), 97–104.

24. Chaudhuri, "Sandhurst Revisited," 202.

25. At Sandhurst there was a room servant for every two to three cadets on the same floor.

26. Ibid., 200.

27. Ibid., 202.

28. Evans, *Thimayya of India*, 60.

29. Ibid., 72–74.

30. Cadet N.A.M. Raza noted that as a result his vacation in Switzerland was ruined. See Raza's confidential interview, *Indian Sandhurst Committee: Report of the Sub-Committee*, 100.

31. Evans, *Thimayya of India*, 64. Sant Singh was the 49th Indian cadet to enter Sandhurst (January 1925). He retired as a general in the independent Indian army. BL/IOR, L/MIL/9/319, 111.

32. *Indian Sandhurst Committee: Report of the Sub-Committee*, 104.

33. Chaudhuri, "Sandhurst Revisited," 202.

34. Mohammad Ayub Khan, *Friends Not Masters: A Political Autobiography* (London: Oxford University Press, 1967), 10.

35. Chaudhuri, "Sandhurst Revisited," 201. This opinion is backed by Cadet H.A. Francis, who noted that Indian cadets were refused stripes on the grounds that they were incompetent but that inferior British cadets often were awarded stripes, a point readily attested to by cadet. Thorat, who stated that British cadets inferior to him were given stripes. Cadet Raza pointed out that every British cadet who did not get restriction (punishment) managed to get a stripe. He felt that this was a deliberate policy to prevent Indians from commanding British cadets. See confidential interviews, *Indian Sandhurst Committee: Report of the Sub-Committee*, 99–104.

36. Evans, *Thimayya of India*, 65.

37. See confidential reports on Indian cadets, BL/IOR, L/MIL/9/319.

38. Thorat, *From Reveille to Retreat*, 5.

39. *Indian Sandhurst Committee: Report of the Sub-Committee*, Annexure I, 79.
40. Ibid., 83–84.
41. Ibid., Annexure III, 95.
42. Ibid., Annexure IX, 106–16.
43. C.B. Otley, "The Social Origins of British Army Officers," *The Sociological Review*, vol. 18, no. 2 (July 1970): 216.
44. Maurice G. Garnier, "Changing Recruitment Patterns and Organizational Ideology: The case of a British Military Academy," *Administrative Science Quarterly*, vol. 17, no. 4 (December 1972): 503.
45. C.B. Otley, "Social Affiliations of the British Army Elites," in Jacques van Doorn (ed.), *Armed Forces and Society: Sociological Essays* (The Hague: Moutan, 1968), 88–89.
46. Ibid., 102.
47. Garnier, "Changing Recruitment Patterns," 505.
48. Commissions for Indians: Journal of the Army, Letter from General Officer Commanding Southern Army General Sir Edmund Barrow to Major General M.H.S. Grover, military secretary to His Excellency the commander in chief, army headquarters (AHQ) Calcutta, 12 March, Barrow Collection, BL/IOR, Mss.Eur.E.420/9, 2.
49. Chaudhuri, "Sandhurst Revisited," 202.
50. Evans, *Thimayya of India*, 66.
51. Chaudhuri, "Sandhurst Revisited," 209.
52. M.R.A. Baig, *In Different Saddles* (Bombay and Calcutta: Asia Publishing House, 1967), 32–33.
53. Ibid., 34.
54. Chaudhuri, "Sandhurst Revisited," 201.
55. *Report of the Indian Sandhurst Committee*, 14–15.
56. According to General Thorat, who entered Sandhurst in 1924, the total cost of education at Sandhurst including leave expenses was around Rs. 20,000. The amount had to be deposited with the government before the candidate could appear for the entrance exam for Sandhurst. Thorat, *Reveille to Retreat*, 3.
57. Ibid., 16.
58. Ibid., 21.
59. Ibid., 37.
60. Ibid., chapter 2.
61. Philip Mason, *A Matter of Honour: An Account of the Indian Army, Its Officers and Men* (New York: Holt, Reinhart and Winston, 1974), 466.
62. Sinha and Chandra, *Valour and Wisdom*, 134.
63. Dun was also the first IMA GC under officer and was parade commander in 1934.
64. Regulations respecting admission to the IMA Dehra Dun and for first appointments to His Majesty's Indian land forces, 1931, BL/IOR, L/MIL/17/5/2284, 7.
65. In September 1938, the government of India accepted a resolution passed by the Indian Legislative Assembly. It was adopted in terms of the recommendation of the Skeen Committee that the operation of the Indian Sandhurst (IMA) should be reviewed five years after its inauguration. Although the committee could not complete its work, due to the outbreak of the war, its incomplete report does give

interesting insight into the quality of the cadets for the IMA *India: Legislative Assembly Debates*, 1938, 1525.

66. Quoted in Sri Nandan Prasad (ed.), *Expansion of the Armed Forces and Defense Organization, 1939–47* (New Delhi: Combined Inter-Services Historical Section [India & Pakistan], 1956), 179.

67. Ibid., 4.

68. The total number of marks increased from 1,900 in October 1932 to 2,150 in October 1935.

69. Gul Hassan Khan (the last commander in chief of the Pakistan army), *Memoirs*, 9.

70. Pamphlet of the competitive examination for admission to the IMA, Dehra Dun, and the Royal Indian Navy (RIN), October 1935, BL/IOR, L/MIL/17/5/2282, 26.

71. Sinha, *A Soldier Recalls*, 36.

72. While on the special list, Indian land forces, the Indian officers could continue to wear IMA uniform. They were outfitted with camp and kit allowances of up to Rs. 670 and Rs. 100 respectively. They were also issued a revolver, a compass, and field glasses. Ibid., 4–5.

73. Pamphlet of the competitive examination for admission to the IMA, October 1935, 20–37.

74. S.K. Brown lecture to Imperial Defence College (IDC), October 1931, BL/IOR, L/MIL/5/857.

75. Indianization of the army and formation of IAF, New Delhi: Government of India Press, 1938, BL/IOR, L/MIL/17/5/1800, 1, 18.

4

Wogs in the Mess: The Introduction of Indian Officers into the Colonial Indian Army, 1919–1947

On 16 March 1929 a young Indian second lieutenant embarked upon his journey from Nasirabad to Jullunder to join his new regiment, the 7th Light Cavalry. As he approached his destination, Lieutenant Chaudhuri realized "that this was the test, the crucial posting on which the future would depend."[1] Along with other Indian officers commissioned after Sandhurst, Chaudhuri had completed a brief "acclimatizing" one-year stint with a British unit, the 1st Battalion, North Staffordshire Regiment, in Nasirabad. Now he was on his way to join his permanent unit. The "future" that Chaudhuri mentions was not just his own personal future in the Indian army, but that of the entire Indianization policy. Unlike at Sandhurst and the IMA, the new young Indian officers were usually on their own in their new units. The pressures upon them to perform in the field were immensely greater than any they had known in the military schools. These pressures were not only due to the fact that they were isolated, but because they had finally come into contact with the rank and file of the Indian army. Based upon the unsatisfactory performance of the ICC and other direct-commissioned officers who had preceded the Sandhurst and IMA cadets, the British officers and Indian soldiers had a rather jaundiced view of the new aspirants.

Often one of the first distasteful confrontations experienced by Indian officers when they joined a unit was that of blatant racism, very different from the subtle version practiced in Sandhurst. Chaudhuri recalls the second in command of the North Staffordshire Regiment who habitually belted out epithets for Indians, such as *wog*, *niggers*, and *nig-wigs*. When Chaudhuri politely expressed his discomfort at the major's use of such language, the latter expressed genuine surprise, noting that he did not think

Chaudhuri would mind, for he considered him as "one of us."[2] General S.D. Verma also recalls, "I was called a wog in my own mess . . . chaps five to ten years older treated me as a pariah."[3] John Masters, a former British Indian army officer, echoed these views in his memoirs. He notes, "Some British Regiments treated their attached Indian Army subalterns like dirt. One even made them sit at a separate table in the mess."[4] Other British units, however, mindful of the delicate nature of the job of introducing young Indian officers into an army career, seem to have gone the proverbial extra mile to make them feel at home. Thimayya remembered that when he first joined the Highland Light Infantry in Bangalore for his one-year stint, the British officers of that unit were extremely concerned that they not cause him any offense, noting "you're the first Indian officer we've seen. Headquarters said we'd have to handle you tactfully. We mustn't be snide about Indians in front of you. Mustn't give you beef. We want you to like it here, and we're worried we might drop some bricks."[5] Even when the young Indian officers were posted to their permanent units, they continued to face varying degrees of resistance. S.P.P. Thorat was posted to his permanent unit, the 1st Battalion of the 14th Punjab Regiment in 1927, and recalled that

> the attitude of some Britishers towards their brother officers was not what it should have been. This was particularly noticeable in their social behavior which bordered on being hostile. They made no secret that Indians were not wanted as officers. We were forbidden to bring Indian food or play Indian music even in our own rooms. Some British officers did not allow their wives to dance with Indians in the club; in short we were treated as outcasts.[6]

Some Indian officers including Brigadier P.S. Bhagat and General J.S. Aurora believed that the British officers actually tried to segregate the Indian officers in a separate mess. Tony Bhagat noted that,

> at one time it was proposed that the Indian commissioned officers should have a separate mess. But I think it was soon realised that that was going to make it extremely difficult for Indian officers to get the respect that they must have if they were going to command troops. So mercifully it was not put into practice.[7]

Aurora recalled that the British were determined to preserve the Anglo-Indian rituals of the mess, and food became a major point of confrontation. According to Aurora, "The Indian meals were limited to two lunches a week, and the rest of the time the food had to be British, whereas for most of us [Indians] British food did not suit our palate. Therefore we had to find ways and means of supplementing it and even having food from the Jawans' [privates'] messes."[8] At Singapore Aurora was transferred from his post as messing member when he tried to get the cook to fry the vegetables instead of boiling them every day. In Chaudhuri's unit, Sunday lunch was the only occasion when Indian food was served. And he recalls the jubilation among Indian officers of their sister Indianized Regiment, the 16th Light Cavalry, when, after a "long struggle," they managed to introduce a "mildly curried" vegetable dish with every meal. Like Aurora, Chaudhuri and his fellow Indian officers had to satiate their yearning for spice by taking "substantial" samples during inspections of the troops' meals. Other gastronomic tactics used included the tradition of relying upon the culinary skills and hospitality of the wives of married Indian officers. In certain desperate situations, Indian meals were ordered clandestinely to the tent of the temporarily attached Indian medical officer who was not a member of the regiment, and hence not subject to its dietary restrictions. After the official dinner the Indian officers would converge upon their hapless host's tent to devour their curry.[9]

THE MODEL INDIAN OFFICER

Thimayya selected the 4th Battalion, 19th Hyderabad Regiment as his home regiment. The unit was stationed in Bagdhad, and he joined it in March 1927. Here Thimayya discovered that he had to earn the respect not only of his British colleagues, but also of the Indian soldiers. Most of the men associated command ability and education almost exclusively with British/white officers. Their negative opinions of Indian leadership were confirmed with the first batch of Indian officers. However, as more capable officers like Thimayya and Chaudhuri entered the army, the Indian soldiers were quick to give them the same respect and loyalty they had given to their British officers.[10] Thimayya himself proved to be popular with both his Indian soldiers and the British officers of the regiment. While at Bagdhad, Thimayya was the first Indian appointed assistant provost marshal of the British garrison.[11] Thimayya was fortunate in that his first three commanding officers—Colonel Hamilton-Britton, Colonel Nicholls, and Lieutenant Colonel Lewis—treated him fairly, and were even supportive. Under Nicholls, Thimayya was made temporary Battalion Adjutant until he passed his captaincy exams. At a social level, too, Thimayya found that he was well received by his British colleagues. He and his French-educated wife Nina (also from Coorg) were sought after company by British families.[12]

As the Indian officers gained in seniority and experience, their self-confidence increased accordingly. In late 1939 Thimayya's battalion was transferred to Singapore. The new commanding officer (CO) and his second in command were the dreaded *koi-hai* ("anyone there") type,[13] still locked in the 1857 mode of thought, and relations between the unit's Indian and British officers reached a new low. In Singapore the CO's mishandling of the situation led to a mutiny by the Jat and Ahir companies. The situation was prevented from getting out of hand when Thimayya had a personal meeting with the soldiers and convinced them to stop their mutiny. He then went over the head of his protesting CO to the Fortress Commander Major General Fitzsimmons to have the soldiers armed for an exercise on the shooting range. This show of trust worked, just as Thimayya had foreseen, thus nipping the mutiny in the bud. Although Thimayya had to transfer out of the battalion in October 1941 due to an unworkable relation with his CO, his reputation was in no way sullied by the incident.[14] Indeed, in 1942 at the recommendation of General Polk, commander in chief of the Eastern Command, Thimayya (now a major) was sent to Staff College at Quetta.[15] He graduated second in his class of 140 and chose "combined operations" as his first choice and specified a G-2 operations appointment in the field as his second choice. As second ranked in his class, Thimayya had every right to apply for these positions. However, no Indian had ever been appointed to this high-profile operational post, and here the British balked. Thimayya, to his great chagrin, received the usual G-2 staff duty appointment given to all Indian graduates of Staff College. Once again Thimayya stood his ground and refused the appointment. His luck held, and he was posted as G-2 operations in the 25th Division. But Thimayya's appointment as G-2 to the 25th Division created a problem, for the divisional commander, Major General Davies, had been trying for some time to get his G-3, an Englishman who had not yet gone to Staff College, into that post. However, all G-2 appointments were made by army headquarters (HQ), and the Chief of General Staff Lord Claude Auchinleck sent General Davies "a most imperial rocket,"[16] informing him that Thimayya was the man for the job.

Thimayya's arrival at the 25th Division HQ was not exactly welcome, or so he thought. But after a frank discussion with General Davies, Thimayya was relieved to know that the general had nothing against him or Indian officers.[17] Thimayya, like many other Indian officers, was being overly sensitive to any perceived hostility from the British. This, not surprisingly, led to considerable misunderstanding, but his ability to communicate his apprehensions to his British superiors solved any potential problems that might have arisen.

No sooner had Thimayya settled his differences with his CO, the 25th Division found itself confronting the Japanese at Mungadaw in Burma. There Thimayya was promoted to Lieutenant Colonel and took command of the 8th Battalion, 19th Hyderabad Regiment. He recalls that he "felt a marveleous thrill of pleasure at having full command of the battalion . . . but then a sense of responsibility settled on my back like a heavy burden."[18] Thimayya could not have assumed command at a worse time. For various reasons morale in the battalion was very low and little real patrolling was being done. Nevertheless, Thimayya whipped the unit into shape and organized a successful night attack to take the well-defended 400 feet hill that guarded the approaches to the Mayu Range.[19] Thimayya's handling of the battalion in action, probably a first for any Indian, was cause for great relief among the high command who had placed so much trust in the young Indian officer. No less a person than the corps commander himself called to congratulate Thimayya. The corps commander noted that in the entire corps so many Japanese had never been killed in a single engagement.[20] The rewards were quick to follow; after a month's leave in India he was made temporary G-1 of the division.[21] On Thimayya's return, his battalion took part in a crucial battle against Japanese-held tunnels in the Mayu Range. Here for the first time, three Indian battalions commanded by three Indian lieutenant colonels—Thimayya, L.P. Sen, and Thorat—took part in the same battle. Thimayya's battalion took not only its assigned hill feature "Poland," but also "Pt 109," assigned to Sen's battalion, much to the latter's consternation.

The tremendous success garnered by Thimayya came to the notice of the Supreme Commander Lord Louis Mountbatten, who publicly touted Thimayya as the model successful Indian officer.[22] In the ongoing offensive against the Japanese, Thimayya's battalion was assigned, along with those of Thorat and Sen, to support a British commando attack to secure the beachhead at Kangaw.[23] Once again, the three Indian-led battalions performed splendidly and broke the back of the Japanese defenses.[24] After a well-deserved rest period Thimayya returned to Burma to command the 36th Brigade of the 26th Division, becoming the first Indian to command a brigade in the field (Ramri Island).[25] His brigade was the first to enter Rangoon, where it ironically captured his elder brother, who had joined the Indian National Army (INA) there.[26] Months later the Japanese surrendered. His last appointment in the field before independence came as commander of the 268th Infantry Brigade, part of the British-Indian division assigned to the British Commonwealth forces for the occupation of Japan. In January 1947 he returned to India to join the Indian Armed Forces Naturalization Committee.

Chaudhuri's experience as a new officer in the 7th Light Cavalry largely mirrored those of Thimayya. He, too, had to win the confidence of the Indian soldiers of the regiment who were not only unimpressed with the Indian officers preceding him, but also distinctly skeptical about the abilities of a Bengali officer.[27] Although his ascent up the promotion ladder was not quite as dramatic as Thimayya's, it was steady. Just prior to the onset of hostilities in 1939, he qualified for entrance into Staff College, Quetta.[28] After completing the course (December 1939 through June 1940), he was posted as general staff officer (GSO-3) operations to HQ 5th Indian Division in Secundrabad. In his new posting, Chaudhuri experienced the same opposition that Thimayya had to his arrival. Colonel Frank Messervy (the GSO-1 for the 5th Division) informed Chaudhuri that he was being transferred to G-3 Chemical Warfare. The reason given was that "operations had to handle a number of top secret matters and just then he did not think it appropriate to have an Indian officer in the post."[29] Unlike Thimayya, Chaudhuri swallowed his anger and pride and accepted the transfer. Later he practically filled in the more senior position of the GSO-2 operations who was constantly drunk! During the war, Messervy himself went on to win great fame as an armored division commander in the Western desert and as a corps commander in Burma. Years later, in 1946—when Chaudhuri (then a colonel) was director of Armored Corps, HQ Allied Forces South East Asia (ALFSEA) in Singapore—he ran into Messervy who was general officer commander in chief for Malaya. Something about the quiet and efficient Chaudhuri must have impressed him, for by then he had lost all doubts about the quality of Indian officers; after apologizing profusely for his previous actions, he promptly offered Chaudhuri a position on his staff as brigadier in charge of administration. Chaudhuri, taken aback by the sudden and overly generous offer, declined initially, but Messervy insisted and Chaudhuri soon joined his staff in Kuala Lumpur.[30]

In October 1940 Chaudhuri's division sailed for Post Sudan in North Africa where he served in various staff appointments. Although Chaudhuri did not see any action, in 1943 he was posted as instructor to Staff College, Quetta. Here, too, he faced resistance. General Evans, the commandant of the college, said, "I am unhappy to have you here. You are a junior officer and there are many senior British officers in the course. You will have to use all your tact to ensure that there is no trouble." [31] Fortunately, Chaudhuri got along well with all the officers, and General Evans soon had every confidence in his young Indian instructor. After his tour at Quetta, Chaudhuri was posted to the 16th Light Cavalry for operations in Rangoon, Burma, which is where he ended his wartime career.[32] He was selected by General Auchinleck to lead the Indian victory contingent in London in March 1946. Along with Cariappa, he became one of the first Indians to be selected to attend the Imperial Defence College (IDC), London. In November 1947 he returned to Delhi to become brigadier (War Plans Section) at the army Headquarters.[33]

THE BLACK SHEEP

Thimayya and Chaudhuri represent two of the most successful types of Indian officers. Included in this elite group are others like Cariappa, Sen, and Thorat, to mention but a few. However, there were an equal number of less-than-impressive officers. Earlier we learned that the small district of Coorg in South India was responsible for producing two of the most able Indian officers—Cariappa and Thimayya. Unfortunately, Coorg also produced one of the glaring failures of the Indianization process—C.B. Ponnappa.

Along with Cariappa and Thimayya, Ponnappa, too, benefitted from the availability of an excellent Catholic education. He and his brother were educated at St. Alyosis College High School (graduating in 1915).[34] In 1918 he, along with Cariappa, was called up for training at the Daly College, Indore (renamed as the Training School for Indian Cadets). He and Cariappa became two of thirty-nine cadets who were granted temporary King's commissions on 1 December 1919. He was then posted to Tekrit in Iraq, where he joined the 116 Marathas. Ponnappa appears to have taken part in some minor actions against Arab forces and was mentioned in despatches. On 21 May 1921 he and his unit arrived in Lahore to assist the local authorities trying to suppress the Sikh (Akali faction) agitation. It was here that Ponnappa had his first big clash with authority. According to Ponnappa, his battalion commander Lieutenant Colonel Marsh refused him permission to get married, but he was undaunted and corresponded with Major General Black, the commandant of the Daly College cadet wing, and finally secured leave to get married. When Ponnappa returned to his unit in the summer of 1922, he discovered that Colonel Marsh had left him an adverse annual report. The colonel noted that Ponnappa was argumentative, sulky, and unpopular, and recommended that he should not be retained in the Indian army.[35] Despite these troubles, Ponnappa managed to pass his Captain's exam successfully in March 1926. The battalion was then transferred to Quetta, where Ponnappa was made battalion quarter master. Here, too, he appears to have had a number of tiffs with the new commander Colonel Franks.

On 1 April 1933 Ponnappa was posted to the Madras University Training Corps as its adjutant. He rejoined his battalion on 1 April 1936 and was placed on the Special Unemployed List for 1 April 1937.[36] But if it weren't for the onset of the Second World War, it is likely Ponnappa's Indian army career would have ended then and there. When the war broke out, however, he was recalled to duty at the Maratha Regimental Centre in Belgaum. He became commander of the 11th Maratha Territorial Battalion, which spent the war as a railway protection force in India. In 1946 he was made a full colonel and was made president of the Officers Services Selection Board. His job was to select officers for permanent commission in the Indian army from among those who were granted temporary commission during the Second World War. Once again, his actions resulted in controversy. This time he was called to Meerut to meet the director of the Officers Services Selection Board, Brigadier N.A.M. Raza, to answer charges that he was anti-Muslim in his selection duties.[37] This serious problem seems to have been resolved in Ponnappa's favor, for he soon became president of the board himself. It is possible that the partition of India at this time assisted Ponnappa, for Raza opted for service with Pakistan. However, soon afterward he was posted to Allahabad as brigade commander of the subarea. This was followed by a number of similar postings until his retirement in 1952, still with the rank of brigadier.

Ponnappa's career in the Indian army was troubled, to say the least. He appears to have been in constant conflict with his British colleagues and senior officers. Although Ponnappa has claimed that the crux of the issue was their anti-Indian attitudes, it is unlikely that he did not come across a single fair-minded British officer, as his autobiography seems to imply. The problem appears to have been more a question of his own personality. He appears to have been the opposite of his fellow Kodavas, Cariappa and Thimayya, who were quite outgoing and popular with their British colleagues. Another source of the problem might have been the nature of Ponnappa's commission. It appears that, with the exception of Cariappa, few of the graduates from the cadet course at Daly College, Indore, had great success in their army careers. Hampered by the obviously incomplete nature of the military education they received there, most of them were forced to learn the rudiments of military and leadership skills on the job. This was a process that seems to have proved too daunting for Ponnappa. He almost consistently received votes of no confidence from his commanders. His placement on the Special Unemployed List in 1937 was a final and possibly conclusive vote of no confidence on his record. And, while Ponnappa could lay the blame for this on the doorstep of the British, he had little excuse for his subsequent lackluster performance in the independent Indian army. His career ended within five years in the rank of brigadier, a rank he assumed in 1947.

The lack of an effective military education was not the only cause of failed military careers. Take, for example, the case of M.R.A. Baig, a Hyderabadi who claimed descent from Sultan Murad of Turkey.[38] As a result of his family connections and wealth, Baig was educated at Clifton, one of the elite British public schools. In January 1923 he entered Sandhurst, where he encountered racism for the first time in his life (see chapter 3). He graduated in mid-1924 and was attached to the 4/7th Dragoon Guards in Bolaram (twenty miles from Hyderabad) for his obligatory one-year posting. After that he received his permanent posting in August 1925 to the 16th Cavalry. Baig recalls regimental life as being quite unpleasant, for real integration of the unit never took place, and he and his fellow Indian officers never felt that they "belonged."[39] According to Baig, he and the first two Indian officers of the regiment, Faiz Mohammed Khan and Sheodatt Singh, lived together in a house known as "the native quarter." To Baig, who had lived as an "equal" in Britain prior to his Sandhurst years, this type of treatment was unbearable and, by his own admission, he was "outraged and reacted violently."[40]

In 1928 Baig attended the Cavalry School in Saugor for a seven-month course, followed by a course at the Small Arms School in Pachmari. He returned to his regiment in April 1929 expecting to be appointed its adjutant, and was enraged to learn that he had not been considered for the position.[41] Although he subsequently was sent to the Machine Gun School in Ahmednagar, the perceived rebuff had proved too much for the proud Baig, and he had made up his mind to leave the army. This decision no doubt was aided by the fact that at Ahmednagar, too, he found that Indians were being excluded socially.[42]

Some Indian officers became virulently anti-British in reaction to the racism they experienced. Thimayya recalls the Rajput Captain Kanwar Daulat Singh from Kotah, who, unlike the other Indians in the Hyderabad Regiment, was quick to confront the British at every opportunity. According to his biographer,

> From subsequent conversation, Thimayya gathered that Daulat Singh was a[n] intelligent man, and a fine soldier, but his anti-British feelings coloured his whole life. When his daily work was done, he took off the hated uniform and donned a dhoti [Indian lower garment]. He never touched the foreigner's food. He was always doing Pujas [prayers]. He had his family with him, but kept his wife in purdah [seclusion].[43]

Daulat Singh's anti-British sentiments became so pronounced that, when the battalion returned to India, he was finally dismissed after "trumped-up charges" were brought against him.[44]

In some cases the failure of a career meant nothing less than outright desertion and becoming a "traitor." Mohan Singh was among the first batch of Indians to join the IMA in 1932.[45] He had risen from the ranks as a VCO and had been selected to undergo a training course at Kitchener College, Nowgong, to prepare him for entry into the IMA.[46] Commissioned in 1934, he was attached to the 2nd Border Regiment in Ferozepur for a year, after which he was posted to the 1st Battalion, 14th Punjab Regiment at Jhelum. In February 1941 his battalion embarked for Burma, and Mohan Singh was promoted to major and given command of the headquarters company.[47] In September 1941 the battalion, which was part of the 11th Indian Division's 15th Brigade, was involved in constructing defenses at Jitra near the Malay-Thai border. At this point, according to Mohan Singh, he soon began to feel "tired and depressed."[48] When hostilities commenced, Mohan Singh's battalion was entrusted with the defense of the border fifteen miles north of Jitra. Contact with the Japanese was made on 9 December, and, by the 11th, the battalion was under heavy attack. Constant artillery, air, and tank attacks forced the battalion to withdraw to a position two miles to the rear. Here, too, the battalion was subjected to heavy fire and finally was broken. Mohan Singh himself recalls being under direct fire with remarkable candor: "I had a narrow escape [from a Japanese tank]. After that it did not take me even a fraction of a second to decide my next action. I bolted."[49] According to Mohan Singh, he then seriously began to evaluate his "position" in the Indian army and the "role" of the army. He also appears to have been influenced by Japanese propaganda, for he remarks that, "in contrast to the Japanese propaganda, the British had not given even an empty promise to grant us complete freedom after the war."[50] It was then that Mohan Singh decided that the time was right to approach the Japanese for assistance in starting a movement for India's independence.[51] Accordingly, he established contact with the Japanese via Indian civilians and within a year he established the first brigade of the INA.

THE REASON WHY

Mohan Singh's experiences reflect a rather extreme reaction to dissatisfaction with being part of the British-controlled Indianization process. Yet there is no denying the fact that just about every Indian officer had to undergo the trauma of racism at varying stages in this career. Indian officers reacted differently to the often hostile treatment meted out to them in their units depending on their individual personalities. Some, including Daulat Singh, M.R.A. Baig, Osman Baig, and Mohan Singh, refused to accept or ignore this sort of treatment. They remained constantly suspicious of any moves made by the British and were unable or unwilling to communicate with them. Others, including Thimayya, Cariappa, and Chaudhuri, chose largely to ignore those British officers who were hostile and instead sought to cultivate British officers who were friendly. These Indian officers generally tended to immerse themselves in their careers and pay little heed to the controversy surrounding them. Although none of the officers discussed above appear to have capitulated completely to the negative social aspects of regimental life, they did walk a fine line. According to General Dharti Kumar Palit, "some [officers] sold out to the British socially."[52] And then there were those Indian officers who, for various reasons, were proven unsuited or unqualified for the job at hand but attribute all the blame for their failed careers to British racism; Ponnappa and Kanwar Amar Singh (see above) are two such cases. Probably the most curious "failed" career story belongs to General B.M. Kaul. A Sandhurst graduate (from the same batch as John Masters), Kaul actually left the infantry to join the Army Service Corps (ASC). According to Kaul, he was trying to join the higher-paying military police or the border scouts to provide for his ailing mother but, since neither of these organizations took Indians, he was forced to join the ASC.[53] Whatever the reason for his departure, Kaul's old unit did not want him back when he tried to rejoin it later. For most, a career spent in the ASC would have meant no access to higher-command positions in the field army. But Kaul proved to be a masterful politician and later would ally himself with Indian politicians to take his career to dramatic heights in the independent Indian army.

There is little evidence to suggest that there was a conspiracy by the

British officers of the Indian army to destroy Indianization as most writers and some former Indian officers allege. The responses of British officers to Indianization was just as varied as the responses of their Indian counterparts and was similarly a matter of individual personalities and opinions. Some indeed were opposed to Indianization and did all they could to hamper it without directly disobeying orders. Others, like Thimayya's first three COs and Major General Das' company commander Pete Rees, took an active interest in guiding the careers of their Indian subordinates.[54] Generally, British officers maintained a very professional and "correct" attitude toward Indian officers. If the latter proved to be communicative and able, the British would respond with guarded friendliness and respect. Their attitude toward the Indian officers is best summed up by General J.S. Aurora: "If you were somebody who fitted in, they liked you. If you were aloof or wanted to be on your own, they left you alone."[55] Often senior British officers would hesitate to confer any operational responsibilities upon Indian officers but would relent and apologize for their prejudice when the Indian officer in question showed himself to be equal or even superior to his British counterpart. The Messervy-Chaudhuri story is one such classic case (above). Another such incident involves Major General Das, who was posted to Italy during the Second World War as second in command of the machine gun battalion of the famous 4th Indian Division. When he arrived at his unit, the CO flatly refused to accept Das, and he was given the choice of returning to India or staying on with a demotion to a company commander. A lesser individual might have returned to India, but Das remained. Within a few months the CO was replaced and the new CO saw to it that Das became the battalion commander.[56] Overwhelmingly, the fate of the Indian officers lay in their own hands. If they proved to be professionally incompetent or unable to adjust to the underlying racial ostracism in their respective units, their careers usually floundered. If, on the other hand, they were capable officers and had the ability to ignore the racist jibes, they proved to be successful.

As the Indianization program gathered momentum, Indian officers no longer found themselves totally isolated in their units. However, attitudes toward them did not necessarily soften. General Palit recalls that when he joined his unit, relations actually had deteriorated between the Indians and the British. He was "aghast" to see that there was no mixing between the two and that Indians often were referred to as "wogs." Neither Palit nor the other Indians in his unit ever were invited to the house of either the commanding officer or the second in command.[57] Palit's experience was probably an extreme case, but right up to the Second World War there was constant tension between the ever-increasing numbers of Indian officers and their British colleagues. It was only during the war that the situation improved markedly.

This was caused by the influx of working-class noncareer British officers, who appeared not to suffer from the racial and class prejudices to which their well-heeled upper-class British "brethren" of the prewar Indian army had so steadfastly adhered. Years later, Palit was still somewhat amazed when he recounted how this new breed of British officers would mix freely with Indians. Not only did they communicate openly, but also they ate Indian food in the traditional Indian style (with their fingers), tried to learn Hindi, and even took to Indian music![58]

The war also seems to have softened the old die-hard senior officers' attitudes toward Indian custom and culture, particularly in regard to food. When Chaudhuri was brigadier in charge of administration of the Malay Command on General Sir Frank Messervy's staff in 1946, the general's young senior aide, young Major John Wainwright, approached Chaudhuri with a plea for curry, claiming that he was "browned off" with English meals. When Chaudhuri had some Indian food brought in from the Indian troops' cookhouse, General Messervy stumbled onto the impromptu feast and joined in with great gusto and relish. After that incident Chaudhuri recalls that curry was served more often at the command house.[59]

The social ostracism that Palit and other Indian officers experienced in the army must be understood in the context of the British "club culture" that existed in India at the time. For many British, the various military and civilian social clubs represented the only avenue for meeting other British colleagues and families in a social setting. They represented an oasis where the British could relax and interact with one another without having to worry about impressing the natives. Thus it is not surprising that the clubs proved to be the last all-white bastions against Indian encroachment. Although most of the military clubs opened up to the Indian officers by the Second World War, the exclusive civilian clubs like the Yacht Club of Bombay, the Punjab Club in Lahore, and the Bengal Club in Calcutta kept their doors closed to Indians right up to independence.[60] As Zareer Masani points out,

> The vast majority of Indians, of course, had no desire to enter European society. And the notion of ethnic segregation was by no means new in a caste-ridden society where many Brahmins would still not eat food touched by the lower castes. What made Anglo-Indian racism unacceptable was that it was practiced by foreign rulers and affected precisely those Indians who were most Westernized and had the strongest aspirations to equality.[61]

Perhaps no Indians were more Westernized as a group than the Indian officers. In their case, the exclusion was all the more painful, for the club often represented their only opportunity for social activity, cutoff as they were from their family and friends. The Indian officers were in reality in much the same position as their British counterparts, but without the support system the latter enjoyed to make a military career in India socially bearable. The problems of the Indian officers were exacerbated by the fact that there were barriers to socializing with their own people. When Thimayya's battalion was posted to Allahabad, he and his fellow Indian officers found that they were barred from joining the Allahabad Club. The Indian officers then tried to cultivate ties with the leading Allahabad families but, to their chagrin, were rebuffed.[62] According to Chaudhuri, "The Indian civilians tended to keep aloof from the army, even from the Indian officers. They were in that era both shy and perhaps a little suspicious of the military community."[63]

In a bizarre way, the outbreak of the war proved even more beneficial to the Indian officers and the Indianization program. As the more experienced British prewar officers either became casualties or rapidly were promoted, the Indian officers, who previously had been perceived as intruders in some British circles, became a precious commodity. The most significant change was the disbandment of the eight-unit scheme. Indian officers now could be posted to any unit within the Indian army. Without the Indian officers it is doubtful that the British would have found enough trained officers from their rapidly diminishing British officer pool to command the largest professional army of the war. It was precisely such a lack of adequately trained British officers for the Indian army in the Great War (1914–1919) that had led to the collapse of many Indian units on the western front.[64] Furthermore, important appointments in operational areas also became more accessible to Indian officers. The requirements of the war meant that more and more positions in Staff College at Quetta became open to Indian officers. Similarly, instructor appointments also became available to Indian officers. In December 1939 two Indian officers, Captains Som Dutt and S.M. Shrinagesh, became the first Indian officers to serve on the staff of the IMA. Captains Khalid Jan and K.C. Khanna also joined the academy in August and September of 1940 respectively. The official history of the academy notes that these appointments were "necessitated by the exigencies of the war."[65] The war also placed intense pressure upon Winston Churchill to remove existing restrictions on Indian officers preventing them from punishing British personnel. In a successful argument to repeal this restriction, the secretary of state for India, Leo Amery, noted that George Washington, a senior colonial officer, had been "mortally offended by being put below the youngest joined subaltern from home [Britain]."[66]

The extent to which relations had improved between British and Indian officers by the Second World War can be gauged by comparing two official welcoming talks given to new officers joining the Indian army in 1927 and in 1942–1943. In February 1927 Second Lieutenant Chaudhuri was returning to India aboard the *Dorsetshire* and had to attend compulsory classes on "habits, manners and hygiene in the Orient."[67] He remembers that

> what was more disconcerting was the talk on how to deal with the indigenous population. The natives had to be firmly handled for familiarity would breed disrespect. Native habits and customs were declared to be incomprehensible and generally unclean. Apart from the men enlisted into the Indian Army, the locals were classed as usually dishonest. . . . [T]he emphasis lay on preserving the prestige of the white man which, linked to the Empire, took precedence over everything else, official or personal.[68]

In 1942 the Indian government printed a compilation of "Four Lectures by a Commanding Officer for Officers Joining the Indian Army." Gone were the distorted and unimaginative injunctions to which Chaudhuri referred. The 1942 orientation made a concession to the growing contribution and sensibilities of the Indian officers. It noted that "the I.C.O. varies in capability just as you young officers do. One brigadier wrote 'I could not wish for a better leader British or Indian'—read accounts of decorations they have, the vast majority of them have done and are doing their job well."[69] In a pointed reference to the Indian officers in his audience, the speaker noted that while the British had often been accused of being insular with strangers, the same "sometimes applied to you [ICOs]," and he asked the Indian officers to "do their best in reaching a happy understanding with the new arrivals from England."[70] A more dramatic shift can be perceived in a 1943 pamphlet for the guidance of British commanding officers, staff, and regimental officers proceeding to India. This confidential note appears to have been prepared for senior British officers only. It cautioned all concerned to "be correct and courteous at all times in dealing with Indians; it is their country and, although it may take some time to know their social grades and customs, if this is remembered it will help in dealings with them."[71]

The war provided the Indian officers with a setting to put into practice the skills they had learned in peacetime. It was time to prove in a most emphatic way that they had the ability to lead men into battle. The Second World War was a watershed period in the operational and doctrinal maturation of the Indian officer corps. Although comparatively few in number, enough Indian officers, particularly from the last Sandhurst batches and the "pioneer" group of the IMA served in important operational and staff positions to provide the postindependent Indian army with a viable and competent leadership core.

Table 4
List of Units Selected for Indianization by 1938[72]

CAVALRY:	3rd Cavalry, 7th Cavalry, 16th Light Cavalry
ARTILLERY:	"A" Field Battery (new), 1st (Madras) Field Battery, 2nd Field Battery, 3rd Field Battery, 4th Field Battery. 2nd Brigade to be formed later - followed by another Field Brigade or Mountain Brigade.
ENGINEER:	1 Field Troop. Q.V.O.* Madras Sappers & Miners. No. 44 Division HQ.Coy., Q.V.O.* Madras Sappers & Miners. No. 15 Field Coy., Q.V.O.* Madras Sappers & Miners. No. 5 Field Coy., K.G.V.O.** Bengal Sappers & Miners. No. 22 Field Coy., Royal Bombay Sappers & Miners.
SIGNALS:	4th Cavalry Brigade Signal Troop, 4th Indian Division Signals.
INFANTRY:	2nd Battalion, 1st Punjab Regiment. 5th Battalion, 2nd Punjab Regiment. 5th Royal Battalion, 5th Mahratta Light Infantry. 5th Battalion (Napier's), 6th Rajputana Rifles. 1st Battalion (Q.V.O.L.I.)***, 7th Rajput Regiment. 5th Battalion (Burma), 8th Punjab Regiment. 5th Battalion (K.G.V.O.)**, 11th Sikh Regiment. 4th Battalion (Sikhs), 12th Frontier Force Regiment. 6th Royal Battalion (Scinde), 13th Frontier Force Regt. 1st Battalion, 14th Punjab Regiment. 4th Battalion, 19th Hyderabad Regiment.
OTHER:	Royal Indian Army Service Corps (R.I.A.S.C.) NO. 6, Distribution Supply Coy, Bolarum. Two Anti-Tank Coys (mule) 3 Troops, Two Anti-Tank Coys (mule) four Troops. Indian Army Observation Corps (I.A.O.C.) partial. Indian Army Vehicle Corps (I.A.V.C.) partial. Military Farms - Army Remount Department.

*=Queen Victoria's Own, **=King George the Fifth's Own, ***=Queen Victoria's Own Light Infantry.

NOTES

1. B.K. Narayan, *General J.N. Chaudhuri: An Autobiography, As Narrated to B.K. Narayan* (New Delhi: Vikas, 1978), 58.

2. Ibid., 49.

3. Stephen P. Cohen interview (henceforth Cohen interview) with (retired [henceforth retd.]) Lieutenant General S.D. Verma, Midhurst, Sussex, 28 November 1963.

4. John Masters, *Bugles and a Tiger: A Volume of Autobiography* (New York: The Viking Press, 1956), 15.

5. Evans, *Thimayya of India*, 83. Some British units, while angered by the presence of Indian officers, managed to hide their feelings. General S.D. Verma was posted to the Royal Welch Fusiliers at Quetta. It was only when he had settled into the unit that he learned that there was a good deal of resentment about a "bloody wog being thrust upon us." Verma, *To Serve with Honour*, 14.

6. Thorat, *From Reveille to Retreat*, 21.

7. Zareer Masani, *Indian Tales from the Raj* (Berkeley, Los Angeles: University of California Press, 1987), 25.

8. Thorat, *From Reveille to Retreat*, 26.

9. Narayan, *General J.N. Chaudhuri*, 72–73.

10. The 4/19th Battalion's companies came from North India and included Kumaonis, Jats, Rajputs, and Ahirs. See Evans, *Thimayya of India*, 102–3.

11. Ibid., 106.

12. In Quetta, Nina was the only Indian wife not in *purdah* (veil). Ibid., 146.

13. The Hindu term is translated as "anyone there," and was often the only Hindi words used by the British in India.

14. Singapore fell two months later. Ibid., 171–72.

15. Thimayya was one of six Indians out of 140 students.

16. The 25th Division was then training in Madras and preparing for deployment to Burma. Ibid., 182–84.

17. Ibid., 188.

18. Ibid., 194.

19. Earlier a British battalion had launched a costly and ineffective daytime attack with artillery against the same position. Ibid., 196–200.

20. Ibid., 201.

21. General Davies, who had cracked physically and mentally, was replaced by Major General Sammy Wood, who immediately asked Thimayya to become G-1. Ibid., 201.

22. Ibid., 213.

23. In fact, the 51st Brigade was known as the "All-Indian Brigade." Thorat, *Reveille to Retreat*, 64.

24. Of the half-dozen or so Indian officers who commanded battalions in the Second World War, only one, Lieutenant Colonel Sarvajeet Singh Kalha, was commissioned from the IMA; all the others came from Sandhurst. Unfortunately, Kalha, who was part of the first batch of Indian officers coming out of Dehra Dun, was killed in action in Surabaya in 1946 fighting Indonesian insurgents. Had he sur-

vived, he may well have been the army chief in 1971 instead of Jemi H.F. Manekshaw. Verma, *To Serve With Honour*, 71.

25. Prior to the Kangaw landings, Thimayya had taken over temporary command of the 53rd Brigade replacing its sick commander. Evans, *Thimayya of India*, 224.

26. The INA was established after the fall of Singapore by Major Mohan Singh with the cooperation of Indian civilians and the Japanese army. Its basic objective was to liberate India from British rule with Japanese help (see below).

27. Chaudhuri himself was six feet tall and rather fair, the antithesis of the image of a typical Bengali "babu." Narayan, *General J.N. Chaudhuri*, 69.

28. His nomination to Staff College was facilitated by the close relations he had with his brigade commander, "Mo" Mayne, who later became General Sir Mosley Mayne, general officer commander in chief of the Eastern Command. Mayne provided invaluable guidance to Chaudhuri in his formative years. Ibid., 105.

29. Ibid., 119.

30. Ibid., 119–20.

31. Ibid., 133.

32. The regiment was attached to the 17th Infantry Division under Major General Cowan.

33. Ibid., 141.

34. Brigadier C.B. Ponnappa, *Soldier and Citizen: And Other Writings* (Bangalore, India: Hosali Press, 1971), 3.

35. Ponnappa claims, "I was the assertive type, and the British did not like my attitude." Ibid., 9, 11.

36. The Special Unemployed List scheme was part of the British government's effort to reduce the military budget. Ponnappa was hired as battalion commander in the state forces of Travancore, where he promptly clashed with Lieutenant Colonel Watkins, the commander of the state forces. Ibid., 18–19.

37. This apparently had been brought to Raza's notice by the Commander in chief General Claude Auchinleck. Ibid., 28.

38. Baig, *In Different Saddles*, 2.

39. The other officers were Faiz Mohammed Khan and Sheodatt Singh, who had arrived before him, and Hiralal Atal, Idris, Khalid Jan, and Shiv Verma, who came with and after him. Ibid., 54.

40. Ibid.

41. He was informed by the colonel that this was automatic, for he had obtained a second-class (Q-2) grade at Saugor. Ibid., 70–71.

42. Baig's younger brother Osman, who had followed him into the army, suffered a similar fate. Chaudhuri remembered that, when he joined the 7th Cavalry in 1929, Osman, then a lieutenant in the unit, greeted him with the remark, "you must be mad to join this Regiment, it is the worst bloody regiment in the Army." Like his elder brother, Osman soon left the army. Narayan, *General J.N. Chaudhuri*, 15.

43. Evans, *Thimayya of India*, 97.

44. Ibid., 115.

45. Sinha and Chandra, *Valour and Wisdom*, 138.

46. Mohan Singh, *Soldier's Contribution to Indian Independence: The Epic of the Indian National Army.* (New Delhi: Army Education Stores, 1974,) 34. The objective of the college was "to assist officers in preparing young NCOs for promotion to commissioned ranks and in educating them up to the standard required for a platoon commander." See note setting forth scheme for Kitchener College at Nowgong, Letter from Chief of General Staff Major General Kirke to general staff, 30 August 1927, BL/IOR, Mss.Eur.E.396/11.

47. Singh, *Soldier's Contribution*, 48.

48. Ibid., 50.

49. Ibid., 61.

50. Ibid., 66.

51. The Japanese appear to have tortured many captured Indian officers in an attempt to get them to defect. Captains Dhargalkar and Badhwar of the 3rd Cavalry regularly were beaten and hung up in cages for weeks on end for refusing to join the INA. Captain Ghanshyam Singh of the 16th Cavalry went through many mock beheadings for his refusal to cooperate. However according to S.D. Verma, some Indian officers simply relented to this pressure and joined the INA. Verma, *To Serve with Honour*, 45–46.

52. Taped interviews with Gillian Wright, November 1987-January 1988, BL/IOR, Mss.Eur.R. 193/9. General D.K. Palit, along with some other Indian officers in his unit apparently forced into a tight-knit group of their own by British ostracism, began to perceive any Indian officer who still went out of his way to make contact with the British as a "toadie." See Masani, *Indian Tales from the Raj*, 25.

53. Cohen interview with Lieutenant General B.M. Kaul, New Delhi, 19 December 1964.

54. See Ibid. and also Wright interview with Major-General M.N. Das, BL/IOR, Mss.Eur.R. 193/9. Das remembers that Pete Rees, who was his company commander, was instrumental in guiding him through his delicate first year in the Indian army. Following the war, Rees was promoted to major general and became the commander of the boundary force that was responsible for overseeing the flow of refugees to and from the newly created India and Pakistan. Allan Campbell-Johnson, *Mission with Mountbatten* (London, New York: Robert Hale, 1951), 176.

55. Masani, *Indian Tales from the Raj*, 25.

56. Interview with Major General M.N. Das, BL/IOR Mss.Eur.R. 193/9.

57. Interview with General D.K. Palit, Ibid.

58. Ibid.

59. Narayan, *General J.N. Chaudhuri*, 73.

60. One of the reasons some clubs opened their doors to Indians was because of the actions of the British officers. When S.D. Verma and other Indian officers were rejected membership in the Peshawar Club, the CO of the regiment (16th Cavalry) decided not to hire out any horses to the club, forcing it to end its exclusion of the Indian officers. Verma, *To Serve with Honour*, 22. Thimayya's CO in the Highland Light Infantry (HLI) also tried to get the United Services Club in Bangalore to let Thimayya become a member. When he failed, the officers of the HLI threatened to resign en masse from the club, but Thimayya, who was only attached to the unit for a year, managed to persuade them not to do so. Evans, *Thimayya of India*, 88.

61. Masani, *Indian Tales of the Raj*, 53.

62. Narayan, *General J.N. Chaudhuri*, 111.
63. Ibid., 74.
64. See chapter 1.
65. Sinha and Chandra, *Valour and Wisdom*, 150.
66. Leo Amery to marquess of Linlithgow, India Office, 1 September 1942, BL/IOR, Mss.Eur.F. 125/11. vol. 2, 673.
67. Narayan, *General J.N. Chaudhuri*, 45.
68. Ibid., 45–47.
69. Four letters by a commanding officer for officers joining the Indian army, BL/IOR, L/MIL/17/5/2225, 26.
70. Ibid.
71. (Not to be published) notes for the guidance of commanding officers, staff and regimental officers proceeding to India with a brief summary of the more important regulations and instructions applicable, General HQ India, WO, January, 1943, BL/IOR, L/MIL/17/5/2330, 8.
72. Indianization of the army and formation of the IAF, BL/IOR, L/MIL/17/5/1800, 21–22.

5

The Roots of Doctrine: Modernization of the Indian Army, 1919–1939

In the years preceding the First World War, critics of the Indian army and particularly the Cardwell system had described it as an "albatross" around the neck of the British army. When the system was reintroduced after the war in the 1920s, a new generation of critics took up the anti-Cardwell torch. To many of them it appeared that the British army was essentially "regulated by the conditions prevailing on a portion of one of the frontiers of the Empires' constituent parts."[1] The chief concern was that the Indian army, with its sights firmly set on frontier warfare, would hamper any progress the British army might make toward *mechanized warfare*, the buzzword of the "progressives" in the interwar British army. An older concern was that imperial commitments, to India in particular, would sap the strength of the small postwar British army.

This pessimism about the Indian army's ties with the British army became the chief concern of a younger generation of British reformers—including Fuller, Ironside, Hobart, and Lindsay—all of whom saw the Cardwell system as a major barrier to change in the British army.[2] However, running concurrently with this negative view of the Indian army was another radically different appreciation of its utility. This opinion, held primarily by senior officials at Whitehall, began to regard the Indian army as nothing less than an indispensible partner to the smaller British army in the defense of the entire British Empire, a view no doubt consolidated by India's considerable contribution in the Great War. These optimists won the debate on military modernization in the interwar period. They helped initiate events that would not only better integrate the Indian army into the greater scheme of imperial defense, but also dramatically influence the military doctrines of the two armies. This chapter is an attempt to analyze the doctrinal evolution of the Indian army in the post-1919 era. It will seek to demonstrate just how changing perceptions of the Indian army altered its role from that of internal and border security to that of a conventional "medium-power" army capable of intervening in any theater of combat throughout the world.

A MATTER OF MONEY

The 1919 appointment of the Army in India Committee, led by Lord Reginald Esher, signaled the first moves toward integrating the Indian army with the British army. The committee considered among other things the impact dominion status would have upon India's contribution to imperial defense. According to the Esher Committee report,

> India has now been admitted into partnership with the Empire, and the Indian Army has fought, alongside troops from other parts of the Empire, in every theatre of war. Its responsibilities have thus been greatly widened, and it can no longer be regarded as a local force, whose sphere of activity is limited to India and the surrounding frontier territories. It must be treated as part of an Imperial Army, ready to serve in any part of the world.[3]

The committee's report, submitted in 1920, put forth the radical recommendation that the Indian army be made directly responsible to the British government rather than to the viceroy. The report suggested that the Indian army could be used to bypass restrictions on the size of the British military as agreed upon in the postwar negotiations. The Esher Committee essentially called for the all-important appointment to the post of the military secretary of the India Office be made by the chief of imperial general staff (CIGS). Furthermore, the committee suggested that the appointment of the commander in chief for India should be made only after taking the "advice" of the CIGS. The proposals merely served to alarm the Indian government, which had no intention of handing over control of the army to the British government and the Committee for Imperial Defence (CID). Fortunately for it, unexpected help came from the nascent Indian Legislative Assembly. One of Esher's ill-thought-out plans had been to make extensive use of the Indian army to police the British Empire and the mandated territories. This proposal immediately ran afoul of the Indian politicians. Sir P.S. Sivaswamy Aiyer introduced fifteen resolutions, basically rejecting the entire Esher Committee report. The resolutions also emphatically rejected any proposal to make the Indian government relinquish control of the army to Whitehall. The new Legislative Assembly declared

> That the Army in India should not, as a rule, be employed for service outside the external frontiers of India except for purely defensive purposes, or with the previous

consent of the Governor General-in-Council in very grave emergencies, provided that this resolution does preclude the employment on garrison duties overseas of Indian troops at the expense of His Majesty's Government and with the consent of the Government of India.[4]

Indeed, as far back as 1919 when the Esher Committe was formulating its report, Lord Chelmsford had insisted that, "so long as India pays,—and I do not suppose the War Office are going to propose to the English Treasury to take over the charges of the Indian Army,—India must control its own Army."[5] The next year the Secretary of State for India Edwin Montagu also declared, "We must definitely get it out of our heads the vague idea too often entertained that India is an inexhaustable reservoir from which men and money can be drawn towards the support of Imperial resources or in pursuance of Imperial strategy."[6]

The Indian government led by the Viceroy Lord Chelmsford gratefully accepted the Sivaswamy Resolutions passed by the Legislative Assembly in 1921. The Indian government and the Indian politicians had no intention of paying to police the rest of the empire. Upon this particular issue, at least, the two traditional rivals could agree fully. In fact, relations between the Indian government and the Indian legislators were so good at this time that the Commander in Chief Lord Rawlinson was of the opinion that the Legislative Assembly's attitude was one of "pleasing moderation." He noted that the budget, which included some extra taxation to fund army spending, passed through "without much serious difficulty."[7]

Despite this unlikely cooperation to defeat the Esher proposals, in reality the Indian government found itself pushed inexorably into the orbit of increasing imperial defense commitments. In 1927 contingency plans were initiated for sending Indian troops to protect the Persian oil fields, with the understanding that "no financial liability whatsoever will fall upon India."[8] In 1928 the Indian army was committed to sending a division to Iraq and two independent brigades to Singapore.[9] By the 1930s the Indian army had much of its strength scattered in outposts ranging from the Far East to Africa, just the sort of situation the Indian government had intended to avoid. Even worse, until 1933 the army received no financial assistance from the British government. How, then, did this come about? In order to answer this question we must examine the shift in the strategic perception of the leadership of the Indian army during the interwar period.

The lack of funds posed the main stumbling block to any enhanced Indian involvement in imperial Defense. Indeed, in 1922, soon after the Great War, the Retrenchment Committee led by Lord Inchappe effectively froze any prospects of the army's expansion or modernization.[10] If, therefore, the army was to modernize for its role as an imperial defense force, the British treasury would have to help. A CID subcommittee report on Indian defense requirements supported this view by noting in June 1922 that it "recognized that the Indian Army cannot be treated as if were absolutely at the disposal of His Majesty's Government for service outside India." The committee accepted the Indian government's view that "the Indian Army should not be required to permanently provide large overseas garrisons." The cost of such a garrison, moreover, "should be borne by His Majesty's Government, or by the dependency or colony requiring their services."[11] In 1933 the British Cabinet–appointed Garran Tribunal allotted an amount of 1.5 million pounds to India from the British treasury to finance the portion of the Indian army that would act as an imperial intervention force.[12] With the prospect of British government financial backing for a modern intervention force, the Indian government's attitude toward imperial defense softened considerably. As Viceroy Lord Linlithgow noted in 1937, "You have the money—we have the men."[13]

In March 1938, amidst a worsening security situation in Europe and at the urging of the Secretary of State for War Hore-Belisha, the CID set up a committee led by Major General H.R. Pownall to look into the reorganization and modernization of the Indian army.[14] The committee acknowledged that the system of collective security had failed and that the empire was seriously threatened by the axis powers. Yet, on the other hand, the committee noted that the frontier menace to India from Afghanistan and Russia had decreased. The committee noted that, "there are grounds for the belief that on the present scale of her defence forces India is less under insured than are other parts of the British Empire. Moreover, the degree of readiness of the forces in India is in some respects higher than elsewhere, and she maintains a large standing army in peace." The committee noted that the Indian government felt willing to place one division at Britain's disposal "contingent upon effect being given to certain measures reorganizing and reequipment of the army in India."[15] In order to implement the new role of the Indian army successfully, the committee deemed it essential that those Indian units slated for the imperial reserve must adhere strictly to the standards of British home units. Thus, modernization of a portion of the Indian army became imperative. At the time of the filing of the report, the Indian army was divided into three categories—covering troops, the field army, and internal security forces—with the allotment of forces described in Table 5.

For the financing of this modernization and reorganization, the committee drew attention to the fact that the government of India had made it clear that no increase could be made in the current (1938) estimates amounting to Rs. 45 crores (33,750,000 British pounds). The Pownall Committee itself estimated that the British government would have to provide an additional 2,285,000 pounds annually and that a further sum of 870,000 pounds from imperial funds might be needed each year.[16]

With general agreement on the Pownall proposal, fueled in part by the deteriorating security situation in Europe, a further committee established

Table 5
Allotment of the Army in India[17]

Units	Covering Troops	Field Army	Internal Security	Total
Cavalry: British	-	4	-	4
Indian (horse)	3	8	5	16
Indian (armoured car)	1	1	-	2
Artillery: R.H.A. Batterys	-	3	-	3
Field	4	40	-	44(a)
Mountain	16 1/2	8	-	24 1/2(b)
Medium	1/2	5 1/2	-	6
Heavy	-	-	2	2
A.A.	-	1	-	1
Infantry: British Bns	7	10	26	43
Indian Bns	46	30	20	96

(a) Includes 'A'(Indian) Brigade
(b) Includes 7th Light Battery

Abbreviations: R.H.A, Royal Horse Artillery; A.A., antiaircraft; Bns, battalions.

in the summer of 1938 under Admiral of the Fleet Lord Chatfield sought to examine just how the modernization scheme would be paid for and implemented. The Chatfield Committee, while agreeing with the general conclusions of the Pownall report, felt that the whole Indian army, not just a single imperial reserve division, needed modernization. The committee proposed a more elaborate reorganization of the army, detailed in Table 6.

In addition to the reorganization plan, the committee submitted an estimate of the finances needed to modernize and expand certain key defense industries:

Metal and Steel factory, for the manufacture of heavy and light bombs (Rs. 80 lacs).

Gun and Shell factory (Rs. 73 lacs).

Rifle factory (Rs. 73 lacs).

Ammunition factory (Rs. 10 lacs).

Gun Carriage factory (Rs. 6 lacs).

Table 6
Detailed Distribution of Units[18]

Unit	Permanent Garrison	Northern Command Reserve	Coast Defence	Internal Defence	General Reserve	Total
British Cavalry: Light Tank Regt	-	-	-	-	2	2
Indian Cavalry Light Tank Regt	-	-	-	-	4	4
Indian Cavalry Armd Regt	4	-	-	-	-	4
Field Arty Regt (British)	2	2	-	-	1	5
Field Arty Regt (India)	-	-	-	-	2	2
Mountain Arty Regt (India)	4	1	-	-	-	5
Medium Arty Regt (British)	1	-	-	-	-	1
Heavy Arty Btty (India-Coastal)	-	-	2	-	-	2
A.A. Btty (India)	-	-	-	-	3	3
A.Tk. Btty (British)	-	-	-	-	1	1
Ind Field Pack Co: Sappers&Miners	1	1	-	-	1	3
Ind Field Co: Sappers&Miners	7	3	1	-	3	14
British Infantry Bns	-	-	-	-	2	2
British Infantry Bns	5	4	5 1/2	15 1/2	4	34
Indian Infantry Bns	45	10	3	8	9	75

Abbreviations: Regt, regiment; Arty, artillery; Btty, battery; A.A., antiaircraft; A. Tk., antitank; Bns, battalions.

Cordite factory (Rs. 24 lacs).
Filing factory (Rs. 32 lacs).
TNT factory (Kirkee) (Rs. 70 lacs).[19]

On the crucial financing estimate, the committee calculated that the total cost would be:

Army—Rs. 36.26 crores = 27.20 million British pounds.
Air Force—Rs. 6.21 " = 4.66 " " "
Navy—Rs. 2.62 " = 1.96 " " "
Total—Rs. 45.09 " = 33.82 " " "

The committee felt that, while India should bear some of the burden, the bulk of the 33.82 million pounds for the initial modernization cost must come from Britain over a five year period.[20]

India generally welcomed the sweeping proposals by the Chatfield Committee. Generals S.F. Muspratt (military secretary, 1931–1933) and Auchinleck (DCGS, India, 1936–1938) noted that the "conclusions of the Chatfield Committee are far-reaching and the recommendations made in report are likely to influence profoundly the future of the forces in India."[21] Their only objection was to the committee's proposal to reduce the army size,[22] a longtime goal of British reformers, including the secretary of state for war. As Muspratt and Auchinleck observed, "Coming at a time when the rest of the world is furiously increasing its armed forces, the proposed reductions of the army in India on the score of then being surplus are certain to prove controversial."[23] They were correct. With the imminent outbreak of war, the British general staff refused to approve any troop reductions. In June 1939 the British Cabinet agreed to assuming the added cost in the Chatfield report. The same year, the general staff in India issued its first modernization plan. The plan detailed the peacetime unit strength of the army and allocated units for deployment in either the external defense force, based in the Deccan, or the general reserve headquartered at Meerut and Lucknow. The plan called for a major expansion and modernization of defense-related production facilities, including gun and shell, metal and steel, and ammunition and explosive factories. It also called for an immediate conversion from the obsolete Berthier section machine gun to the more modern Czech-inspired Bren section machine gun.[24]

THE OBSTACLES

While the various official committees attempted to modernize and reorganize the Indian army and its supporting British units within the existing framework of the Cardwell System, the radical reformers were in complete opposition to it. According to B.H. Liddell Hart, "So long as the Cardwell system is maintained they [British battalions in India] are worse than superfluous, since not only are they preserved in a form that does not meet the conditions of modern war, but a similar number of units of the same type have to be maintained at home."[25] The proposed remedy of the radical reformers was the separation of the two armies. According to J.F.C. Fuller, "If mechanised arms cannot operate in this [Afghanistan] theatre of war, the reorganization of the army at home will either be seriously delayed, or two armies will have to be maintained, one for European warfare and the other for Oriental."[26] The most common scheme proposed was the creation of two separate active armies: the first one of long service (twenty years) for colonial duty and the second of shorter service for continental duty in the event of a major war.[27]

The reformers complained vociferously that the Cardwell system forced the British army at home to maintain similar units to reinforce those in India, thus deflecting it from mechanization. There is, however, no reason to believe that the reformers would have gotten their wishes had the British garrison (45 battalions) in India been cut drastically. After all, the British battalions in India were maintained wholly by Indian taxpayers' money. In the event of them being removed from India, they in all probability would have been disbanded, further reducing the emaciated British army. One British official noted morosely that a reduction in British units would throw those units "on to the Imperial Budget, or, as the only alternative, force us to disband them and so to weaken the armed strength of the Empire as a whole without any relief to the British taxpayer."[28] So even without these battalions, no extra money or forces would be made available in Britain to contribute toward the military modernization as the reformers had hoped. The main obstacle to the mechanization of the army was not the Cardwell system, but rather the extreme paucity of funds.

When Lord Rawlinson (1920–1925) succeeded Sir Charles Monro (1916–1920) as commander in chief for India in the autumn of 1920, he was plunged into "the old problems of military efficiency and financial stringency."[29] Although Rawlinson considered that

> the provision for internal defence is already dangerously small, he had reluctantly suggested a reduction in the British establishment of 6,000 troops to 59,000 in all, but this would not be possible before 1922. As it was the British contingent was under-strength and required an actual increase of 7,000 men even to reach the proposed reduction total.[30]

The Viceroy Lord Chelmsford (1917–1921) concurred with the above views and noted that recruitment and organization of the British army always took into account the fact that India maintained a minimum strength of British troops. Hence, any reduction of the British garrison in India would raise a vast number of difficult and complex questions.[31] India saved the British taxpayers from supporting no less than a quarter of the British army. Of the 252,000 British troops in 1921, 65,501 (26%) were stationed in India (including Aden Garrison) and supported wholly by Indian tax money.[32] Not surprisingly, opposition to any massive reduction of the forces in India came not only from India alone, but also from the British general staff. The Chief of Imperial General Staff General Sir Cyril Deverell (1935–1937) staunchly opposed any attempts by the Secretary of State for War Hore-Belisha (1937–1940) to reduce the India garrison. In a letter to the prime minister in November 1937, Hore-Belisha noted, "The elimination of the Indian obsession, which refuses to allow objective examination of the proper disposition and organization of our Imperial Forces, and assumes that the Indian commitment is fixed for all time on unchanging traditions and that it must govern the pace and capacity of development of the rest of the army."[33] In another letter he noted, "A cardinal feature of readaption of the Army is an impartial examination of whether India's share of our personnel is not disproportionate. Such an examination he [Deverell] is unwilling to undertake."[34] Having reached an impasse with Deverell, Hore-Belisha decided to replace him with General Gort, "who is the most dynamic personality I have met in the Army, and who is bred in an independent school. He could devote most of his time to executive reorganization of the Army."[35] With Deverell out of the way an exuberant Hore-Belisha delivered his first army estimates speech at the House of Commons in March 1938. He outlined a total sum of 108,500,000 pounds, the highest since 1914–1918, and repeated his view that "India must no longer govern Army organization and distribution. For this reason the Prime Minister was prepared to initiate discussions between the War Office and the India Office."[36]

In reality the Indian army was not as averse to reductions as critics have made it out to be. The military budget was in fact placing a great strain on the economy. In 1920 the Indian government spent more than 40 percent of its budget on the military.[37] In May 1921, the new Viceroy Lord Reading appointed a committee under the Commander in Chief (India) General Rawlinson to examine "Indian military requirements." Rawlinson, despite the objections of his general staff, acquiesed to the committee's plan for the removal of three British cavalry regiments and five battalions of British infantry.[38] However, as soon as the committee submitted its report, the Muslims of the Madras presidency began a violent anti-British agitation—"the Moplah rebellion"—which postponed consideration of it.[39] A similar rejection of the proposal by the British Cabinet quickly followed.[40] Although Rawlinson was pleased by the cabinet's decision, with the help of the Inchappe Committee's report he did manage to push through some reductions in both the British and Indian components of the army. "It is," he argued, "more important for the internal peace of India that we should balance our budget, than we should keep extra troops."[41] By 1925 the army in India had been reduced to an establishment of 197,000: 57,000 British soldiers and 140,000 Indian troops—respectively 24,000 and twelve thousand fewer than in 1914.[42]

It is also important to note that India was neither the only nor the most draining region in terms of imperial commitment. Restoring order in Ireland remained the single largest burden that the British army had to bear in the early 1920s. The "Irish Ulcer" more than anything else prevented the Cardwell System from functioning effectively and upset traditional patterns of training and deployment. At the height of the conflict in Ireland, on 10 December 1920 when martial law was proclaimed in four Irish counties—Cork, Tipperary, Kerry, and Limerick—no less than fifty-one British battalions were deployed in Ireland.[43] In August 1921 the British Cabinet actually decided to hold back troops destined for India in order to deploy them in Ireland if necessary.[44] Only after the Anglo-Irish agreement in December 1921 did a gradual removal of the British garrison in the Irish Free State begin.[45]

THE DOCTRINE

While the Indian army lagged behind the British army in terms of equipment, the same deficiency did not necessarily apply to doctrine. When Sir Giffard Martel arrived in India in the late 1920s prior to taking an instructor's position at Staff College, Quetta, he wrote to Liddell Hart—a fellow military reformer and staunch critic of the Indian Army—that the "army in India is in no way the dud show that people at home suggest—a real live show in many ways though short of equipment."[46] Even though the Indian army did not take to armored warfare as enthusiastically as the reformers would have wished, it certainly did not stop its Staff College at Quetta from planning and war-gaming the latest mechanized warfare doctrine.

In fact, ever since the Indian army established Staff College at Quetta, it had kept abreast of the latest doctrines from Europe. A joint entrance exam for the staff colleges at Quetta and Camberley indicates that these two vital operational training centers closely coordinated their educational programs. Candidates had to be well versed in the latest debates on military modernization. Their questions covered British military strategy during the Great War ("Westerners" vs. "Easterners"), the possession of mobility for a fighting force, the role of armored fighting vehicles and planes in policing the empire, and the impact of the Cardwell system and ideas to change it.[47]

Significantly, the more "realistic" of the many inter- and postwar British officers who propagated mechanized warfare doctrines spent a significant portion of their formative years at Quetta. Even Martel, who often chaffed at what he perceived to be the army's foot-dragging on mechanization, conducted numerous mechanized war games at Quetta. In 1932 he and his students drafted a bold plan for taking Kandahar (in Afghanistan) in seventy days with light tanks and aircraft.[48] General Percy Hobo Hobart, the first commander of the permanent tank brigade in 1933, also served as an instructor at Quetta, where he developed many of his radical views on armored warfare.[49] General John Burnett-Stuart, one of the most influential British officers in regard to armored warfare, also spent a considerable portion of his time in India. His biographer records that "he received a sound education in small-units tactics during his service with the Rifle Brigade [1897–1898] in India.[50] In 1920 Burnett-Stuart returned to India as general officer commanding Madras District and was instrumental in putting down the Moplah disturbance. During those operations he became one of the few, and probably the only, interwar British officers to make large-scale use of highly mobile columns of infantry, armored cars, and pack artillery in an operational environment.[51]

Quetta contributed to the doctrinal maturation of another British officer, General B.L. "Monty" Montgomery. In June 1934, freshly promoted to the rank of full colonel, Montgomery assumed the post of chief instructor at Quetta. His brother Brian and close friend General Dudley Ward felt that it was in Quetta that Monty's "tactical concept of war had . . . fully matured." General Ward noted, "People like Liddell Hart I think are vastly overrated. They were obsessed with mobility—which is fine if you can have it. But it isn't often so; and the only way you can win battles is to defeat the enemy who wants to deprive you of that mobility. It was Monty who taught us how to do this."[52]

Service in India tended to give many of these reformers (with the exception of Hobart) a more realistic approach to mechanization. As commander of the 3rd Division, Burnett-Stuart believed that mechanization was an inevitable but slow process. He recognized the continued existence of the Cardwell system and felt favorable toward partial mobility: four armored divisions with at least one in Egypt and one in India.[53]

Furthermore, the image of an Indian general staff obsessed with frontier soldiering as painted by the reformers and critics of the Indian army is inaccurate. The majority of the interwar Indian army commanders, including Rawlinson, Chetwoode (1930–1935), Auchinleck (1941, 1943–1947), and A.P. Wavell (1941–1943) were all dynamic and progressive military leaders. Chetwoode, in fact, served as the general officer commanding of the Aldershot Command prior to becoming commander in chief for India. In September 1925 Chetwoode commanded one side in Britain's first large-scale peacetime maneuvers since 1914. This was the first exercise to test the new concepts of mechanized warfare. It predictably turned into a fiasco and strengthened Chetwoode's caution against rapidly adopting such a radical new method of fighting without adequate preparation.[54]

As commander in chief for India (1930–1933) Chetwoode stood alongside the ranks of cautious modernizers, but he had no intention of being a defender of the status quo. In an address to the cadets at Staff College, Quetta, he bitterly criticized the intellectual stagnation of the officer corps in both the British and Indian armies:

> I do not think that, as a class, they [officers] have improved in general education, or military instinct and leadership, since the war. I have found men all over India who evidently scarcely read the papers, and quite unaware of the larger aspects of what is going on in India around them, and still less of a stupendous events outside this country. I am rather afraid that quite a number of the average Staff College students aim at being correct, methodical, 'sealed pattern' staff officer, ground out to pattern by the Quetta and Camberley mill. Am I altogether wrong in thinking that, to many Englishmen, to be independent in thought, to have imagination, to go outside the obvious, to be different to others, is to be almost un-English, or even that more frightful 'not sound.'[55]

Even Brian Bond, who labels Chetwoode as one of the conservatives on mechanization, felt compelled to describe Chetwoode's Quetta address as "the most devastating indictment of the military profession by a senior-ranking officer in the inter-war period."[56]

Prior to taking over as army chief in India, Wavell served as commander of the experimental 6th Infantry Brigade, during which time he penned an article in the *Journal of the Royal United Services Institute*, noting that while mechanization was inevitable, it would happen gradually. More importantly, Wavell noted that a mixed combined-arms unit of tanks and highly trained infantry would be the way of the future.[57] Wavell's emphasis on infantry support was actually a step ahead of the solely armor-based concepts of his fellow reformers and would play an important role in his efforts to modernize the Indian army during his tenure as its commander in chief from 1941–1943.[58]

The caution of these Indian commanders in chief toward rushing headlong into a new system of warfare has often been seized upon by the reformers and researchers as evidence of their lack of progressive ideas. In reality the Indian general staff more often than not had a far better idea of the true capability of their army and officers and of the limitations of resources and finances than did reformers.[59] This came about due to the fact that the Indian army was deployed almost permanently in operational conditions from the Far East to the Middle East. Constantly embroiled in coping with unexpected situations, the Indian general staff had to make the best possible use of a significantly smaller financial budget than its British counterpart. An excellent example of this commonsense approach is evident on the question of whether tanks should be used in India or not. Tanks, as Fuller pointed out, may well have been useful on the frontier, but were they necessary? The Indian army had already secured a firm handle on the tribesmen with a combination infantry, armored cars, and a few RAF squadrons. In view of the financial situation, would it have been possible or even desirable to establish tank regiments on the frontier with all the tremendous costs it would have entailed? The first twelve production Carden-Loyd Mk. I light tanks actually arrived in India in July 1932; they were joined by eighteen more in September. Plagued by mechanical failures in the harsh terrain and the high temperature of the subcontinent, the tanks were used primarily as experimental units with two companies being formed: Neither of them saw any service on the frontier.[60]

The metamorphosis of the Indian army's strategic role to that of imperial defense necessitated a radical move toward mechanization. But even at this eleventh hour the level heads of the Indian army led the way in helping to establish the standard doctrine for the British and Commonwealth armies in the forthcoming war. Actual material change in the army was slow, for the need to rearm the British home army first saw to that. But the Indian army was already moving ahead with its own reorganizational plans.

THE ANATOMY OF MILITARY MODERNIZATION

In December 1939, even as the Chatfield Committee worked through its report, the Chief of general staff's office sent a note to all regional command headquarters in India. The note pointed out that the rapid mechanization of armies in Europe had "appreciably modified the theory and practice warfare developed with the older types of forces and now a tactical technique is rapidly being evolved."[61] The note called for the closing of the gap between British and Indian armies. However, the note also stated that "stereotyped higher formations such as corps and divisions which form the basis of organization of European armies are not likely to be needed by a modernized army in India."[62] The note continued that cavalry and infantry brigades were the best formations in peacetime. The last stipulation is puzzling, for it seemed to go against the move to match the Indian army with the British army. The Chatfield Committee, which originally put forth the proposal, felt that such peacetime organization was wasteful and that in time of war these units would be created and organized specially.[63] The note indicated that future modernization plans would enable the cavalry light tank regiments to be equipped with the latest two-pounder (pdr) gun tanks, the artillery would be fully mechanized with modern guns and tractors, and the infantry battalions would get sufficient transport to carry all weapons and unit equipment, bringing it, approximately, up to the 1938 model for British U.K.–based battalions.[64]

All of these plans, coming to fruition as they did on the eve of war, did not transform the Indian army into a well-equipped modern army overnight. As Bond points out:

Table 7
Planned Composition of Indian Units[65]

British or Indian Light Tank Regt:	3 sqdns (squadrons) + sqdn HQ and Regt HQ - 3 troops of 4 light tanks in each sqdn - 4 tank mortars = 41 tanks and 80 wheeled vehicles.
Indian Cavalry Armoured Regt:	Regt HQ + sqdn HQ - 3 troops of 3 armoured cars - 1 sqdn of 3 troops of 4 light tanks each - 4 tank mortars = 14 light tanks, 24 armoured cars, 68 wheeled vehicles.
Indian Cavalry Motor Regt:	Regt HQ + sqdn HQ - 3 sqdn of 3 troops of 3 sections - each section in one 15 cwt trucks - 1 LMG = 46 LMG's, 2 At-Tk rifles, 9 2in mortars, 108 wheeled vehicles.
British and Indian Field Artillery Regt:	Regt HQ - 4 batteries of 4 guns - 113 vehicles.
Indian Mountain Artillery Regiment:	As at present.
British Medium Artillery Regt:	Regt HQ - 3 batteries of 4 howitzers - 80 vehicles.
Anti-Aircraft Battery:	HQ - 4 sections of 2 AA guns - 17 vehicles.
Anti-Tank Battery:	HQ - 3 troops of 2 sections of 2 anti-tank guns - 27 vehicles + supt units.
British and Indian Infantry Battalions:	Bn HQ + Co HQs - 4 companies of 3 platoons of 3 sections each = 49 LMGs, 42 2in mortars, 4 At-Tk rifles, 48 wheeled vehicles.

Abbreviations: cwt, cubic weight; LMG, light machine gun; supt, support; Bn, battalion; Co, company.

Clearly these decisions came too late for any real progress in the modernization of the army in India to be made before the outbreak of the Second World War. Indeed it was weaker and less prepared for war in 1939 than in 1914 with a total of 205,038 British and Indian troops as compared with 269,954 in 1914. As for up-to-date equipment, as late as February 1939 there was still one anti-aircraft battery in the whole of India. The Indian forces fell far short of being able to fulfill the internal and external roles envisaged for them by the Chatfield Committee.[66]

Bond and other researchers including Martin A. Wainwright are quite right in their belief that, in terms of equipment in 1939, the Indian army was woefully short of the lofty goals set for it by the Chatfield Committee. But was the Indian army "less prepared for war" as Bond alleges above? A detailed examination of the tactical doctrines of the British and Indian armies during the war years will reveal that even if the Indian army had lacked the material resources to wage a modern war, in terms of doctrine at least, it had entered the Second World War with a far more realistic appreciation of its capabilities and limitations than it had for the 1914–1919 war. Indeed, the true dynamics of the military modernization in the Indian army are not to be found in the highly visible "material" sphere, but rather in the ideology and mind-set of that army, as will be evident in the following chapter.

NOTES

1. Major B.C. Denning, *The Future of the British Army* (London: Witherby, 1928), 60–61.

2. Robin Higham, *The Military Intellectuals in Britain, 1918–1939* (New Brunswick, NJ: Rutgers University Press, 1966); Brian Bond, *British Military Policy between the Two World Wars* (Oxford: Clarendon Press, 1980).

3. Report of the Army in India Committee [Esher Committee], 1919–1920, BL/IOR, L/MIL/5/1762, pt. IV, 7. In the summer of 1920 the Indian army maintained ten battalions of infantry in Mesopotamia, nine in Egypt, seven in Palestine, six around the Black Sea, and various other smaller garrisons. See 13 July 1920, PRO, CAB 4/7, 252-B.

4. *Legislative Assembly Debates*, vol. 1, no. 15, 1683–762 in BL/IOR, L/MIL/7/10822.

5. Letter from Chelmsford to Edwin S. Montagu, 12 February 1919, Montagu Collection, BL/IOR, Mss.D.523/8, 26. In 1920 the viceroy stated bluntly to the British Cabinet that the government of India "could not accept any obligation to supply permanent overseas garrisons to the mandated territories." See "Supply of Overseas Garrisons from the Indian Army," 3 September 1920, PRO, CAB 24/11, CP 1844. In October the Secretary of State for India Edwin S. Montagu, adding his voice to the chorus of demands calling on the British government to withdraw from Mesopotamia, pointed out to the cabinet that the Dominions had refused help in this matter and that the government of India, including the Commander in Chief (C-in-C) General Rawlinson, was demanding the return of Indian soldiers. "The Mesopotamian Mandate," 9 October 1920, PRO CAB 23/112, CP 1948.

6. "Indian Military Expenditure" memorandum by Montagu, 24 December 1920, PRO, CAB 6/4, CID, 118-D.

7. Rawlinson to Lord Derby, 30 March 1921, Derby Collection, BL/IOR, Mss. Eur.D.605/5.

8. CID minutes, 29 June 1931, PRO, CAB 2/5.

9. Memorandum by India Office, 3 May 1928, PRO CAB 5/7, 318-C.

10. *Report of the Indian Retrenchment Committee, 1922–1923* (London: HMSO, 1923). BL/IOR, L/MIL/17/5/1780.

11. Report of the Indian Military Requirements Subcommittee, 22 June 1922, PRO, CAB 16/38, vol. 1, 130-D.

12. Tribunal on certain questions in regard to defense expenditure in dispute between the government of India and the WO and the air ministry [Garran Tribunal], India Office, November 1932, BL/IOR, L/MIL/17/5/1911.

13. Bond, *British Military Policy*, 112. By October of 1936, as it became evident that British industrial resources would be inadequate for her own rearmament pro-

gram, British ministers were initiating "urgent" inquiries about the possibility of purchasing antiaircraft munitions and weapons from the Dominions and India. See CID minutes, 29 October 1936, PRO, CAB 2/6, 2.

14. Director general of ordnance and intelligence.

15. The defense problems of India and the composition and organization of the army and RAF in India [Pownall Committee], 12 May 1938, BL/IOR, L/MIL/5/886, 331. Earlier that very year it was decided that in the event of a war with Italy, India was to provide two brigade groups and four air squadrons for Egypt, one brigade group and two air squadrons for Singapore, a brigade to Persia, a brigade to Aden, as well as a force of indefinite size to Iraq. CID minutes, 25 March 1938, PRO, CAB 2/7.

16. Ibid., 393–95. See also Rawson, "The Role of India in Imperial Defense," 287–97. At the same time the Pownall Committee was making its report, an unofficial Indian army committee led by the DCGS Major General Auchinleck was reaching much the same conclusion and urging the government of India to set up local munition and weapon-manufacturing facilities to modernize the army. Report of the Modernization Committee [Auchinleck Committee], Simla: Army HQ, October 1938, BL/IOR, L/MIL/17/5/1801.

17. L/MIL/5/886, 360.

18. Reorganization proposal: Detailed distribution of units, BL/IOR, L/MIL/5/886, 463.

19. Ibid., 476.

20. Report of the expert committee on the Defense of India [Chatfield Committee], 1938–1939, Ibid., 451, 459, 463, 477–78. See also "Cabinet Committee on the Defence of India. Report of the Expert Committee on the Defence of India," 23 June 1939, PRO, CAB 24/287; and "Draft Report by Committee on Defence of India," 7 June 1939, ID (38), PRO, CAB 27/65, a.

21. Defense requirements India, 1938–1939, Chatfield Committee: Notes on report by Generals Muspratt and Auchinleck, BL/IOR, War Staff (henceforth WS) 1934—L/WS/1/155, 15.

22. One British cavalry regiment and six British infantry battalions to return to England and three Indian cavalry regiments, four companies of Indian Sappers and Miners, and fourteen Indian infantry battalions to be disbanded.

23. Ibid., 7.

24. Plan for modernization of the army, 1939 (operations), General staff India, BL/IOR, WS 2099—L/WS/1/170.

25. B.H. Liddell Hart, *The Defence of Britain* (London: Faber, 1939), 305–6; See also B.H. Liddell Hart, *Memoirs* (London: Cassell, 1959), 91–97. Liddell Hart, along with Percy Hobart, another radical reformer, felt that the entire British army in India was little more than a police force and that it in fact could be replaced by a police force, which could be supported effectively by a single mobile division. Jacobsen, "Modernization of the Indian Army," 55.

26. This was after his 1927 tour of India. See J.F.C. Fuller, *On Future War* (London: Sifton, Praed, 1928), 262.

27. Harold R. Winton, *To Change an Army: General Sir John Burnett-Stuart and British Armored Doctrine, 1927–1938* (Lawrence, Kansas: University Press of Kansas, 1988), 124; See also Captain J. Kieth Edwards, "Second (Military) Prize

Winning Essay for 1927," *Journal of the Royal United Services Institute*, no. 73 (August 1928), 458–73.

28. Future military expenditure Cabinet Committees, August 1921, PRO, CAB 27/164, GRC (DD) 8.

29. Rawlinson to Derby, 25 November 1920, BL/IOR, Mss.Eur.D.605/1.

30. Secretary of state to viceroy, 18 January 1921, Chelmsford Collection, BL/IOR, Mss.Eur.E.264/14, 50.

31. 22 January 1921, Ibid, 33.

32. Monthly returns: Distribution of the Army, PRO, WO 73/115.

33. Letter from secretary of state for war to prime minister, 1 November 1937, quoted in R.J. Minney, *The Private Papers of Hore-Belisha* (London: Collins, 1960), 66.

34. Ibid., 66.

35. On 1 December 1937 he writes to Deverell asking him to step down. The latter concurs with his comment, "Time will show that your criticisms as far as I am concerned are unjust as they are cruel." Ibid., 69, 72.

36. Hore-Belisha also called for "the new army to be made more flexible." Among other things, he proposed the reduction of personnel by creating a greater number of "smaller" divisions that would be easier to move and support. Ibid., 92–94.

37. Memorandum by Finance Department, India Office, circulated by Montagu, 7 December 1920, PRO, CAB 6/4.

38. Ad hoc Subcommittees of the Committee for Imperial Defence, PRO, CAB 16/38, vol. 2, IMR/14.

39. Viceroy (army department) to secretary of state, 21 July 1921, BL/IOR, L/MIL/3/2513, 1631.

40. Since November 1921, a CID subcommittee had been examining the Rawlinson proposals at a leisurely pace. "The Proceedings of the Indian Military Requirements Sub-Committee," PRO, CAB 16/38, vol. 1. In explaining the British Cabinet's rejection of the proposal, the Secretary of State Montagu stated that the cabinet felt that further reduction of British troops in India was not possible in view of the political condition in India and the frontier situation. Secretary of state to viceroy, 14 February 1922, BL/IOR, L/MIL/3/2534, M.1348/1922, no. 1.

41. Sir Frederick Maurice, *The Life of General Lord Rawlinson of Trent* (London: Cassell, 1928), 313.

42. Ibid, 109. The Viceroy Lord Reading himself was firmly of the opinion that the budget could not be balanced without substantial reductions in military expenditure. Reading to Jonathan Peel, 3 August 1922, Reading Collection, BL/IOR, Mss.E.238, vol. 5, 112.

43. Keith Jeffrey, *The British Army and the Crisis of Empire 1918–1922* (Manchester: Manchester University Press, 1984), 88.

44. Minutes and conclusions of cabinet meetings and conferences of ministers, Cabinet Meeting, 25 August 1921, PRO, CAB 23/26/72(21).

45. The withdrawal began in December 1922. PRO, CAB 23/32/68(22), app. II.

46. Bond, *British Military Policy*, 106.

47. Examination for admission to the staff colleges at Camberley and Quetta, WO: London, HMSO, February 1936-March 1937, BL/IOR, L/MIL/17/5/2281, 2–4.

48. Bond, *British Military Policy*, 106.

49. Kenneth Macksey, *Armoured Crusader: Major General Percy Hobart* (London: Hutchinson, 1967), 82–83.

50. Winton, *To Change an Army*, 65.

51. Although mopping-up operations continued until the second half of 1922, the back of the rebellion had been broken by November 1921, thanks to Burnett-Stuart's mobile columns. A.C.B. Mackinnon, "The Moplah Rebellion 1921–1922," *Army Quarterly*, no. 8 (1924): 260–77. In 1926 he became commander of the 3rd Division at Salisbury Plains and oversaw the development of the Experimental Armored Force from 1927 onward. Bond, *British Military Policy*, 62, 65.

52. While at Quetta B.L. Montgomery met Auchinleck and Alexander, both brigade commanders. He is reported to have remarked that "the best man, was a chap called Auchinleck." Auchinleck had also served as chief instructor at Quetta from 1930–1932 and was three years older than B.L. Montgomery. Nigel Hamilton, *Monty: The Making of a General (1887–1942)* (New York: McGraw-Hill, 1981), 248–49, 258.

53. Winton, *To Change an Army*, 85.

54. Ibid., 33–34.

55. Bond, *British Military Policy*, 67–68.

56. Ibid., 67.

57. A.P. Wavell, "The Army and the Prophets," *Journal of the Royal Services Institute*, no. 75, (November 1930): 671.

58. Wavell also served as commander of the 2nd Aldershot Division from 1935–1937.

59. Recent research indicates that senior British home army generals (including Haig), who also were bitterly criticized and later sidelined by the reformers, were actually enthusiastic supporters of mechanization. However, like their counterparts in India, they had a more realistic understanding of Britain's ability to finance and implement such complex reforms. See J.P. Harris, *Men, Ideas and Tanks: British Military Thought and Armoured Forces, 1903–1939* (New York: St. Martin's Press, 1996).

60. Review of important military events in India, 1932, PRO, WO 32/1285.

61. Chief of General Staff (CGS) army HQ to all commands, 13 December 1938, BL/IOR, WS 2047—L/WS/1/164, 94.

62. Ibid., 95.

63. Letter from army HQ to Southern Command, 15 July 1939, Ibid., 56.

64. CGS army HQ to all commands, Ibid., 96–97.

65. CGS army HQ to all commands, 13 December 1938, BL/IOR, WS 2047—L/WS/1/164, 98.

66. Bond, *British Military Policy*, 123–24.

6

The Crucible of War: The Second World War and the Emergence of the Indian General Staff

The very same day Prime Minister Winston Churchill announced to Parliament that Britain was at war with Germany, the Viceroy Lord Linlithgow informed India over the radio of the circumstances in which "we find ourselves at war with Germany today."[1] The viceroy's declaration set off a political firestorm. The Indian National Congress, angered by the viceroy's lack of consultation with them, rejected his declaration and Congress Party ministers of all seven provinces where the congress held a majority resigned.[2] Although noncooperation and political agitation by the congress represented a potential problem for the Indian army, Linlithgow was more concerned about preventing Hindu-Muslim conflict among the soldiers.[3]

The war itself came as no surprise to the Indian government. Feverish planning (if not action) had been underway for some time to transform the Indian army into a capable modern intervention force. The first real test for the Indian army came in the desert of North Africa. Here two armies—the British Commonwealth and the German—pitted their imperfect doctrines of warfare against each other. At the end of an immense struggle the Afrika Korps was all but wiped out and the British Commonwealth forces emerged with a radically different appreciation of how to wage "modern" war. In the East, in Burma and Malaya, this scenario repeated itself between the British Commonwealth forces and the armies of imperial Japan with the same end result.

By the conclusion of the Second World War, India had become the single largest colonial contributor to the British war effort.[4] During the war India raised a military force of 2,500,000 professional soldiers, sailors, and airmen, the largest force of its kind in the world. This force suffered casualties including 24,338 killed, 64,354 wounded, 11,754 missing, and 79,489 prisoners of war (POWs), for a total of 179,935.[5] It fought in Malaya, Burma, East Africa, North Africa, Tunisia, the Middle East, Sicily, Italy, and in a number of smaller wars ranging from Greece to Indochina. It won 4,028 awards for gallantry, including thirty-one Victoria Crosses (twenty-seven in Burma—including twenty by members of the Indian army). The British 14th Army in Burma became the largest single army in the world with one million men, 700,000 of whom were Indian. It fought along a seven hundred–mile front, almost the equivalent of the eastern front. The Japanese incurred half their total casualties of the entire war in Burma alone![6]

Within this global crucible of war the army of independent India was born. During the course of this conflict the future leaders and architects of the army of independent India developed and honed their skills of warmaking. This chapter is primarily an analysis of how the Commonwealth armies emerged with a winning tactical doctrine in the war. It is also an examination of how the rapidly growing Indian officer corps matured as a professional organization during this period.

THE WAR IN THE WEST

The historiography of the war in North Africa has tended to dismiss the early campaigns against the Italians. Most of the research on this period has dwelled upon General O'Connor's highly mobile campaigns against the Italians with his "Jock" columns. These small motorized units of infantry, artillery, and armor wrought havoc on disorganized and retreating Italian forces. What has passed almost without notice is the excellent use of Indian artillery during these campaigns in the roles of both infantry and tank support. In the December 1940 battles against the fortified Italian camps at Nibeiwa and East Tumar, the division (CRA) chief of Royal Artillery of 4th Indian Division[7] used his entire divisional artillery—fifty-six 18pdrs and 25pdrs, eight 6in howitzer, and eight 60pdrs—as a single group to support each brigade's (three per division) attack in an excellent fire plan.[8]

The same coordination with artillery is evident in the East African campaign when the 4th and 5th Indian divisions took on the Italians at their best—defending well-prepared defensive positions with their best troops.[9] Throughout the campaign and especially during the decisive battle to seize the key stronghold of Keren, the artillery worked in close conjunction with the Indian infantry. At the fall of Keren, the British Commander General Platt praised "the continuous support given to the infantry by the Royal Artillery."[10] The performance of the artillery was all the more creditable because the Commonwealth forces had a limited force of only 124 guns.[11] Indeed, the entire Eritrean campaign ranks as one of the most effective displays of the use of limited firepower resources. The Indian army displayed its traditional flair for making the most of extremely limited resources.

The arrival of Rommel and his Afrika Korps changed the complexion of the desert war in more ways than one. Not only were the Germans a qualitatively superior opponent compared to the Italians, but also the Indian Army no longer constituted the bulk of the 8th Army. The "new" British-dominated 8th Army immediately revealed serious deficiencies in functioning as a cohesive combined-arms force, something at which the Germans were much more successful. Furthermore, mobility—that long-sought goal and the core of many a staff-college war games at Quetta and Camberley—proved as elusive as a mirage in the desert. Successive 8th Army commanders from General Cunningham to General Ritchie failed miserably to concentrate their forces at the decisive point. Even when they achieved such a rare concentration, British armor proved unable to work in concert with the artillery and infantry and was mauled repeatedly by German antitank defenses.[12]

In his authoritative three-part study in the *Journal of Royal Artillery* of British field artillery tactics, Brigadier R.G.S. Bidwell comments extensively on the misuse of artillery by the British army in the early period of the North African campaign against the Germans. Yet he notes with some puzzlement that "this, however, does not explain why it was from India, the most starved and backward of commands, that two divisions [the 4th and the 5th] came who at Keren and in the early desert operations showed how artillery should be handled. It was later that the decline began."[13] The obsession with mobility deflected the 8th Army from appreciating the need for "true" combined-arms operations with infantry and artillery. Under the influence of the radical reformers the British army entered the war with a gross over-appreciation of the capabilities of armor-only formations.

The British 7th Armored Division—a division trained by General Percy Hobart, who was a great believer of armored-only formations—entered the war in June 1940 with a ratio of about 330 tanks (two armored brigades) to only two infantry battalions and two artillery regiments. At the Sidi Rezegh battle there were no less than five hundred tanks (three armored brigades) backed by a support group of only three infantry battalions.[14] After Sidi Rezegh, General Auchinleck, commander in chief in the Middle East, proposed measures to create a parity between armor and infantry. He specifically wanted to reduce the number of armored brigades in a division to one and replace the ad hoc support group with a full infantry brigade.[15] In addition, Auchinleck said,

> We must, therefore, while retaining the divisional HQ organization, ensure that it is capable of handling a collection of brigades of varying numbers and types. That is to say, the real basic tactical unit must be the brigade group, whether armoured, motorized or lorried, and that each brigade group must be capable of being transferred from one divisional command to another as a matter of course and habit,

and without having to resort to a last minute improvisation which must occur with our present divisional organizational whether it be armoured corps or infantry.[16]

Auchinleck also proposed mobile field divisions of mixed armor and infantry for the army of maneuver to regain the initiative from the Germans.[17] The main problem he faced was that Ritchie (his 8th Army commander) was unable to carry out his directives. Auchinleck finally sacked Ritchie and took personal command of the army on 25 June 1942. With an Indian army officer in command, the desert campaign's effect was immediate. At the first battle of Alamein the German Commander Rommel noted,

General Auchinleck, who had meanwhile taken over command himself at El Alamein, was handling his forces with considerable skill and tactically better than Ritchie had done. He seemed to view the situation with decided coolness, for he was not allowing himself to be rushed into accepting a "second best" solution by any move we made.[18]

Indeed by June 1942 Auchinleck had stabilized a defensive line at Alamein. Here he reverted to the positional warfare tactics utilized so successfully in the East African campaign against the Italians. For possibly the first time in the campaign against the Afrika Korps, the 8th Army was successful in concentrating its artillery resources for a major defensive battle. At the battle of First Alamein in July 1942, the 8th Army concentrated the fire of nine artillery regiments on more than one occasion. In the midst of the raging battle on 15 July, the 8th Army Chief of General Staff T.W. Corbett, declared, "The artillery is being restored to its rightful place in the battlefield."[19] Unfortunately for Auchinleck, Churchill and the Chief of Imperial General Staff General Alanbrooke failed to see the true measure of his achievement and sacked him! The immediate reason given was his failure to punch through German lines in the subsequent counterattacks. However, these counterattacks, launched under tremendous pressure from Whitehall, collapsed as a result of the demoralized state of the British armor, which simply refused to advance in support of the infantry! Alanbrooke, who was well aware of the tremendous difficulties confronting Auchinleck, was not prepared to take on Churchill on his behalf as he would on many later occasions for General Montgomery.

Nevertheless, Auchinleck's brief stint as commander of the 8th Army marks a sea change in British military operations during the war.[20] Henceforth all British operations would center on positional warfare tactics, the centerpiece of which was the battle of attrition. Massed artillery, airpower, and infantry would dominate henceforth. The armor would operate as a supporting arm of the infantry. This "change" represented a return to the operational style favored by the Indian army, a style dictated not out of any orthodoxy, but by a realization that British and Indian armies quite simply lacked the training and equipment to carry out complex combined-arms mobile operations.[21]

Historians only now are beginning to appreciate the fact that Montgomery's assumption of the leadership of the 8th Army was not a revolution in British military leadership or tactics, but rather an evolution of the system introduced (*reintroduced*, to be precise) by Auchinleck when he was army commander. The second Alamein battle was predominantly an artillery and infantry offensive by the British. The armor came into play much later in the battle, after the infantry had broken through the German defenses. Even with Rommel on the run, Montgomery dared not send his armor in pursuit, so complete was the British disillusionment in their own ability to conduct even basic maneuver operations with armor.[22] It is not surprising that the artillery that played such a vital role in second Alamein battle was literally a continuation of Auchinleck's organization. As General Tuker recalls, "On the night of 23 October, 30th Corps attacked under a barrage on a four division front, the barrage co-ordinated by the good gunner, Brigadier Meade Dennis, the same officer who had well served Auchinleck as artillery commander on the northern sector of the Alamein front. He was now used to handling hundreds of guns."[23]

The second battle of Alamein proved significant for the artillery as it saw the introduction of complex artillery fire control. "Fire-plans could be arranged quickly, and what is more important, modified in mid-career to match the ebb and flow of battle."[24]

According to Colonel G.R. Stevens, the official historian of the 4th Indian Division, the new system of fire planning in all probability originated by the divisional CRA Brigadier Dimoline, who by

> constant training and experiment evolved a technique for crash saturation shoots well in advance of current practice. Gun surveys and the artillery communications grid were elaborated until the C.R.A. could sit in his battle headquarters with trace sheets which blended like a musical score, from which he could play his weapons singly, in unison or in harmony.[25]

The effect on the battlefield was startling; as General Sir Francis Tuker notes,

> Lacking an efficient armoured force, Eighth Army was now using much of its field artillery in a mobile role to halt the Axis advance, a role which was properly that of self-propelled artillery but nonetheless most effective in country where a few heights afforded such wide observation for the gunners and where mechanical traction enabled them to concentrate at speed. The records of the 9th Light and other [German] formations bespeak the punishment they received from South African and British guns, field—and medium. The method showed a reading of circumstances, of ground, resources and enemy which was refreshing after so many months of

neglect. Throughout July the application of artillery in the sector from Ruweisat northwards was about as good as it could be.[26]

The techniques used by Dimoline continued to evolve throughout the desert campaign. In fact, they represent the early manifestation of time-on-target (TOT) synchronized shoots and seventy-gun battery (divisional artillery) "stonks," which became very common in the European theater.[27]

The 8th Army Montgomery inherited from Auchinleck was by no means a lame duck. Tuker, who commanded the 4th Indian Division at the time of Montgomery's assumption of command, agreed with Montgomery's assertion that the 8th Army was ill-trained, but wondered to what he was comparing them, as troops from the U.K. were even less competent. Tuker felt that the best-trained allied infantries came from Australia, New Zealand, India, and South Africa.[28] British units entering the North African theater showed considerable inexperience and doctrinal rigidity. Tuker noted that during the battle of Medjerda, Tunis in May 1943, the British units refused to execute a night attack, a standard procedure for Indian units. During the same battle, the British 1st Army, who were strangers to Brigadier Dimoline's new artillery fire plans, hesitated before allowing him to take charge of a four hundred plus artillery concentration.[29]

When the war moved from Africa to Italy, so too did the Indian army, with the 4th, 8th, and 10th infantry divisions. Here, also, it became obvious that the Indian army's emphasis upon infantry was not misplaced. The campaign in Italy proved that "even in modern combat infantrymen were often more relevant than either tanks or planes."[30] General Alphonse Juin, commander of the Free French Forces, even went so far as to remark "that the widespread mechanization of the British and American forces constituted a serious obstacle to any swift progress up the Italian peninsula."[31] Under the circumstances it was not surprising that the Indian infantry divisions representing some of the most experienced infantry divisions in the theater saw almost continuous action right up to the German surrender in Italy in September 1945.[32]

THE WAR IN THE EAST

The campaign in Southeast Asia witnessed the largest use of Indian troops during the war. No less than nine Indian infantry divisions and a large number of independent brigades (armor and infantry) plus support groups became involved in that theater of conflict. Included in this force were the only Indian tank units to see extensive action during the war, the 50th, 254th, and the 255th Indian tank brigades.[33]

Early in the conflict, the excellent mobility of the veteran Japanese forces and their total disregard for flanking security took the British/Indian forces completely by surprise. Hong Kong, Singapore, and Malaya fell in quick succession. In Singapore alone 85,000 Commonwealth troops surrendered to the Japanese! Only in Burma did the British manage to slow the Japanese momentarily and to stage a fighting retreat. Outmaneuvered and outfought by a remarkably lightly armed, albiet experienced, Japanese army, the Commonwealth and Chinese forces fell back into India. Here, at last, the indomitable imperial Japanese forces paused to regroup and consolidate their overextended supply lines.

In India the battered Commonwealth forces built up their strength and planned for the next phase of the war under the guidance of the Indian army officer, Lieutenant General Sir William Slim. The significance of Slim's assumption of command of the 14th Army is comparable to Auchinleck's takeover of the 8th Army in North Africa. The effect in terms of both the course of the war and allied military doctrine proved to be the same. However, Slim, unlike Auchinleck, was under less pressure from Churchill to produce instant victories and had the luxury of being able to mold his forces into the best possible condition before going on the offensive. One of his first acts was to issue an eight-point training directive to all of his units to "get used to having Japanese parties in their rear, and when that happens, regard not themselves but the Japanese as 'surrounded.' " Point five of the directive cautioned infantry on Japanese style tactics: "There should rarely be frontal attacks and never frontal attacks on narrow fronts. Attacks should follow hooks and come in from flank or rear, while pressure holds the enemy in the front." On the issue of armor, Slim sought to change the prevalent view that tanks were useless in the jungle. He argued that "tanks can be used in most country except in close country they must always have infantry with them to defend and reconnoitre for them. They should always be used in the maximum numbers available and capable of being deployed."[34] Slim was in fact laying the framework for allied tactics in the coming campaign whereby superior allied firepower and logistics would deflect Japanese mobility and ultimately destroy their lightweight infantry-based army.

In the allied counteroffensive against the Japanese in Burma, infantry bore the main responsibility of assaulting the enemy, closely supported by tanks when available, and always heavily backed by artillery and air strikes. Although artillery and air support never reached the numbers employed in North Africa and Europe, divisional artillery concentrations like those used to support the 37th Brigade's (of the 23rd Indian Division) assault on Tamu in July 1944 became commonplace.[35] The Japanese, by contrast, rarely managed to concentrate more than a battalion's worth of artillery. At Kangaw, for instance, the heaviest reported Japanese artillery concentration of the war comprised of only one battalion firing six hundred rounds per day.[36] "Cab-Ranks" provided close air support whereby forward observers (FOs) called down fire from fighters circling over the advancing troops.[37]

The campaign in Burma witnessed some of the best all-arms coordination of British and Commonwealth forces in the entire war. This was particularly true in the case of armor and infantry, whose cooperation exceeded the level reached in Africa and Europe. Undoubtedly this was due partly to the weakness of the Japanese, who could deploy only a fraction of the tanks and artillery the Germans had in Africa and Europe. This has led some observers to conclude that, due to the Commonwealth's overwhelming superiority in material and men, "tactics were not so important as the logistics of manoeuvering such a force into position."[38] This, however, is inaccurate, for the mere sustaining of logistics and the concentration of forces would not have been enough to defeat the extremely mobile Japanese forces. This was accomplished through relentless pursuit of the enemy by all Commonwealth forces operating as a well-oiled combined-arms team of air, artillery, tanks, and infantry. Mobility—the quality sought in the pre-Auchinleck 8th Army and a concept that found little place in Monty's set-piece battles—became a vital element in Slim's Burma campaign.

APPRENTICES OF WAR

The small group of Indian officers were caught in the midst of this catastrophic struggle; for them the Second World War proved a defining moment in their military careers. While peacetime training and education had given them a largely theoretical grasp of warfare, actual combat enabled them to mature considerably as military leaders. The lessons learned by the young Indian officers during the war years formed the core of Indian military doctrine in the postindependence period and continues to play a major role in the evolution of the Indian army today.

Individual Indian officers who later rose in their careers to assume senior positions in the independent Indian army participated in the often painful learning process that the Indian and other allied armies endured during the war. In the deserts of North Africa Indian officers took part in the well-orchestrated campaign against the Italians. Early during the campaign in East Africa the advancing 4th Indian Division encountered large, well-situated minefields left behind by the retreating Italians. Second Lieutenant Premindrah Singh Bhagat (later major general) of the 21st Field Company, Royal Bombay Sappers and Miners, spearheaded the advance through the minefields relying solely on his eyesight and a bayonet. Despite an ambush and two mine explosions which destroyed his vehicles, Bhagat stuck to his task for five days, enabling the pursuit to flow smoothly. For his actions, Bhagat became the first Indian commissioned officer to be awarded the Victoria Cross.[39]

Indian officers also participated in the chaotic early campaigns against the German Afrika Korps. Many learned firsthand the disastrous consequences of being unable to concentrate forces and the artillery. Quite early in the campaign against the Germans in 1942, Major (later General) P.P.

Kumaramangalam's 7th Field Battery put up a tremendous defense against the attacking Germans at Bir Hachiem, and he received a Distinguished Service Order (DSO) in the process.[40] In the confused retreat following this battle, the Germans took four Indian artillery officers, including Kumaramangalam, prisoner.[41] Other Indian officers also became embroiled in the chronic indecision that infected the 8th Army during this period. In June 1942 Major S.D. Verma (later lieutenant general) of the 10th Indian Division held a position along the tenuous defensive line on the coast road at Mersa Matruh. He recalled that they "kept getting conflicting reports and orders. One day it would be that we were to stay and 'fight to the last man last round.' The next day's rumours would announce that we would have to make a breakout."[42] The division eventually broke out of the German encirclement with heavy casualties. Verma himself became separated from his convoy, but managed to find his way back to British-held territory (El Daba). Amidst defeat he learned a lasting lesson on military leadership: "The memory of the dishevelled and dirty uniforms the men were wearing and the vacant looks in their eyes is still fresh. The fact that some of their officers were slowly locating them and trying to cheer them up must have been a great morale booster for them, because soon they were showing their normal spirit."[43]

The few Indian armored units that took part in this campaign became part of the debacle. Many learned of the urgent need for artillery support in the face of German armored superiority. In April 1941 Major (later army chief) Rajendra Sinjhi organized a two-squadron rear guard of the 2nd Lancers to cover the retreat of the remnants of the 3rd Indian Motor Brigade after its gallant defense against the Germans at El Mekili. The rearguard action ended quickly and relied mainly on artillery to keep the German tanks at bay. In the retreat to El Adem, Rajendra Sinjhi's column surprised and captured a German encampment. For his actions he became the first Indian officer to be awarded the DSO.[44]

For most of the Indian officers who fought on the western front, and the North African desert in particular, their primary wartime memory involved defeat by the Germans. These officers learned firsthand the disastrous consequences of a British-led Commonwealth army engaging the Germans without a coherent military doctrine. These experiences no doubt molded their attitudes toward warfare in the postindependent Indian army. Rajendra Sinjhi and Kumaramangalam both became army chiefs of the independent Indian army. S.D. Verma and P.S. Bhagat also rose in the hierarchy to become senior general officers. The underlying theme in all of the actions and writings of these officers in the postindependent Indian army rested on a firm belief in the infantry-artillery, defensive-offensive doctrine originated by Auchinleck in North Africa.

The main theater of war where most Indian officers saw action lay in the East with the 14th Army. In this conflict with the cream of the Japanese imperial army, the seeds of the independent Indian army's tactical doctrine emerged. The majority of the senior commanders of the postindependence army also gained their war experience on this front. In the early part of the campaign against the Japanese, many Indian officers became Japanese POWs with disastrous consequences for their military careers. In chapter 4 we examined in some detail the wartime career of Captain Mohan Singh, who joined with the Japanese to establish the INA. In all, four hundred Indian officers joined the INA, and about 250 of them came from the medical corps.[45] The independent Indian army had no use for these deserters, despite the "nationalistic" motives for their desertion and cooperation with the enemy. There were, however, many Indian officers who, as prisoners of the Japanese, refused to join the INA. The treatment of these officers was often much worse than those of other British and Commonwealth officers.

The Japanese tortured many officers, including Captain Dhargalkar and Badhwar, for weeks on end.[46] Their unit, the 3rd Indian Cavalry, had been operating in support of the 11th Indian Division in Malaya during the Japanese invasion of November 1942. The unit's armored cars could put up little resistance against the fast-moving Japanese infantry and armor. On 31 January 1942 its remnants retreated into Singapore, where it, along with the rest of the garrison, surrendered on 14 February. Two Indian officers of the unit, Captains Dhargalkar (later lieutenant general) and Badhwar (later major general) became Japanese POWs.[47] The trauma of prolonged detention in Japanese POW camps no doubt sapped the morale and resilience of these and other officers. It also deprived them of valuable combat experience. Dhargalkar and Badhwar were two of the few officers, who rose to high-command positions in the independent Indian army.

Not all Indian officers, however, fell prey to the early Japanese offensives. Captain Jemi H.F. Manekshaw (later field marshal) launched one of the few successful British counterattacks in the early part of the war to retake Pagoda Hill during the battle of Sittang River.[48] Manekshaw became one of the few Indian officers to see extensive action against the Japanese throughout the war. His tremendous drive and energy eventually resulted in the award of a Military Cross (MC) in June 1942.[49] Manekshaw rose in the Indian army to become not only army chief, but also India's first field marshal. He commanded the Indian army during its very successful campaign in East Pakistan in 1971. The tactics of that campaign bore remarkable similarities to Slim's successful campaign against the Japanese in Burma and Malaya.

In addition, Indian officers had the opportunity to command battalion- and brigade-level units in combat in the eastern theater. These officers became very involved in implementing General Slim's radical eight-point plan to carry the war to the Japanese. The most visible example is, of course, that of Brigadier Thimayya. His first action as battalion commander (colonel) in which he seized a heavily defended Japanese hill in a night attack with a brief artillery shoot undoubtedly would have earned high marks from his instructors at Staff College, Quetta.[50]

Colonels L.P. Sen and S.P.P. Thorat also commanded battalion-level formations in the field during the war. Like Thimayya before him, Thorat's entry into the war was preceded by a stint at Quetta (1941). After a brief posting to the army HQ, Thorat joined the 4/14th Punjab, which, as part of the 114th Brigade of 7th Indian Division, played a role in clearing Japanese forces from the Naga hills. After a short stay, which involved taking part in many "small but savage" actions, he moved to 9/14th Punjab part of the 20th Indian Division engaged in fighting in the Imphal plains.[51] Here Thorat, replacing his commanding officer who had been struck down with dysentery, took over temporary command of the battalion. Unaccustomed to his newfound rank, Thorat accompanied his troops on a lengthy reconnaissance mission. The brigade commander, while happy with Thorat's initiative, did not approve of his involvement in patrol actions. In November 1944 Thorat received his first official battalion command—the 2/2nd Punjab part of 51st Indian Infantry Brigade. This particular brigade became known as the "Indian Brigade," for unlike other Indian army brigades, it had three Indian battalions instead of one British and two Indian. More significantly, all three battalions had Indian commanders—Thimayya, Thorat, and Sen.

In January of 1945 the battalion took part in the bloody battle of Kangaw. The 51st Brigade had the assigned task of clearing the strongly fortified Japanese rearguard positions. In this action Thorat had to coordinate his battalion attack with artillery and air support. Despite such firepower, his battalion suffered heavy casualties as it advanced through the rice paddies to close with the Japanese. At one point Thorat flung himself into the intense hand-to-hand combat to bolster his men. (During this action Thorat killed a young Japanese officer and seized his sword.) The battle only ended when Thorat called in air strikes to smash a Japanese counterattack. Thorat appears to have been fully aware of the Japanese tactic of evacuating a position under attack and then swiftly counterattacking to retake it thus inflicting maximum casualties on the enemy. After his initial attack had succeeded, Thorat limited any extension of his advance and consolidated his position on half of the hill feature. The inevitable Japanese counterattack followed and was thrown back by the well-prepared battalion defenses. Thorat's battalion played a key role in the bloodiest battle of the Arrakan campaign and emerged from it as battle-hardened veterans.[52]

Along with Sen and Thimayya, Thorat was one of the few Indian officers above the rank of major to see such intense action during the war. His maturation as a professional and veteran officer is clearly evident from the first limited action he saw at Kohima to the culminating brutal battle at Kangaw. His firm grasp of his soldiers' mentality, his easy ability to inspire them to Herculean efforts by his sheer presence, and his cool, calculating appreciation of the tactical solution and the enemy's likely moves are all hallmarks of a budding commander, a role he fulfilled as chief of the army in independent India. Thimayya, too, became army chief, and Sen became a senior general officer.

It was in the eastern theater rather than the western front that the Indian Armored Corps (IAC) came of age. The Burma/Malaya campaign involved the only extensive combat use of large brigade and regiment-sized Indian tank formations in the entire war. Large tank divisions so popular in Africa and Europe were not useful in the East. A staff report in 1945 outlines the Indian army's approach toward armored corps formations:

> As a result of the outstanding success of the German Panzer divisions in France in 1940, military opinion swung strongly in favour of the creation of numerous armoured formations. Under pressure from the prevailing military thought, it was decided in India to embark on a program of mechanization and expansion which included the formation of a I.A.C. of 3 armoured divisions. . . . It was [then] decided in 1944, to abolish the remaining Indian armoured division in the India Command, and to concentrate on the production of Indian tank brigades to suit conditions of possible operations against the Japanese.[53]

The senior-most Indian cavalry officer of the war was Lieutenant Colonel J.N. Chaudhuri who became the first and only Indian to command a cavalry regiment, the 16th Cavalry (armored cars).[54] Chaudhuri's greatest challenge came when the general officer commander (GOC) 17th Division established a special mobile column, including Stuart light tanks and Sherman medium tanks of 7th Light Cavalry and Probyn's Horse under his command. The aim was to take Rangoon before the 26th Indian Division got there. Although the column failed to beat the 26th Indian Division to the punch, it showed a remarkable degree of tank-infantry cooperation in sweeping aside Japanese bunkers and roadblocks.[55] In addition to providing reconnaissance and fire support to the 17th Indian Division, the 16th Cavalry saw extensive action after the war fighting communist nationalist in Indochina.[56] Several Indian officers, including Captain Sheodatt Singh of the Deccan Horse (part of 255th Indian Tank Brigade), saw extensive action with tank units in the East. These officers and their units performed invaluable fire support tasks for attacking Indian infantry, gaining invaluable experience in combined-arms operations as a result.

More so than that in North Africa, the fighting in Burma and Malaya laid the foundation for the future tactical doctrine of the Indian army. It was in Burma that the combined-arms battle concept reached its zenith for the British Commonwealth forces. Artillery, although fewer in number than in the European or North African theater, played an equally crucial role in the conflict.[57] Many future senior Indian artillery officers learned their trade in the jungles and mountains of Burma. Captain J.K. Khanna won the MC while serving with the 3rd Indian Field Regiment at Palel. His sixth Indian Field Battery moved a troop of guns over steep mountains so that Japanese positions on the reverse slopes could be engaged. This initiative operation involved the partial dismantling of heavy 25pdr guns, as well as literally carrying them by hand over the mountains amidst torrential monsoon rains.[58]

The Second World War resulted in the lifting of most of the time constraints on the Indianization program and dramatically altered its careful progress. Thousands of emergency commissioned Indian officers (ECIOs) now flooded into the Indian army. For many of them service in the war provided an ideal opportunity to consolidate and enhance their career prospects in the postindependence period. One such officer, S.K. Sinha, became the 11,555th ECIO during the war. He joined the 4/12th Frontier Force Rifles—part of 17th Indian Division in Burma—and took part in "low key" operations until the war's end. At the close of the war most of the ECIOs were not given permanent commissions. Out of a grand total of about thirteen thousand ECIOs, only 450 were selected for permanent commission in 1945 and 1946. Sinha and Captain B.N. Sarkar were the only two selected from their batch of forty.[59]

More often than not, it was only after the war that many of the now permanently commissioned ECIOs began to see extensive action as "peacekeepers." Sinha was posted as general staff officer as the G-3 operations to HQ 15th Indian Corps at Batavia (Jakarta), Indonesia. This corps HQ was redesignated HQ Allied Forces Netherlands East Indies (AFNEI). It had three Indian divisions, two Dutch divisions, an independent armored brigade, and an independent parachute brigade. The original purpose was to take over from the Japanese forces and release the thousands of allied POWs and civilian European captives. However, the mission soon turned into a war against Indonesian nationalist forces led by Sukarno, who had no desire to see a Dutch reoccupation of the islands.

Since the Dutch divisions were still being raised and trained, it was the veteran Indian 5th, 23rd, and 26th infantry divisions that bore the brunt of the fighting and secured the port towns of Batavia, Semarang, and Surabaya in Java; Medan, Pedang, and Pallembang in Sumatra; and Macasser in the Celebes. Here the Indian officers were exposed to intense guerilla warfare, and several Indian officers—including Lieutenant Colonel Sarvajeet Singh Kalha, who had won the DSO in Burma—were killed. Sinha recalled feeling awkward about the role the Indian troops were playing in subduing Indonesian nationalists while India herself was on the threshold of independence.[60] But most Indian officers, well aware of the fact that independence for India was imminent, were more interested in maintaining high professional standards. The British in India were not complacent about the use of Indian troops in such situations. In the first of a series of letters to the Secretary of State for India Pethick-Lawrence, Wavell urged him to make it clear to the British government the serious repercussions likely to arise from using Indian troops to suppress the Indonesian nationalists.[61]

Major T.N. Raina with the Kumaon Battalion at Macassar in the Celebes, and a close friend of Sinha, said that

> Indian officers must maintain the highest standard of discipline and ensure that their troops did the same. We should not allow ourselves to get swayed by emotion or by the contradiction inherent in the role we are asked to perform in Indonesia. This was necessary not only in our individual interest but also in the interest of our country.[62]

It is doubtful if the British policy makers who had despatched the Indian troops to Indonesia could have come out with a better statement to highlight the long-term goal of establishing a professional and obedient Indian officer corps. Raina's commitment to his professional ethos seems to have worked, for he retired as chief of army staff, and Sinha himself retired as a senior general officer. Indeed in Vietnam, when the 20th Indian Division moved in to accept the Japanese surrender and to keep the peace until the arrival of the French, the Viet Minh issued propaganda leaflets urging the "heroic sons of Gandhi" not to wage war against the Viet Minh. This appeal, however, fell on deaf ears, since all the Indian soldiers were well aware that the British were preparing to leave India.[63] In September 1946, even after the withdrawal of 20th Indian Division from Vietnam in March, there were 44,800 Indian troops in Burma, 59,000 in Malaya, 16,000 in Iraq, 12,500 in the Middle East, 11,400 in Japan, 5,800 in Hong Kong, 1,500 in Ceylon, 1,000 in Borneo, and 400 in Italy. All told the total number of Indian troops deployed overseas in September amounted to 274,900.[64] On the eve of independence the Indian army was one of the few armies in the world that emerged with extensive experience in guerilla warfare as a result of its extensive deployments from Vietnam to Indonesia. This experience proved invaluable in enabling the postindependence Indian army to wage a successful if protracted campaign against communist separatist movements in northeast India.

Not all Indian officers participated in combat operations during the war. Indeed, many of them sat out the war behind a desk or as an ADC to a British general. One such officer was Gul Hassan Khan, who spent most of the war as an ADC to various British generals, culminating with General Slim. His most challenging task seems to have been the organization of an impromptu meal for the Army commander and his staff at Monywa, Burma.[65] Despite this fact, a substantial number indeed did gain considerable experience in the field.[66] In the process they imbibed many of the tactical and strategic doctrines that the Indian army helped evolve during the course of the war. On the eve of Indian and Pakistani independence, all that remained to be answered was whether these officers were mature enough to take over the reigns of command in the Indian army from their departing British mentors.

NOTES

1. *Gazette of India*, 3 September 1939, 1.

2. B.R. Tomlinson, *The Indian National Congress and the Raj, 1929–1942: The Penultimate Phase* (London: Macmillan, 1976), 144. Although most Indian political parties, including the congress, were eager to see the end of British rule in India, they were decidedly anti-Nazi and roundly denounced fascism and racism. See Sir Albion Bonerji, "The Indian Attitude towards the War Aims of the Allies," *Asiatic Review* 36 (1940); 312.

3. The congress had decided not to give any support for the war effort unless the British promised to grant independence immediately. The Muslim League responded with a call for the partition of India to enable Muslims to have an independent state of their own. Linlithgow to Zetland, 8 March 1940, Linlithgow Collection, BL/IOR, Mss.Eur.F.125/28, 141.

4. This includes Dominions.

5. This is a very conservative "official" estimate.

6. India and the war 1939–1945: The facts, Information Department, India Office, 1 January 1946, BL/IOR, L/MIL/17/5/4263.

7. They were known as "Red Eagles."

8. Major P.C. Bharucha, "The North African Campaign 1940–1943," in Sri Nandan Prasad (ed.), *Official History of the Indian Armed Forces in the Second World War 1939–1945* (New Delhi: Combined Inter-Services Historical Section [India & Pakistan], 1956), 91–93; G.R. Stevens, *Fourth Indian Division* (Toronto: McLaren & Son, n.d.), 16.

9. The HQ of the Deccan District, which had proceeded to Egypt to form HQ 4th Indian Division, was reconstituted, and these new brigades plus Poona Horse were formed into the 5th Indian Division. India's part in the war 1940, General staff India, Simla: Government of India Press, 1940, BL/IOR, L/MIL/5/4261, 5.

10. Individual battalion attacks, like those by 4/16th Rajputana Rifles during the first battle of Keren, received the support of the entire divisional artillery—forty-four 25 pdrs, eight 6in howitzers, and four 3.7in howitzers. Sri Nandan Prasad (ed.), *Official History of the Indian Armed Forces in the Second World War: East African Campaign 1940–1941* (New Delhi: Combined Inter-Services Historical Section [India & Pakistan], 1956), 68, 121.

11. Stevens, *Fourth Indian Division*, 46.

12. An Indian army circular issued in 1942 acknowledged that minefields and German 88mm high-velocity antitank guns posed a serious obstacle to tank/infantry cooperation. War information circular No. 26A, General Staff, New Delhi: Government of India Press, 1942, BL/IOR, L/MIL/17/5/4265.

13. Brigadier R.G.S. Bidwell, "The Development of British Field Artillery Tactics 1940–1942," *Journal of Royal Artillery*, vol. 94, no. 2 (September 1967): 92.

14. I.S.O. Playfair, *The Mediterranean and the Middle East*, vol. 1 (London:

HMSO, 1954), 103; J.A.I. Agar-Hamilton and L.C.F. Turner, *The Sidi Rezegh Battles* (Cape Town, South Africa: Oxford University Press, 1957), 474–75.

15. These proposals were accepted by the WO, and a circular was sent to all commands specifying the following composition for armored and infantry divisions:

> Infantry division—two infantry brigades, one tank brigade, plus supporting arms (armored brigade was later replaced by infantry brigade).
>
> Armored division—one armored brigade, one lorried infantry brigade, plus supporting arms.

WO letter to various commands and theaters, 20 May 1942, BL/IOR, WS 12048-L/WS/1/616, 264.

16. Proposals from C-in-C in the Middle East: extensive reorganization of armored division in that theater, BL/IOR, WS 6385-L/WS/1/448, 281. Auchinleck also proposed to give brigades more supporting arms to make tham a self-sufficient tactical unit—the so-called Brigade Group—capable of fighting independent of a division. This proposal was in part influenced by similar independent formations frequently utilized by the Afrika Korps. Playfair, *Mediterranean and the Middle East*, vol. 3 (London: HMSO, 1956), 213–15, 254, 286–87. This proposal, however, was not well received. The secretary to the India Office, Military Department, felt that independent brigade groups would not be an economic use of force and that if supporting arms were decentralized to brigade groups permanently they would be difficult to withdraw. Major General R.M.M. Lockhart to General S.W. Kirby, 9 April 1942, GHO New Delhi, BL/IOR WS 6385-L/WS/448, 218–19.

17. John Connell, *Auchinleck, a Biography of Field-Marshall Sir Claude Auchinleck* (London: Cassell, 1959), 684.

18. Erwin Rommel, *The Rommel Papers, 1891–1944*, ed. B.H. Liddell Hart, trans. Paul Findlay (New York: Harcourt, Brace, 1953), 248.

19. Agenda and minutes of Commanders' Conference, Meeting at GHQ BTE, 15 July 1942, PRO, WO 201/2050.

20. There is a considerable debate among "pro-Auchinleck" and "pro-Montgomery" historians about just which of these commanders played a pivotal role in determining the emergence of a "winning" British tactical doctrine for the rest of the war. Recent work reveals that both sides are beginning to take compromised positions, which would seem to suggest that the evolution of British military doctrine in North Africa was an evolutionary process, with both Auchinleck and Montgomery making important contributions. However, even Michael Carver, a "pro-Monty" scholar (and former 8th Army officer) has acknowledged that, unlike Montgomery, Auchinleck was never given the luxury of time to prepare adequately for battle. Michael Carver, *Dilemmas of the Desert War: A New Look at the Libyan Campaign, 1940–1942* (Bloomington: Indiana University Press, 1986), 132, 145.

21. Indeed, with the exception of the United States Army, none of the combatants in the Second World War had the necessary material to conduct large-scale mechanized operations.

22. Carver notes that when Montgomery arrived in Egypt, he had an overly optimistic plan as far as the role of the armor was concerned. He subsequently changed his plans to a less ambitious one. As a result, his pursuit of the Germans was "over-insured." Ibid., 138–39.

23. Stevens, *Fourth Indian Division*, 191.
24. Bidwell, "Development of British Field Artillery Tactics," 90.
25. Stevens, *Fourth Indian Division*, 191.
26. General Sir Francis Tuker, *Approach to Battle* (London: Cassell, 1963), 153.
27. J.B.A. Bailey, *Field Artillery and Firepower* (Oxford: The Military Press, 1989), 185–86, fn. 44. It must be noted here that 8th Army's artillery tactics in turn were derived largely from artillery techniques evolved toward the end of the First World War. See Ibid., 184.
28. Tuker, *Approach to Battle*, 224.
29. Ibid., 361–64.
30. John A. English, *A Perspective on Infantry* (New York: Praeger, 1981), 175.
31. Alphonse Juin, *Memoires*, vol. 1 (Paris: Fayard, 1959), 232.
32. The Indian army experienced considerable difficulty in trying to pry its divisions away from the Italian theater. In a letter to the allied HQ in Algiers, the C-in-C's office in New Delhi pointed out that the 4th Indian Division was needed in Burma and that the Indian government had never contracted "to keep three or any other number of Indian divisions in the Mediterranean theatre—the fact that five Indian divisions are there is purely fortuitous." Telegram C-in-C India to WO and armed forces HQ in Algiers, 13 June 1944, BL/IOR, WS 5725—L/WS/1/431, 3–4. The 4th Indian Division never went to Burma; it was transferred to Greece in September 1944 to try to put a damper on the budding civil war.
33. See Annexure 9, *Report to the Combined Chiefs of Staff: By the Supreme Commander South East Asia 1943–1945* (London: HMSO, 1951), 265–72.
34. Viscount William Slim, *Defeat into Victory* (New York: David McKay, 1961), 116–17.
35. Sri Nandan Prasad (ed.), *Official History of the Indian Armed Forces in the Second World War: The Reconquest of Burma, 1941–1942*, vol. 2 (New Delhi: Combined Inter-Service Historical Section [India & Pakistan], 1958–59), 48.
36. A.L. Pemberton, *The Development of Artillery Tactics and Equipment* (London: The War Office, 1950), 308–9.
37. FOs were then called visual command posts (VCP) Ibid., 341, fn. 67.
38. Brigadier Michael Calvert, "Victory in Burma", in E. Bauer, *The History of World War II* (London: Orbis, 1979), 631.
39. Charles Chevenix Trench, *The Indian Army and the King's Enemies* (London: Thames & Hudson, 1988), 143–44.
40. *The Statesman*, 30 August 1942. 2nd Field Battery was part of the 2nd Indian Field Regiment, which was in turn part of the 3rd Indian Motor Brigade Group.
41. Y.B. Gulati, *History of the Regiment of Artillery: Indian Army* [Published under the authority of the director of artillery, Army HQ, New Delhi] (London: Leo Cooper, 1972), 71.
42. Verma, *To Serve with Honour*, 33.
43. Ibid., 36.
44. The delay imposed by the 3rd Indian Motor Brigade upon the Afrika Korps between 6 and 8 April allowed the Australian forces enough time to reach and fortify Tobruk. Major General Gurcharan Singh Sandhu, *The Indian Armour: History of the Indian Armoured Corps 1941–1971* (New Delhi: Vision Books, 1987), 77–87.

45. Cohen interview with Lieutenant General K.P. Dhargalkar, London, 9 December 1963.

46. Chapter 4, n. 51.

47. Sandhu, *The Indian Armour*, 118–23.

48. Prasad, *Reconquest of Burma 1941–1942*, 167.

49. Sinha and Chandra, *Valour and Wisdom*, 150.

50. Evans, *Thimayya of India*, 196–201. See chapter 4, n. 19.

51. Thorat, *From Reveille to Retreat*, 54.

52. Ibid., chap. 6.

53. GHQ India to BGS, India Office, 8 February 1945, BL/IOR, WS 12048—L/WS/1/616, 3.

54. Sandhu, *Indian Armour*, 212.

55. The 26th Indian Division preempted Chaudhuri's move into Rangoon with a seaborne landing. Ibid., 233.

56. Ibid., 241.

57. An army circular, however, noted that the Japanese were even weaker in artillery and relied primarily on mortars for fire support. "War Information Circular, Foreign Armies," GHQ Inida, New Delhi: Government of India Press, 1943, BL/IOR, L/MIL/17/5/4266.

58. Gulati, *History of the Regiment of Artillery*, 78.

59. Sinha, *A Soldier Recalls*, 67.

60. Ibid., 68.

61. Wavell to Pethick-Lawrence, 1 October 1945, in N. Mansergh, E.W.R. Lumby, and Penderel Moon (eds.), *India: The Transfer of Power 1942–1947*, 12 vols. (London: HMSO, 1970–1983), 6: 46, 306, 323–24, 337.

62. Sinha, *A Soldier Recalls*, 75.

63. Peter M. Dunn, *The First Vietnam War* (London: C. Hurst 1985), 168.

64. The Indian government was placed in a predicament by this deployment, because 250,000 Indian soldiers were due to be released by 31 March 1947. See "Note on a Wholesale and Urgent Withdrawal of All Indian Troops Serving Outside India," Wavell to London, 8 September 1946, in Mansergh, Lumby, and Moon, *Transfer of Power*, vol. 8, 464–65.

65. Khan, *Memoirs*, 39–41.

66. A fact readily acknowledged by the Secretary of State Leo Amery, who, in a triumphant letter to Churchill on 27 April 1945, declared that Indianization was a success, with most Indian officers performing "extraordinarily well in the war." See Amery to Churchill, 27 April 1945, L/WS/1/924, in Mansergh, Lumby, and Moon, *Transfer of Power*, vol. 5, 427.

7

The Indian Army and the Colonial Legacy

In addition to its considerable combat role, India served as a major allied assault base during the Second World War. India accommodated 1,320,000 men (British and American) and built 42 million square feet of covered storage area. The Indian government established seventy new training establishments to take up to 470,000 men at a time. Over two hundred fully equipped airfields were built, as were seven major air bases with one mile long runways for the American air force to fly supplies to China. The total value of the supplies given to the U.S. forces in India totalled 129,180,000 British pounds or $516,720,000. India also supplied vast quantities of food and material to Commonwealth forces all over the world. In many cases it was the sole supplier of certain equipment; for example, India produced all the jungle-green uniforms and battle dress worn in Burma.[1] It is hardly surprising then that, at the end of the war, India's debt to Britain had been eliminated and that India actually had built up a credit for $1,240 million.[2]

India emerged from the war as a regional military power. Its contribution to the British war effort and the resultant size of its military forces and defense infrastructure left it in an ideal position to fulfill the goals the Chatfield Committee had set for it in the interwar period, that is becoming the bulwark of British imperial defense. The subsequent onset of the Cold War only served to further enhance India's strategic potential in the eyes of British defense analysts in both New Delhi and Whitehall.

The volatile political situation in India, however, remained the main stumbling block to this rosy future. Political events in India were fast outstripping the understanding of the governments in India and Britain. That the British ultimately would leave India no longer remained doubtful. The Labour government elected in August 1945 already had declared publicly its intention of giving India independence. The problem looming was how to implement the transfer of power. Would there be one undivided India or two independent states of India and Pakistan? While the politicians attempted to thrash out this intractable issue, the soldiers, led by the Commander in Chief General Auchinleck (reappointed Commander in Chief, India in June 1943) worked feverishly to prepare the Indian army for independence. Initially Auchinleck and his staff had felt that the Indian army would not be partitioned. A unified Indian army was, after all, the core of the Commonwealth's future defense strategy. The British, even at this eleventh hour, had hoped that, although India and Pakistan may well be partitioned, the two dominions would continue to maintain an undivided military establishment. This, however, proved to be wishful thinking, and on 3 June 1947 Auchinleck and his staff had to confront the fact (after Mountbatten's speech) that they had only seventy-two days within which to "reconstitute" (Auchinleck preferred this word to *partition*) the Indian army.

WHERE ARE THE GENERALS?

One fact remained constant regardless of whether the army would be divided or not: The Indian army was desperately short of senior Indian officers. Even the most favorable of prewar estimates on the schedule for Indianization had projected the mid-1950s as the period when senior Indian officers would assume high rank in the army. Independence had preempted this goal by almost a decade. An official memo from the British chiefs of staff highlighted the dilemma: "If the present standard is to be maintained, complete nationalization should be spread over at least ten years, which for political reasons is considered to be too long."[3]

Initially Auchinleck resisted efforts to accelerate the process. In response to a resolution—moved in the Council of State by Pandit Kunzru—that a time limit be set down for the nationalization of the entire officer corps, Auchinleck reiterated that, while complete Indianization remained his final goal, he did not want to accomplish this by lowering the very high standards of efficiency attained by the Indian army. He pointed out that there was no automatic correlation between an officer proving himself to be a good junior leader in war and an officer being a good senior officer in peace. He further opined that the Indian army "needed the best regular officers to maintain the essential minimum of efficiency in peace, officers with the ability to judge men and events soberly and with a deep knowledge of men and things, which can only come from long experience." Auchinleck presented statistics proving that of nine thousand regular officers needed, only 5,100 could be found within the next years without recourse to some unpalatable temporary expedients. These included the secondment of British officers from the British army to fill the gap; the retention of ECOs,

British and Indian, who might be willing to extend their services for a year or two; and the conferment of a number of short-service commissions on Indians already serving in the army.[4]

The political pressure, however, proved too much, and in November 1946 Auchinleck decided to give Indian regular officers, none of whom had progressed beyond the rank of brigadier, accelerated promotion over the heads of British officers.[5] However, he continued to express doubts about promoting Indian officers to senior positions while they had less than nine years of service. He pointed out that in regular European armies candidates for such senior appointments would have no less than twenty years of service. Furthermore, most of the eight thousand or so junior officers who made up the bulk of the officer corps had less than eight years of service instead of the usual twelve to fourteen years.[6] To ensure that newly commissioned Indian officers received the best possible training, Auchinleck gave the IMA top priority for people, ensuring that its staff could be "filled with the best officers who could be spared."[7]

Auchinleck's task was complicated further by the fact that the quality of Indian candidates coming up before the selection board was very poor and the percentage of rejections very high, resulting in the filling of only half the new vacancies at the first regular course of the IMA.[8] Auchinleck, determined not to lower the standards of admission, called for a drastic overhaul of the selection process, including the establishment of a preselection training school. Indeed, as early as April 1945, at a session of the National Defence Council in New Delhi, Auchinleck had made it clear that, while all efforts were being made to increase the number of Indians in command positions, only the best men available would be selected.[9] Brigadier Nathu Singh, the newly appointed director of officer selection, was given the express task of publicizing the IMA to capable candidates. He also had the onerous task of convincing Indian cabinet members that this was the best possible course.[10]

To implement further the goal of preparing Indian officers for senior command positions and to consolidate the links with Commonwealth defense, the British decided to send Indian officers to the IDC. The IDC had been established to train "selected members of the armed forces and civil services of the United Kingdom, the Dominions, and British overseas territories in the broadest aspects of strategy; and the study of the organization and direction of the whole resources of the Commonwealth and Empire for war."[11] Two Indian officers—Brigadier K.M. Cariappa and Brigadier J.N. Chaudhuri, both of whom were officers of the Order of the British Empire (OBE)—completed the second postwar course at the academy from January to December 1947.[12] They were fortunate to have General Slim as their commandant during the course. Chaudhuri, who was impressed greatly by Slim, recalled his opening lecture: "You have been sent on this course as you are good workers. There are no examinations and tests on this course. We only present you the material."[13]

Meanwhile, back in India, Staff College at Quetta prepared to train Indian officers for midlevel command positions. The first postwar course placed a heavy emphasis on preparing officers for the function of command. In addition to providing a thorough grounding in staff duties, all officers were to have frequent opportunities of acting as the appropriate commander in "syndicate exercises and schemes, so that they may gain an insight into the responsibilities and functions of command."[14] At a tactical level, too, Indian officers were introduced to various aspects of handling and maintaining all types of division-sized formations. The instructors placed particular emphasis upon "detailed staff planning of all phases of the battle, and will incorporate all arms of the service and such elements of the Navy and Air Force which are capable of cooperation or supporting the division."[15] The last requirement would enhance and reinforce the considerable experience gained in combined-arms operations during the Second World War.

Concurrent with the desire to shore up the Indian officer corps, the British had an additional and urgent need to further modernize the Indian army. This requirement would ensure that the army of independent India could continue to play an important role in the defense of the British Commonwealth. Right up to the very eve of independence the British Cabinet in London and the British authorities in India remained convinced that military ties between Britain and India basically would remain unchanged. At one point the government of Clement Richard Attlee considered having the congress sign a defense treaty as a condition for granting independence.[16] This has led at least one researcher to allege a conspiracy theory: that India's right to secede from the Commonwealth was only theoretical.[17] However, the fact that this directive was never carried out leads one researcher to suggest that the British were confident that India's military inferiority in regard to equipment and officers would ensure Indian dependence on Whitehall.[18]

Indeed there is some evidence to support this view. Auchinleck himself seems to have been convinced of this. Writing to the CIGS Lord Alanbrooke in January 1946, Auchinleck stated that it was unlikely that the autonomous Indian government would decline the invitation to maintain British troops in India.[19] In an August speech to the students of Staff College, Quetta, he continued to assume that India would remain in the Commonwealth as a fully autonomous dominion. He pointed out severe shortages in the army, navy, and air forces, and suggested that if the British and Indian governments were mutually agreeable, British troops could be retained in India and organized in independent brigade groups. Auchinleck obviously anticipated little change taking place in the military relationship between India and Britain after Indian independence. The emphasis continued to be placed upon training Indian officers and creating a "smaller, highly protected, extremely mobile, very hard hitting and self-contained" Indian army. It would be just the sort of intervention force the military planners in the interwar period had envisioned.[20]

Not all British policy makers, however, were entirely confident of India's continued cooperation in Commonwealth defense after independence. The British chiefs of staff, including the new CIGS, Field Marshal Viscount B.L. Monty Montgomery, were extremely worried about sharing secret defense-related material with Indian officers attending the IDC. The British chiefs of staff, including the director of military intelligence, felt that Indian officers should be excluded from courses at the IDC for security reasons. At the eleventh hour the chiefs of staff decided not to ban the Indians from the course. Instead, General Slim, the commandant of the college, was told to arrange things so that "super-secret information was not divulged."[21] An enraged Auchinleck declared,

> The D.M.I. and all his clan are of course merely running true to their usual form of never running any risk at all! They are just the same everywhere!! They can't help themselves. . . . My ideas have not changed. So long as India is part of the Commonwealth, Indian officers must be accepted [to the IDC] on an equality with any other regular officers.[22]

Montgomery was unmoved and, in a letter to Auchinleck, he reaffirmed the ban on releasing top secret information, noting that there was concern in London about Jawaharlal Nehru's recent resolution in favor of an Indian republic and the fact that this had been passed in the Indian assembly. Not only did Montgomery reinforce the ban on attendence by Indian officers at the IDC to "certain highly secret lectures," he also declared his intention not to send top secret papers in connection with recent Camberley exercises to India, as requested by Auchinleck.[23] By March 1947, Auchinleck himself was forced to come round to this point of view, noting that it would be logical to ban Indian officers from the IDC until the future constitutional status of India became more clearly defined.[24]

In early 1947 the Indian Armed Forces Nationalization Committee had set 1 July 1949 as the goal for the complete nationalization of the Indian army. This program, based upon "Plan 287," called for an officer cadre of nine thousand Indian officers (excluding medical and veterinary). A February 1947 meeting of the Chief of Staff Committee—which included Lieutenant General Sir Arthur Smith, the Chief of Staff (COS)—deliberated this plan. The committee concluded that

> It is our considered opinion that, by 1 January 1949, there will NOT be enough Indian officers fit by experience to be given all the higher command and senior staff appointments without accepting a very big drop in the present high standard. This

Table 8
Ratio of British and Indian Officers from 1926–1947[25]

Date	British Officers	Indian Officers	Total
1926	-	74	-
1931	3033	108	3141
1 Oct 1939	4028	396	4424
1 Jan 1940	4028	415	4443
1 Jan 1941	7194	596	7790
1 Jan 1942	13833	1667	15500
1 Jan 1943	25565	3676	29241
1 Jan 1944	29740	6566	36306
1 Jan 1945	32344	7546	39890
1 Sept 1945	34590	8340	42930
1 Oct 1945	34100	7800	41900
1 Apr 1947	11500	8400	19900

applies in even greater force, to the technical posts in both lower and higher grades. Officers qualified for these posts will NOT exist.[26]

According to the COS's own figures, there were 34,100 British officers to 7,800 Indian officers on 1 October 1945. This ratio changed dramatically by 1 April 1947: 11,500 British officers to 8,400 Indian officers (it must be noted that the Indian army had reduced substantially its strength during the same period). This would seem to suggest that the goal of nine thousand Indian officers by 1949 could have been met easily. However, a considerable number of these officers were ECIOs with little experience, most of whom would not obtain permanent commissions.[27]

On 5 July 1946 the COS Committee issued a final report addressing the strategic advantages and disadvantages should India become a sovereign state outside the Commonwealth. The committee noted that the only advantage to be seen in the existence of independent India was that it would relieve Britain of considerable manpower commitments. The disadvantages, on the other hand, were numerous. The committee noted that an independent and unfriendly India—influenced by powers hostile to the Commonwealth, such as Russia, China, or Japan—would make it impossible to move freely by sea and air in the northern part of the Indian Ocean area, which was of supreme importance to the Commonwealth.[28] The committee urged that in order to plan for such a contingency the Andaman Islands should be retained as an outpost to Burma and Malaya.[29]

PARTITION

On 3 June 1947, Lord Mountbatten, the last viceroy, announced that power would be transferred to the two independent Dominions of India and Pakistan on 15 August 1947. In May Nehru rejected a last attempt to maintain an undivided defense establishment, giving Auchinleck little more than ten weeks to divide the armed forces between the two emerging nations. The Indian government established the Joint Defence Council (JDC) to facilitate this task. According to Wainwright, this was yet another last-ditch attempt by Mountbatten "to retain the unity of and British influence over the command structure of the two dominions."[30] The same month that Mountbatten made this historic announcement, he set up the Armed Forces Reconstruction Committee (AFRC) to suggest just how defense resources could be divided between the two dominions.[31] The JDC, chaired by Lord Mountbatten, supplanted this role by 15 August. It controlled all the military assets and manpower until they were divided between the two dominions.

On 30 June the interim cabinet accepted the COS's proposal that the armed forces and defense assets be divided along a seventy to thirty ratio in favor of India. However, this clean mathematical divide proved difficult to implement. First, many of the army regiments were ethnically diverse (there were no Muslim-only units). So it was decided that, while units would be divided along the seventy to thirty ratio line, the personnel of these units would have the option of transferring to the other dominion's armed forces. Second, a different problem arose over the division of military establishments. For various but primarily strategic reasons, most of the defense establishments were located in the interior of the subcontinent. It obviously would be impractical physically to uproot these facilities in order to transfer them to Pakistan, so it was decided that only movable assets would be divided. Consequently, India walked away from the partition with one of the largest defense-production establishments in the world.[32]

Once the division of political power had taken place, it became increasingly difficult for the JDC to coordinate the division of military resources. One of the problems was India's reluctance and slowness in complying with the redistribution of military stores. Auchinleck, however, considered this a minor point and felt most of the JDC's task had been completed. Yet it was becoming increasingly apparent that the JDC was becoming a defunct body. The two dominions simply could not agree on anything substantial. Any high hopes Mountbatten might have had for continued cooperation finally were dashed on 22 October 1947, when Pakistan launched Operation Gibraltar, its covert guerrilla war to wrest control of the princely state of Kashmir. In November and amidst escalating conflict in the Kashmir valley, the supreme commander's HQ was dissolved, and Auchinleck left India.

INDEPENDENCE

Although in strict legal terms Britain's control of the armies of India and Pakistan ended on 15 August 1947, she continued to exercise considerable influence over these armies well into 1950, and even beyond that in the case of Pakistan. This was a direct result of the severe shortage of senior officers in both of these armies. Both India and Pakistan embarked toward their independent future with British army commanders: General Douglas Gracey for Pakistan and General F.F. Roy Bucher for India. Furthermore, for several years after independence in India's case and a half decade in Pakistan's case, both the armies utilized several senior British officers at various command/advisory-level positions in their armies; this was particularly so in the case of technical arms (the same was the case with the navies and the air forces). These deficiencies meant that actual colonial military disengagement from in the subcontinent came about only in the mid-1950s.

Soon after independence the British found themselves in a unique position in regard to the two armies. They were no longer saddled with the heavy responsibilities of managing these armies and of coping with the accompanying thankless political consequences. However, they were in a situation where they could watch most closely the evolution of these armies, and, if the situation demanded, exercise subtle yet significant influence upon them. The presence of a number of senior British officers who continued to be employed by these armies made this situation possible. These officers, although nominally under the control of either the Indian or the Pakistan governments, would in the final analysis be answerable only to the British government.

The undeclared war over Kashmir posed the main postindependence crisis for the emerging nations. This war provided the British with an opportunity—unwelcome though it might have been—to witness firsthand the military performance of their erstwhile protégés. The main focus of their attention not surprisingly was the nascent officer corps and in particular the senior commanders of the two armies. The war in Kashmir quickly highlighted the deficiencies in the officer corps of the two armies. The British were determined to ensure that no serving British officer in either of these armies would become involved in the fighting. To guarantee this the British government was prepared to withdraw all its officers by issuing a stand-down order if either army sought to utilize its British officers in combat.[33] Such an order would have had a disastrous effect upon the Pakistani army, and, just as the British had intended, this threat did considerably restrain Pakistani activity in Kashmir for some time.[34]

During the early stages of the Kashmir conflict (26 October 1947), the Pakistani leader M.A. Jinnah ordered the British Commander in Chief of the Pakistan Army General Gracey to seize the strategic Kashmiri locations of Baramulla, Srinagar, and Banihal Pass. Gracey refused to comply and informed the Supreme Commander Auchinleck (27 October 1947). The next day Auchinleck flew to Lahore and informed Jinnah of the "incalculable consequences" of the military violation of "what is now territory of the Indian Union." General Gracey emphasized Pakistani weaknesses, including no doubt its lack of officers. Jinnah, although "angry and disturbed," withdrew the order that Gracey in any case had refused to obey. According to a British intelligence report, the Pakistani army had a "clear 36 hours between the time Mr. Jinnah issued orders for their move to Srinagar and Banihal and the arrival of Indian troops by air in Srinagar." The report suggested that the presence of even a few Pakistani troops at Srinagar would have dissuaded the Indians from landing there. As the report concluded, "We know that the air move of Indian Army to Srinagar was completely unpremeditated and carried out on a non-tactical basis."[35] Indeed, the shortage of officers in the Pakistani army was so serious that in the process of raising four new divisions, it became necessary to reduce the number of regular officers in the battalions from twelve to eight and to increase greatly the responsibility of the JCOs.[36] The shortage of officers in the Pakistani air force was even more urgent, forcing the latter to engage Polish flying officers from Britain in order to avoid using British officers in the conflict.[37] The main problem Pakistan faced with its officer corps was that most Pakistani officers, unlike their Indian counterparts, had little combat experience and lacked the "necessary background."[38]

According to Auchinleck, at partition there were few good Muslim officers, as most of them had been sidetracked to support units, while at the same time there was a great number of able Hindu officers in the fighting units.[39] In General Gracey's view, the reason for this was that Muslims did not do well in competitive exams with Hindus. Gracey, who became the first commander in chief of the Pakistan army, pointed out that at partition Pakistan had only four lieutenant colonels: Ayub Khan, Akbar Khan, M. Hayyauddin, and N.M. Sher Ali Khan.[40] Another British officer, Brigadier John Stephenson, also noted that Hindus on the whole were better staff officers than Muslims.[41]

The British opinion of the Pakistani army's senior leadership was equally gloomy. Mr. A.H. Reed, a British junior councilor reporting on the issue of the future Pakistani army commander, noted that Major General N.A.M. Raza, "a born intriguer, had been lobbying hard for the Commander-in-Chief position." Reed felt that Raza had neither the ability nor the personality for the job. He was feared by his juniors and disliked by the majority of the British and senior Pakistani officers. Reed's own "two favorite bets" were the respective commanders of the 10th and 9th divisions, Iftikhar-Ud Din and Nazir Ahmed Khan.[42]

The British did not enjoy a similar leverage over India. Brigadier J.F. Walker, the military adviser to the U.K. high commissioner in Pakistan, drew attention to the fact that there were no British officers serving in the fighting forces of India and that most of the British officers in the Indian army were employed only in an advisory capacity.[43] Once the replacement of British junior and midlevel officers with Indian officers had begun proceeding fairly smoothly, the British became obsessed almost entirely with the senior Indian army officers. In 1948 the main question occupying the minds of the British was who would succeed General Bucher as the commander in chief. Brigadier Walker quoted General Gracey as saying that the post would go to General Rajendra Sinjhi, who commanded the successful police action to incorporate the princely state of Hyderabad into the Indian Union. In his conversation with Gracey, Walker noted that Rajendra Sinjhi was not considered to be "too able," to which Gracey replied, "Yes but Reggie is a Gentleman."[44]

Apparently professional qualification alone was not enough for some senior British officers to approve the appointments of senior Indian officers. Personality traits, in fact, played a major role in British opinions of the Indian general staff in the postindependence period. In a secret telegram to the Commonwealth Relations Office almost a year after General Cariappa had been appointed as the first Indian commander in chief of the Indian army, Sir Terence Shone, the British high commissioner to India, complained that the departing British commander, General Bucher, had not been consulted about Cariappa's appointment. In Shone's view, "there is no officer in the Indian Army fit to be Commander-in-Chief but there are some probably better qualified than Cariappa. He is vain, superficial, impetuous, lacking in stability, moral courage and above all military judgement."[45] This scathing vilification of India's senior-most military officer by Sir Shone is somewhat puzzling, for although Cariappa is not thought of as a great field commander, he is considered by many qualified observers within and outside of the Indian army to have done a commendable job as its first Indian commander in chief. Shone's attacks on Cariappa are all the more remarkable when one considers the fact that his own military adviser, Brigadier W.W. Loring held a most favorable opinion on Cariappa's appointment. In his first report as military adviser, Brigadier Loring noted with "pride and pleasure" that an Indian commander in chief had at last been appointed. He noted that there were no anti-British feelings in the Indian high command; in fact, there was a desire to keep liaison with British officers. In citing an example, Loring felt that "the Government of India have behaved extremely generously towards General Bucher in making him a full General in the Indian Army."[46] Loring also noted that Cariappa was the officer with more staff experience and was senior to Rajendra Sinjhi, and, had the government of India not chosen him, the army could have been split into Cariappa and Sinjhi factions. As for Cariappa as commander in chief, Loring was very impressed by his "firm" assumption of command.[47]

This strong assumption of command is very much in evidence in Cariappa's first set of Indian army orders. He declared,

> It has been noted that the military bearing of personnel in certain units is below the required standard. This is mainly due to the insufficient time being devoted to drill, with and without arms, and to insufficient attention being paid to precision in drill movements. In order to bring military-bearing to the standard requirement throughout the Army, a period of not less than ten minutes will be spent during each days parade hours on close order drill, by every unit in the Army. The term unit will be taken to include detachments of Army or Corps, wherever they may be employed. When practical to do so, this drill will be carried out with arms. Alertness and precision will be insisted upon.

Cariappa went on to note that many junior officers in Kashmir lacked experience. He recommended a "period" of guidance by senior officers and also suggested that whenever possible plans be "vetted" by seniors. Cariappa also noted that many senior officers were not conversant with their duties in the new appointments. He called for senior general officers to initiate training of their immediate subordinates; for example, brigadiers who in turn would train colonels.[48] The press' reaction to Cariappa was equally favorable. Reuters news of India and Pakistan Service described him as a "lithe 6 footer . . . like Monty he rates the 'human factor' a top priority in any campaign . . . speaks in clipped, effective sentences."[49]

Sir Shone's virulent, albeit behind the scene, attack on Cariappa stemmed partly from his belief that, "although my relations with Cariappa, whom I have known for many years is friendly, I think it unlikely he will seek my advice, and, I would naturally be very cautious of offering it gratuitously. Our influence in military circles will therefore diminish or disappear altogether."[50] Sir Shone's views, however, flew straight in the face of Brigadier Loring. He stated that Lieutenant General Dudley Russell, the senior British adviser to the Indian army, had been sought constantly for his advice and that he—Russell—enjoyed an influential position in the army.[51]

Loring's endorsement of Cariappa notwithstanding, he did note several problems in the Indian general staff. In fact, his first report of 1949 is a comprehensive and qualified review of the performance of the Indian army's senior leadership in the two years since independence. Commenting on Lieutenant General J.M. Shrinagesh, who left 5th Corps in Kashmir to take over for Cariappa as general officer commander in Chief (GOC-in-C) of the Western Command, Loring noted that "he is an extremely nice little man with a good deal of common sense but has very little experience as a senior commander." Of Major General Hira Lal Atal, the new Adjutant General, Loring said,

> Atal is a curious officer who for many years was suspected of being extremely anti-British. . . . British officers [were] wrong in thinking he was anti-British—probably pro-nationalism. . . . However, as Commander of 18th Cavalry he seemed to mistrust all the British officers serving under him, the regiment was an extremely unhappy one and I, as Brigade Commander, had to ask for him to be transferred elsewhere. This fact will make my dealings with him somewhat delicate.

Regarding Major General Lakhinder Singh, the master general of ordnance (a newly created position) Loring expressed his doubts as to whether the general would be able to cope with his new job. Loring also noted that Brigadier Dillon had been appointed as director of movements and quartering because Brigadier S.D. Verma, the incumbent, had not been up to the task. On the other hand, Loring felt that Brigadier N.D. Bilimoria, the director of personnel selection, was an extremely capable officer. In regard to General J.N. Chaudhuri, Loring noted that he was extremely ambitious with the backing of an equally ambitious wife. He foresaw a diplomatic appointment for him after his posting as military governor of Hyderabad.

Commenting on the army HQ, Loring pointed out that very little proper planning about the final setup of the army (then 372,000) existed at their level. At least one serving British officer, Brigadier N.J.B. Stuart, told Loring that he was "extremely depressed because there appeared to be no planning whatsoever and that everything was done on an ad-hoc basis." Summing up his report, Loring stated,

> Taking into consideration the partition of the army in August 1947 and what has happened since, the extremely rapid promotion of most of the officers in the army, I think the army has put up an extremely creditable performance. I have seen no deterioration in discipline, turn out or saluting. General Cariappa himself is extremely keen on maintaining a very high standard.[52]

ENDGAMES

The Indian army marched into independence a creature quite different from what the British had intended. Not only was this army no longer the bastion of a greater Commonwealth defensive alliance, but also it was no longer a single entity. In many ways the partition of the Indian army, and not Nehru's decision to make India a republic, came as the greater shock to the British. The division itself, without a doubt, weakened the subcontinent's military potential. Did this unforeseen calamity then destroy decades of painstaking effort by the British to modernize the Indian army? The answer has to be "No," for the Indian army emerged relatively unscathed from the partition. In regard to the most important asset of any emerging army—the officer corps—the Indian army easily emerged in a superior position compared to Pakistan (see Table 9). Not only did the new Indian army have many more officers than Pakistan, but it had the most capable and experienced officers. Indeed it is in the Indian officer corps that we see the true measure of success of the British efforts.

Although most Indian officers were not prepared for senior command positions in 1947, after an initial process of trial and error, they did settle down to do a fairly competent job. Their professional competence combined with the maturity of the Indian political system ensured that the they would continue to remain one of the few officer corps in the developing world to be untainted by involvement in politics. The military action in Kashmir (1947–1950) also indicated that these senior officers had absorbed fully the cautious defensive-offensive military doctrine of their British mentors. This is a doctrine to which the Indian military continues to adhere even to this day with reasonable success. Furthermore, with the exception of the conflict with Pakistan, recent Indian military involvement in Sri Lanka and the Maldives does seem to indicate that India is at last fulfilling the stabilizing role in the Indian Ocean region envisioned by the British in the years leading to independence.

Pakistan, on the other hand, followed a different road. Not only did it end up obtaining a fraction of the defense material and establishments of undivided India, but also, and more crucially, its officer corps was woefully inadequate in both numbers and seniority. The reports of the British military advisers in Pakistan in the early years after independence bemoaned the fact that promotions were coming fast and furious at the cost of professionalism and quality. Pakistan's senior-most army chiefs and generals found themselves catapulted virtually overnight into positions of tremendous responsibility and authority with little or no training for the jobs. An immature military leadership along with a relatively weak political system resulted in the Pakistani army's involvement in politics. In terms of military doctrine, too, the Pakistani army diverged from the Indian army. In the place of the defensive-offensive military doctrine, the Pakistanis adopted an offensive-defensive military doctrine. Evidence of such a doctrine is revealed in the planning of Operation Gibraltar. Pakistan's adherence to such a doctrine without having the necessary resources and skills resulted in repeated failure, culminating with the disastrous 1971 war against India. Although this doctrine was in part necessitated by India's superiority in resources and manpower, it was engendered mainly by a Pakistani army leadership that had few—if any—doctrinal links to its British past. The Pakistani military leadership, seduced by the high-tech military technology and doctrines of the United States, became convinced that a technologically advanced Pakistani army could easily defeat a numerically superior Indian

Table 9
List of Officers of the Rank of Colonel and Above in the Pakistani Army (1948)[53]

GHQ

Commander in Chief: General Sir Douglas Gracey
COS: Lieutenant General R.C. McCay
Offg. Dy. COS: Major General W.J. Cawthorne

MS Branch

Military Secretary: Brigadier Rahman Kallno
Deputy Secretary: Colonel K.C. Campbell-Meiklojohn

GS Branch

Chief of General Staff: Major General R.A. Hutton
DMO: Brigadier M. Sher Khan
DMI: Colonel M.A. Latif Khan
DSD: Brigadier S.W. Packwood
DWE: Colonel M.H. Hussain
DMT: Brigadier C.J. Jerrard
Dir. Arty.: Brigadier R. Morley
Dir. Sigs.: Brigadier H.L. Lewis

AG's Branch

Adjutant General: Major General N.A.M. Raza
D of O: Brigadier C.P. Murray
DPS: Brigadier H.L. Hill
DGMS: Major General S.M.A. Faruki
DDGMS: Colonel W.A. Burki
JAG: Colonel S. Sherjan

QMG's Branch

Quarter Master General: Major General S. Greeves
Brig. "Q": Brigadier Nasir Ali Khan
DST: Brigadier M.J.A. Sheehan
DDST: Colonel Jamal Dar
DRV&E: Brigadier Malik Gulsher Khan

MGO's Branch

Master General Ordnance: Major General A. Whiteside
CTD: Colonel J. Browne
DOS: Brigadier E.C.O. Morphy
D. DOS: Colonel N.L. Crumby
D. Dos (Stores): Colonel M.A. Khanzada
DEME: Brigadier W.P.B. Ashton
Offg. DDEME (Tech): Colonel D.F. Bartlett

E-in-C's Branch

Engineer in Chief: Major General Sir Willis R. Jeffries
Dy. E-in-C & Dir. Works: Brigadier W.L.B. Veitch
Col. Eng. Staff: Colonel D.R. Martin

Table 9 (continued)

7th Division

Commander: Major General F.J. Loftus-Tottenham
2 i/c: Brigadier M. Hayauddin, MC
CRA: Brigadier J.M.L. Crawford
10th Bde. Cmdr.: Brigadier H.I. Ahmad
25th Bde. Cmdr.: Brigadier Mohammed Azam Khan
2 i/c: Colonel F.W. Gibb
101st Bde. Cmdr.: Brigadier Akbar Khan, DSO (transferred to 9th Div.)

8th Division

Commander: Major General Mohammed Akbar Khan, MBE
2 i/c: Brigadier P.W. Parker
CRA: Brigadier P.H.L. Findlay
51st Bde. Cmdr.: Brigadier H.I. Majid

9th Division

Commander: Major General Nazir Ahmed
110th Bde. Cmdr.: Brigadier K.M. Sheik
101st Bde. Cmdr.: Brigadier Akbar Khan, DSO (Trg. and Admin.)
102nd Bde. Cmdr.: Brigadier Mohammed Yousuf Khan

10th Division

Commander: Major General Mohammed Iftikhar Khan
2 i/c: Brigadier F.H. Stevens
14th Bde. Cmdr.: Brigadier Nawalzada Mohammed Sher Ali Khan
103rd Bde. Cmdr.: Brigadier Mohammed Musa
2 i/c: Colonel K. Ata Mohammed Khan
114th Bde. Cmdr.: Brigadier C.H.B. Rodham
2 i/c: Colonel S.M. Afzal

Instructional Establishments, Etc.

Comdnt. Staff College: Brigadier I.C.A. Lauder
Assistant Comdnt. & Comdnt.:
Staff Wing, Staff College: Local/Colonel R.T. Prince
Comdnt. T&A Wing Staff College: Local/Colonel J.E.G. Malsey
Comdnt. Pak. Inf. School: Colonel N.J.G. Jones
Comdnt. Pak. Military Academy: Colonel F.H.B. Ingall
Comdnt. Pak. Signal Corps Centre & School: Colonel P.H. Smitherman
Comdnt. Pak. Trg. Center/School: Colonel G.M. Stroud
Comdnt. PEME Regtl. Trg. Center: Colonel A.L. Ellison
Comdnt. PAOCC Center: Colonel G. Murphy
Comdnt. RPASC Center & Records: Colonel A.B.M. Way
Admin. Comdnt. Karachi: Colonel C.F. Featherstone
President 52SS Board: Colonel Malik Mohammed Khan
President 53SS Board: Colonel Faiz Mohammed Khan
Comdnt. Baluch RC: Colonel R.E. Fellows
MS to Quaid-i-Azam [Jinnah]: Local/Colonel G. Knowles
IG Frontier Corps: Brigadier D.H.J. Williams
Dy. IG Frontier Corps: Colonel W.H. Fitzmaurice
Comdnt. RPA Center: Colonel W.G.P. Stirling
CRE, Quetta: Colonel E.J. Palairet
DCE, Quetta: Colonel N. Boddington
Comdnt. RPE Center: Colonel J.R. Connor

Table 10
List of Officers of the Rank of Colonel and Above in the Indian Army (1948)[54]

Army HQ India

Commander in Chief: General F.F.R. Bucher
MS: Major General P.N. Thapar
CGS: Major General J.N. Chaudhuri (being replaced by Major General Kalwant Singh)
DMO: Brigadier Jemi H.F. Manekshaw
DMI: Brigadier Chand Das
DSP: Brigadier Som Dutt
DMT: Brigadier J.H. Wilkinson
Dir. Sigs.: Brigadier C.H.I. Akehurst
Dir. Arty.: Brigadier P.S. Gyani
DCGS (W&E): Brigadier H.D. Bilimoria
DME: Brigadier R.F. Worthington
DTD: Brigadier H.C. Parcell
Military Adviser-in-C, State Forces: Major General Himatsinjhi

AG's Branch

Adjutant General: Major General S.M. Shrinagesh
DPS: Brigadier P.C. Banerji
D of O: Brigadier C.D.L. Turner
JAG: Brigadier W.G.H. Wells
DMS: Major General K.S. Master

QMG's Branch

Quarter Master General: Major General B.S. Chimni
DST: Major General G.S. Dhillon
Dir. Movt. & Qrtrng.: Brigadier K.K. Verma
DOS: Brigadier F.A. Rodrigues
Dir. Remount, Vets & Farms: Brigadier Gurbachan Singh

E-in-C's Branch

Engineer in Chief: Major General H. Williams
CES: Colonel R.E. Aserappa
Dir. Tpt.: Brigadier Arjan Singh
Dir. Works: Brigadier F.B. Pigott

Western Command

Commander: Lieutenant General K.M. Cariappa
BGS: Brigadier M.S. Wadalia

HQ J&K Force

Commander: Major General Kalwant Singh (Jammu—being replaced by Major General K.S. Thimayya)
Colonel GS.: Colonel J.T. Satarawalla
Brig. Admin: Brigadier Umrao Singh
CRA: Brigadier S.J. Sathe
HQ 19th Inf. Bde.: Brigadier Usman Khan (Jhangar)

Table 10 (continued)

HQ 80th Bde. Grp.: Brigadier V.D. Jayal, DSO (Akhnur)
HQ 161st Bde. Grp.: Brigadier L.P. Sen (Uri)
HQ 268th Bde.: Brigadier Bikram Singh (Jammu—Miran Sahib)
Poonch Bde.: Brigadier Pritam Singh (Poonch)
HQ 50th Para. Bde.: Brigadier Yadunath Singh (Rajauri)
HQ 77th Para. Bde.: Brigadier Sankaran Nair (Jasmigarh)
HQ L of C Subarea: Brigadier Jai Singh (Pathankot)

HQ East Punjab Area

Commander: Major General K.S. Thimayya (Jullunder—being replaced by Major General S.P.P. Thorat)
HQ Ambala Subarea: Brigadier Roy (Ambala)
HQ Jullunder Subarea: Brigadier Lakhinder Singh (Jullunder)

4th Infantry Division

Commander: Major General Sant Singh (Ambala)
HQ 5th Bde.: Major General Sant Singh
HQ 11th Bde.: Brigadier Henderson Brooks (Anglo-Indian)—(Gurdaspur)
HQ 123rd Bde.: Brigadier M.S. Chopra (Amritsar)
HQ 43rd Lorried Bde.: Brigadier K.O. Dhargalkar (Ferozepore—moving to Poona)

HQ Delhi Area

Commander: Major General Tara Singh Bal (Delhi Cantonment)
1/5 Gurkhas (Delhi Fort), 6/5 Gurkhas (New Delhi), 2 Mahar Regt. (Delhi Cantonment)

Eastern Command

Commander: Major General Nathu Singh (Ranchi—Panagar Base)

1st Armored Division

Commander: Major General Hira Lal Atal (Jhansi—being replaced by Major General J.N. Chaudhuri)
HQ 1st Armd. Bde.: Brigadier S.D. Verma (Babina)
HQ 2nd (Indep.) Armd Bde.: Brigadier Daulat Singh (Meerut)
HQ 9th Inf. Bde.: Brigadier Atma Singh (Bangalore)
BGS: Brigadier N.J.B. Stuart

HQ Bengal, Bihar, and Orissa

Commander: Major General F.R.L. Goodby (Calcutta)
HQ Bihar & Orissa Sub Area: Brigadier Paranjpe (Dinapore)
HQ Shillong (Indep.) Sub Area: Brigadier Habibullah (Shillong)

HQ UP Area

Commander: To be commanded by Major General Hira Lal Atal (Lucknow)
HQ Meerut Subarea:
HQ Lucknow Subarea: Brigadier K. Sherif (Lucknow)
HQ Allahabad Subarea: Brigadier C.B. Ponnappa (Allahabad)

Table 10 (continued)

Southern Command

Commander: Lieutenant General E.N. Goddard (Poona—being replaced by Lieutenant General Rajendra Sinjhi 1.5.48)
Brig. BGS: Brigadier H.M. Mohite (being replaced by Brigadier Dillon 12.5.48)
HQ 7th Inf. Bde.:
HQ Bombay Area: Major General D.R. Bateman (Bombay—being replaced by Brigadier D.S. Brar)
HQ Bombay Subarea: Brigadier D.S. Brar
HQ Poona Subarea: Brigadier J.D.S. Keenan (Poona—being replaced by Brigadier H.M. Mohite 12.5.48)

HQ Madras Area

Commander: Major General A.A. Rudra (Madras)
HQ Madras Subarea: Brigadier Madhur Sinjhi (Madras)
HQ Bangalore Subarea: Brigadier G. Creffield (Bangalore)
HQ Jubbulpore (Indep.) Subarea: Brigadier Sheodatt Singh (Jubbulpore)

5th Infantry Division

Officiating Commander: Brigadier Kripal (Ranchi)
9th Inf. Bde.: Brigadier Atma Singh (Bangalore)
Other Units Forming

Instructional Establishments, Etc.

Staff College, Wellington: Major General W.D.A. Lentaigne
IMA, Dehra Dun: Brigadier Mahadeo Singh, DSO
Inf. School, Mhow: Brigadier N. MacDonald, DSO
Tac. & Admin., Mhow: Brigadier J.C. Hudson
Armd. Corps School: Colonel Aspinall
Arty. School, Deolali: Brigadier A.W. Littlefield
School of Military Eng. Kirkee: Colonel J.S. Forbes
RIASC School, Baraeilly: Colonel J.S. Grewal
RIASC Trg. Centre (North): Colonel P.R. Broadway
RIASC Trg. School (South): Colonel G.S. Gill
IEME School, Kirkee: Colonel I.H. Reeves
IEME Trg. Centre, Katni: Colonel Newton King
IAOC School, Jubbulpore: Colonel J.M. Blyth
Army Medical Trg. College, Poona: Colonel P.P. Choudry

army with speed and surprise. The Pakistani military was also a firm believer in the martial races theory and felt that their numerical inferiority was more than offset by a decided "martial" dominance over the Hindu masses.

In vain, the Pakistani military tried to fulfill its ambition of becoming a bastion of "freedom" from communism in southern Asia by joining the United States–inspired anticommunist military alliances: South East Asia

Treaty Organization (SEATO) and Central Asia Treaty Organization (CENTO). The politicization of its officer corps, its adherence to a military doctrine beyond its capabilities, and its long-standing obsession with India ensured such failure. Although the legacy of the old British-Indian army in regard to its professional officer corps and an operationally sound military doctrine continue to live on and evolve primarily in the Indian army today; the Pakistani army and even the Bangladeshi Army do maintain a high degree of professional competence, especially in comparison to most other developing world armies.

NOTES

1. India and the war 1939–1945: The facts, Information Department, India Office, 1 January 1946, BL/IOR, L/MIL/17/5/4263.
2. T.W. Wallbank, *A Short History of India and Pakistan* (New York: Scott, Foresman, 1958), 208, 214–15, 219.
3. Nationalization of the armed forces of India, Memorandum 214–15, by General Sir Geoffrey Scoones, 5 March 1947, BL/IOR, WS 17089—L/WS/1/1096, 134.
4. Speech made by Auchinleck, 8 April 1946, in Margaret M. Wright, "The Military Papers, 1940–1948, of Field-Marshal Sir Claude Auchinleck," *Bulletin of the John Rylands University Library of Manchester*, vol. 70, no. 2 (Summer 1988): doc. 1147 312–13.
5. Heathcote, *The Military in British India*, 252.
6. Auchinleck to Mountbatten, 8 March 1947, Correspondence and memoranda on the Indian armed forces, Mountbatten Collection, BL/IOR, Mss.Eur.F. 200/6.
7. The last IMA wartime course ended on 2 February 1946, and the regular courses began on 25 of the same month. Sinha and Chandra, *Valour and Wisdom*, 169, 174.
8. During the war the standards for entry into the officer corps were relaxed greatly. This opened the door for a large number of less educated and unmotivated Indian candidates, who continued to flood the selection board after the war. After the war, however, the selection process was tightened up to the prewar standards, resulting in the rejection of many of these candidates.
9. Colville to Amery, L/PO/10/22 Secret. 16 April 1945, N. Mansergh, E.W.R. Lumby, and Penderel Moon (eds.), *India: The Transfer of Power 1942–1947* (London: HMSO, 1970–1983), 5: 393.
10. Army Commanders Conference at GHQ, October 1946: C-in-C's opening address, BL/IOR, WS 13023—L/WS/1/1523, 30.
11. Schools: IDC, Annex VII Charter of the IDC (revised), 23 June 1948, BL/IOR, WS 14044—L/WS/1/806, 7.
12. Ibid., 10.
13. Narayan, *General J.N. Chaudhuri*, 137.
14. Training: Staff College, Quetta, BL/IOR, WS 14066—L/WS/1/824, 17.
15. Ibid.
16. Anita Inder Singh, "Imperial Defence and the Transfer of Power in India,

1946–1947," *International History Review*, vol. 4, no. 4 (1982): 568–88; Anita Inder Singh, "Keeping India in the Commonwealth: British Political and Military Aims, 1947–1949," *Journal of Contemporary History*, vol. 20, no. 3 (1985): 469–81; Anita Inger Singh, "Post Imperial British Attitudes to India: The Military Aspect, 1947–1951," *Round Table*, no. 296 (1985): 360–75; Ayesha Jalal, "India's Partition and the Defence of Pakistan: An Historical Perspective," *Journal of Imperial and Commonwealth History*, vol. 15, no. 3 (1987): 290–310.

17. Singh, "Imperial Defence," 574–76.

18. Wainwright, *Inheritance of Empire*, 62.

19. Auchinleck suggested that British troops might be put into independent brigades to make their stay more acceptable. Wright, *Military Papers*, no. 1136, 308.

20. Address by Auchinleck to students of Staff College at Quetta, 2 August 1946, Ibid., no. 1191, 320–21.

21. Schools: Imperial Defence College, Attendance of Indian officers at Imperial Defence College, 11 December 1946, BL/IOR, WS 14044—L/WS/1/806, 41.

22. Extract from letter from His Excellency Field Marshal Sir Claude Auchinleck, C-in-C India, 3 December 1946, Ibid., 43.

23. Montgomery to Auchinleck, 30 January 1947, Wright, *Military Papers*, no. 1213, 328.

24. Auchinleck to Sir Geoffrey Scoones, principal staff officer to under secretary of state for India, 2 March 1947, Ibid., no. 1215, 328–29.

25. This data has been gathered from a variety of sources: BL/IOR, WS 17096—L/WS/1107, 75; *Report of the Indian Sandhurst Committee* [Skeen Committee], app. 2 56: Prasad, *Expansion of the Armed Forces*, 170, 180–82; "Report of Sub-Committee VII, Indian Round Table Conference (Defence)," quoted in Sinha and Chandra, *Valour and Wisdom*, 29. The fall in the number of Indian officers between September and October 1945 may be explained by the fact that the army was getting rid of a number of the ECIOs between 1945–1946.

26. COS India papers, COS Committee's 207th meeting, 13 February 1947, BL/IOR, WS 17089—L/WS/1/1096, 216–19, 221–31.

27. Lieutenant General Arthur Smith to Lieutenant General Frank Simpson, 9 June 1947, CGS monthly liaison letters, vol. 2, BL/IOR, WS 17096—L/WS/1/1107, 74–76.

28. COS Committee: Appreciation on the strategic value of India to the British Commonwealth of nations, in Wright, *Military Papers*, no. 1188, 319.

29. COS (India) Committee. "Appreciation of the Strategic Value of India," July 1946, Mansergh, Lumby, and Moon, *India: The Transfer of Power*, 8: 53–57. These views were echoed at a meeting of the defense committee of the British Cabinet on 20 October, when the CIGS Montgomery noted that if India did not remain in the Commonwealth, then the U.K. should maintain a prime interest in the Andaman and Nicobar Islands. Cabinet Defence Committee, DO (46) 26th meeting, ibid., 646.

30. Wainwright, *Inheritance of Empire*, 68.

31. It was one of ten expert committees set up to cover every aspect of government.

32. Wainwright, *Inheritance of Empire*, 77.

33. Stand-down in India and Pakistan, Commonwealth Affairs (henceforth CA) Committee 47 2nd meeting, No. PRO, 4 CAB 134/54.

34. Report of the military advisers to the U.K. high commissioners in India and Pakistan, 12 April 1948, BL/IOR, WS 17169—L/WS/1/1187, 13.
35. Ibid., 106.
36. Brigadier Walker [military adviser to the U.K. high commissioner of Pakistan] to Major General Redman [Director Military Operations WO], Ibid., 37–88.
37. Reports from the air advisers to the U.K. high commissioner in India and Pakistan, Ibid., 84.
38. First periodical report from the Military adviser to the U.K. high commissioner in Pakistan to undersecretary of state, WO, 2 April 1948, Ibid., 168–72.
39. Cohen interview with Field Marshal Sir Claude Auchinleck, London, 7 December 1963.
40. Cohen interview with General Douglas Gracey, London, 25 November 1963.
41. Cohen interview with Brigadier John Stephenson, Director Royal United Services Institute (RUSI) London, 3 December 1963.
42. Letter from Mr. A.H. Reed—office of the U.K. High Commission, Flashman's Hotel, Rawalpindi—to S.J.L. Oliver—office of the U.K. high commission, Karachi, 14 June 1949, BL/IOR, WS 17169/II—L/WS/1/1188, 30–31.
43. Second periodical report: Military adviser to the U.K. high commissioner in Pakistan to under secretary of state, WO No. 1000/MA, 24 April 1948, Ibid., 153–65.
44. Brigadier Walker to Major General Redman, DMO, WO 24 September 1948, Ibid., 42.
45. Secret telegram from the U.K. the high commissioner in India to Commonwealth Relations Office, No. 4183, 6 December 1948, BL/IOR, WS 17196—L/WS/1/1217, 8b.
46. First periodical report of 1949 from military adviser to the U.K. high commissioner in India to Brigadier Barker, Commonwealth Relations Office, 5 April 1949, BL/IOR, WS 17215—L/WS/1/1234, 39.
47. Ibid.
48. Reports from the military adviser to the U.K. high commissioner in India to Commonwealth Relations Office, No. 4193, 6 December 1948, BL/IOR, WS 17215—L/WS/1/1234, 14–17.
49. Press clippings; Reuters India and Pakistan Service, 5 December 1948, BL/IOR, WS 17195—L/WS/1/1217, 8a.
50. Sir Shone even suggested that Cariappa may regard his new appointment as an opportunity for achieving personal military glory. Secret telegram from the U.K. high commissioner in India to Commonwealth Relations Office, No. 4193, 6 December 1948, BL/IOR, WS 17195—L/WS/1/1217, 8b.
51. First periodical report of 1949 from military adviser to the U.K. high commissioner in India to Brigadier Barker, Commonwealth Relations Office, 5 April 1949, BL/IOR, WS 17215—L/WS/1/1234, 40.
52. Ibid., 38–42.
53. Brigadier Walker to under secretary of state, WO, 17 May 1948, WS 17169—L/WS/1/1187, 120–23.
54. I have excluded officers below the rank of colonel who are mentioned in the original report. See Report of Brigadier W.W. Loring, military adviser to the U.K. high commissioner in India, 6 May 1948, Ibid., 145–51.

Conclusion

The dramatic transformation of a small British-led colonial force into a large modern national army is a unique event, without parallel anywhere in the world. Indeed, this evolution of the Indian army flies straight in the face of many current theories about the nature of British colonial rule in India. The fact that it actually occurred forces us to reexamine aspects of the British Raj from a different perspective.

We now know that from 1919 onward, and quite possibly before that, a substantial element of the British civilian and military leadership in India had begun to envision a highly professional and nationalized Indian army, an army that would be one of the primary assets of India when it emerged as a "responsible" dominion of the greater British Commonwealth of nations. Indian nationalist politicians who railed against alleged British stalling tactics on Indianization were in reality almost irrelevant to this process, and may even have hampered its progress. Their main concern was not so much the welfare of the budding Indian officer corps, but rather their realization that they could do little to influence British military policy in India. In the midst of this highly visible if ineffective political maelstrom surrounding Indianization, the Indian army continued to evolve and adapt. It established its own military academy in 1932 and eventually consolidated its own military doctrine independent of that of the British army. Herein lay another problem, for opposition to modernization also came from radical military reformers in Britain. These reformers misidentified India as the main cause for the stifling of their own efforts to mechanize the British army, a view no doubt fueled by the knowledge that the Indian army was becoming an independent entity of its own.

Beginning around 1919 the Indian army did in fact work and evolve separately from the British home army. Although the senior officers of the Indian army were British, they often acted in the best interests of the Indian and not the British army. These officers and the British civil servants who worked with them had a specific vision of a professional Indian army and they determined to see it through, regardless of the opposition from either the British army and government or the Indian politicians. It is thanks mainly to the determination of these individuals that the Indian army officer corps emerged in 1947 with at least the bare minimum strength and experience necessary to assume the mantle of command. Another positive side effect of the Indian army's intellectual independence from the British "Camberley" school of thought is manifest in the emergence of the military leadership core that helped guide Britain and India to a winning and sustainable military doctrine in the Second World War. As a result of this independence, independent India inherited not only a professional officer corps, but also a proven military doctrine well adapted to its limited defensive needs.

THE OFFICER CORPS' POSTINDEPENDENCE

In the postindependence period the Indian officer corps has undergone a startling evolution, reflecting both continuity and discontinuity with its colonial past. In the former category, the most visible and crucial example has been the evolution of Indian military doctrine. In all the three major campaigns fought by the Indian army since independence—1947–1948, 1965, and 1971—the army has relied almost exclusively on the positional warfare or defensive-offensive tactics perfected during the Second World War. In all three conflicts the army achieved a fair degree of success in attaining the limited military-political objectives set out for it by the Indian government, namely the defense of Indian territorial integrity. The army did in fact undertake limited offensive actions in all of these three wars, especially in 1971 when several corps seized East Pakistan in a swift fourteen-day campaign. On the whole, however, the army's operations have been essentially reactive in nature, counteroffensive, to be precise. Even the campaign to liberate Bangladesh was a painstakingly planned operation, executed in a "controlled military environment" extremely favorable to the attacking Indian forces.

The reasons for this continued adherence to what is seen by many to be an obsolete, infantry-based fighting doctrine are quite complex. The army's main opponent in these wars has been the Pakistani army, which, of course, evolved from the partition of the British-Indian army in 1947. From the early 1960s onward, however, the Pakistani army has shifted its doctrinal sights from positional warfare to an offensive warfare doctrine based on highly mobile mechanized forces. Consequently, prior to the 1965 War, the Pakistanis amassed a reasonably powerful armored strike force with U.S. M-47 Patton tanks and M-113 armored personnel carriers (APCs). The reasoning behind this was that the more mobile Pakistani forces could outmaneuver the larger infantry-based Indian forces. The tactic failed. The Indian forces, operating behind a screen of antitank defenses—which included dig-in tanks and recoilless guns backed by artillery—devastated the attacking Pakistani armor in much the same way the British 8th Army's guns and tanks had destroyed attacking German armor in the latter half of the Desert War. This scenario essentially was repeated in 1971 on the western front of the Punjab. The Pakistani failure to integrate successfully and to put into effective use the complex mechanisms of a highly mobile mechanized doctrine no doubt strengthened the Indian general staff's cautionary approach to such doctrine. On the other hand, the Indian army has taken an evolutionary approach to mechanized warfare. Successive seminars conducted at the United Services Institute, Delhi, in 1973 and 1976, reveal a general satisfaction with the infantry-based structure of the Indian infantry divisions.[1] At the same time, the Indian infantry formations have continued to evolve to meet changing conditions. An expert independent research team noted that "there are a number of variations in the organization of India's infantry divisions, based on their roles. Weapons and equipment have kept up with modern technology and modern war fighting skills been assimilated as they emerged."[2] Rather than transform many of its infantry divisions into mechanized formations, the Indian army has gone in for "Reorganized Army Plains Infantry Divisions" (RAPIDs). These divisions have a single mechanized brigade and two infantry brigades, thus retaining a strong link to the infantry-dominated armies and doctrines of the past. In fact, the Mechanized Infantry Regiment is one of the newest arms of the Indian army, having been established as recently as 1979.[3] Most of the Indian armored forces continue to be deployed in a defensive role to the infantry divisions and in independent brigades.[4]

This cautious approach (some would refer to it as *stagnation*) to mobile warfare is very much in character with the mind-set of the army's general staff during the interwar period (1919–1938), and, like the general staff, the independent Indian army's doctrine, too, has critics both within and without the army.[5] Regardless, there is no denying the fact that the Indian army has had its greatest operational successes when it has carried out carefully planned defensive-offensive movements. In 1962, when the ill-prepared Indian army sought to take on the veteran Peoples Liberation Army (PLA) along the Himalayas in a dangerous borderline confrontation, the result was a humiliating defeat. Similarly, in 1988 when the army initiated a hurried offensive against the Tamil Tiger rebel army in northern Sri Lanka, it found itself embroiled in a bloody and indecisive three-year guerilla campaign. Offensive-defensive military operations of the type described above, especially against an opponent of unknown quantity, have not been one of the Indian army's strengths.

The doctrinal conservatism of the Indian army's general staff must, however, be placed within the context of a frequent paucity of funds to carry out the sweeping reequipment and, more importantly, the constant military exercises needed to transform units into effective, mechanized fighting forces. Thus, in many ways the budgetary problems confronting the postindependence Indian army are once again similar to those faced by its interwar colonial predecessor. Military innovation and modernization, even when attempted on a very modest scale, has often been dependent upon the availability of funds rather than on the will of the general staff to accept change.

To make matters worse for the army, its doctrinal and operational evolution in many cases is held hostage to conflicts in the political arena. In this respect, the postindependence army differs radically from its colonial predecessor. The latter had the luxury of being able to alter and even reject civilian policies that affected it adversely. The postindependence army, on the other hand, all too frequently has had to surrender even its tactical decision-making processes to the civilian leadership. The most startling example, of course, is the Nehru cabinet's insistence that the army initiate an ambitious tactical push to establish new border posts along the disputed Himalayan border with Chinese-controlled Tibet (1961), despite strong opposition from many of the commanders on the ground. In the late 1980s a rather naive (and some even would say complacent) Indian high command was once again thrust into a so-called peacekeeping role in northern Sri Lanka by the ruling Congress Party–led government. With the Indian army's tactical/operational plans once again being controlled overwhelmingly by dictates from the civilian leadership in Delhi and Columbo, the army jettisoned all its hard-learned lessons from decades of counterinsurgency in northeast India and suffered heavy casualties as a result.

Civilian interference has not been restricted to tactics and operations. Indian governments often have dictated what the army could and could not acquire in terms of big-budget military hardware. By itself, government control of the military's finances is not surprising and, indeed, is to be expected.[6] What stands out in the Indian army's case is that, even when financial considerations have not been in dispute, the civilian leadership has forced the army to acquire weapon systems it considered to be inferior and often too expensive and unnecessary. A case in point is the tank acquisition debacle in the 1960s. The Indian army was in the market to acquire a main battle tank to reequip its obsolete armored fleet. The new tank also would be license produced by the thousands in India, making this one of the most lucrative military contracts in the world. The army's expert committee recommended that the West German Leopard-I tank was by far the most superior tank available in the market. However, the Indian government, led by Defense Minister Krishna Menon, rejected the committee's recommendation and acquired instead the new and unproven British Vickers medium tank.[7] This tank has proved to be a disaster in Indian Army service.

Its chronic mechanical unreliability and inadequate armor protection eventually led to it being sidelined by massive acquisitions of Soviet-designed T-54/55 medium tanks. In the mid-and late 1980s the army's long-awaited acquisition of 155mm medium artillery guns almost was scuttled when a major scandal erupted over the payment of dubious commissions by the Swedish firm Bofors (which manufactured the guns) to middlemen and to unnamed Congress "Indira" faction chiefs in the government.[8]

To a large extent, the dislocation of the army's interests with that of the civilian authorities has been due to a vast communication gulf between the Indian general staff and the important civilian policy-making bodies. The Indian army is unique among former colonial armies in that it has had a virtually nonexistent role in the security policy–making process in the state. The civilian leadership has a tight reign on the military, which results in the micromanagement of all security policy both within and without the army, as outlined above.[9] At least one retired general has taken this to mean that the civilian leadership, and the Gandhi family in particular, have had a low opinion of the Westernized and elitist officer corps and consider it to be at best an antinationalist remnant of the British Empire and at worst a potential threat to continued democracy in India.[10] While there is considerable evidence to support that this view was valid in the era of Nehru's administration, there is no real basis for such a claim in India today. Especially since as I shall explain later, the Indian army is no longer the socially elite institution it was prior to independence, but rather a more heterogenous body broadly representative of the middle–to lower-middle–class strata of Indian society. It seems that the debacle in 1962 and the many scandals surrounding equipment procurement only have strengthened the resolve of the civilian leadership to micromanage even further all aspects of defense policy making. Within the past decade the post of defense minister in the Indian Cabinet all but has become defunct, with the prime minister often reserving for himself the defense portfolio. Similarly, all attempts to establish a national security council (NSC) to evolve Indian security doctrine with substantial input from the three defense chiefs has come to naught.[11] The secretive Cabinet Committee on Political Affairs (CCPA), first established in 1971, remains the only institutional establishment for defense/security–related decision making in the country. And, even in this case, the most important decisions are made exclusively by the prime minister's officer (PMO) at the expense of the cabinet.[12]

The most radical difference between the pre- and postindependence officer corps, however, comes from within the corps itself. Today the social composition of the Indian officer corps is very different from its colonial past. In 1937, for example, the Indian officer corps was comprised of no less than 22.5 percent recruits who came from either princely or landed aristocracy. By 1985 this figure had declined to 0 percent.[13] Indeed, there is some evidence to suggest that the declining pay scale of the army and the corresponding rise in private-sector jobs has drained the upper-middle–class and middle-class recruiting base of the army. In fact, the government contributed to this situation in 1947 when it arbitrarily cut absolute pay by 40 percent. Further erosion of the military's status developed in 1955 when the government abolished the office of commander in chief. The warrant of precedence places the army chief of staff in twenty-fifth place, behind a host of relatively minor civilian officers, such as the comptroller and auditor general, chief justices of the state courts, members of the planning commission, and state cabinet ministers.[14] The subsequent inability or reluctance of the government to maintain army pay scales to the level of not only the private sector, but also the Indian administrative services, has stymied further middle-class interest in army careers. Some studies have indicated that many of the officers joining the army from the late 1960s are in fact sons of the former "other ranks" (ORs), or rank-and-file soldiers, and junior commissioned officers (JCOs).[15] Data also indicates that the number of candidates who are sons of gazetted officers (senior civil servants) has dropped from 30 percent in 1932 to 14.94 percent in 1987, while the number of candidates who were sons of nongazetted officers (junior-level civil servants) rose from 0 percent in 1932 to 25.4 percent in 1987.[16] Further evidence of the decline in the social standing of the Indian officer from this period comes from studies that have indicated that the demand for Indian officers in the marriage market had declined considerably![17] Another study has indicated that in 1985 students graduating from many of the top-ranked Indian high schools rated the military eleventh out of fifteen listed professions.[18] In 1987 the government attempted to rectify the worsening situation by nearly doubling the pay for officers and giving the enlisted men free food allowances.[19] But this move seems to have been too little, too late. In any case, the floating of the rupee in the international currency market in the early 1990s has meant inflation, and there is an even greater disparity between the pay for officers and that for professionals in the private sector.

This transformation of the social origins of the Indian officer corps, however, has not prevented critics from accusing the army and the government of continuing to perpetuate recruitment of "martial races" cadets into the Indian army. According to data from Sandhurst and the IMA, the overwhelming number of Indian cadets admitted into Sandhurst between 1919–1925 and into the IMA between 1932–1936 came from northwestern India. This region contributed no less than 68 percent of the cadets to IMA in the 1932–1936 period. This figure fell to 57 percent in the 1978–1982 period (see table 12), but so did the Northwest's share of the Indian population, which meant that the region was still overrepresented by a factor of 2.5 to 1 in 1978–1982 compared to 2.6 to 1 in 1932–1936. In other words, traditional colonial recruitment patterns have remained the same.[20]

The critics assume that various Indian military academies continue to maintain the same preference quotas that the British initially (and unsuccessfully) had for martial races cadets. While the numbers certainly support this supposition, there is no evidence to suggest that this is in fact government policy or, for that matter, desired by the government. The government has admitted to a policy of actively trying to diversify the officer-recruiting base by appealing to the "non-martial" lower castes and tribal communities of India.[21] In 1961 the government established the first of many Sainik, or military, schools throughout the country. With the establishment of these schools the Indian government hoped to bring "public school education of a high standard within the reach of the common man."[22] The Sainik schools (eighteen of them in 1985) are located mainly in remote and economically backward regions of the country. The government's policy set aside 22.5 percent of the seats for scheduled caste (15 percent) and scheduled tribe (7.5 percent) students; 25 percent of the seats for children of defense personnel, including ex-servicemen, and 67 percent of the seats for students from the home state. Very few middle-class parents chose to send their children to these schools, and most of the students enrolled came from poor socioeconomic sections of Indian society. After completing their high school equivalency at the Sainik schools, the students continued their academic studies for the three years at the National Defence Academy (NDA) at Khadakvasla. This education culminated in a degree from Jawaharlal Nehru University. The students, having become cadets, then undergo selection to be trained as officers in the army, navy, and air force military academies.

By 1985 the Sainik schools provided 40 percent of the cadet intake of the NDA. Nevertheless, despite these vigorous attempts by the government to introduce the underprivileged classes into the officer corps, only 9 percent of the output of the Sainik schools actually enter the army.[23] So, even though the majority of officer candidates still continue to come from traditional recruiting areas, this is probably due to the socioeconomic conditions relating to the officer corps as described above. Since a substantial number of Indian officer candidates are sons of ORs and JCOs, or are the sons of officers who were themselves sons of ORs and JCOs, it is not surprising that most of the officers do come from the traditional "martial races" recruiting area of the Northwest.[24]

The change in the social composition of the Indian officer corps has been accompanied by a general perception—both within and without the army—that the corps, in addition to losing its appeal to the "best and the brightest" of India's youth, is falling prey to careerism and corruption.[25] As early as the early 1970s senior Indian officers criticized the "intellectually mediocre" caliber of officer candidates.[26] These problems have been particularly worrysome for the general staff, and in 1986 the new Army Chief of Staff General K. Sundarji sent out a letter to all officers condemning their "increasingly careerist, opportunistic, and sycophantic" behavior.

Table 11
Intake of Indian Candidates into RMC, Sandhurst (1919–1925) by Region[27]

Province or State Agency	Number of Candidates	Percentage of Total number of candidates
Punjab	35	41.8
Bombay	12	14.12
United Provinces	9	10.59
Bengal	9	10.59
NWFP	5	5.88
Hyderabad State	3	3.53
Rajputana Agency	3	3.53
Burma	2	2.35
Coorg	2	2.35
Bihar	1	1.18
Assam	1	1.18
Central India Agency	1	1.18
Other/Unknown	2	2.35
Total:	85	100.63

He went on to note that "standards of integrity have fallen and honor and patriotism are becoming unfashionable." His criticism also targeted the senior officers, whom he accused of failing to set a "right example."[28] Sundarji's complaint about the officer corps is not without precedent; in many respects it has amazing similarities with a biting attack on the intellectual and professional apathy of the largely British-dominated Indian officer corps during the interwar period by the Army Commander Sir Philip Chetwoode.

Despite the many problems undermining the Indian officer corps' professional integrity, it has remained a professional institution on the whole. While low- and mid-level nepotism is frequent, the selection process for senior officers—barring a few scandals—has remained impartial and based purely on merit and seniority.[29] It is this senior leadership core that seems to be guiding the corps through these turbulent evolutionary changes. Even the much-criticized junior officer cadres have performed rather well in pro-

Table 12
Intake of Officers in the IMA, Dehra Dun (1932–1936) by Region[30]

Province State or Agency	Number of Candidates	Percentage of total number of Candidates
Punjab	165	41.67
NWFP	50	12.63
United Provinces	41	10.35
Delhi	13	3.28
Bombay	19	2.27
Central Provinces	6	1.52
Madras	6	1.52
Bengal	4	1.01
Gujarat	4	1.01
Kerala	3	0.76
Burma	3	0.76
Bihar	2	0.51
Orissa	1	0.25
Other	1	0.25
Princely States	88	22.22
Total:	406	100.01

longed and brutal campaigns in Sri Lanka (late 1980s) and on the Siachen Glacier (ongoing in 2003). It does appear that highly motivated and capable young men in the mold of Thimayya and Chaudhuri continue to join the army and sustain the viability of the corps.

CONCLUSION

One of the greatest imbalances between the militaries of the developed and the developing worlds is not a technical one, but rather an intellectual one. Most armies of the developing world simply lack the necessary leadership and training required to conduct modern conventional warfare. This is not all that surprising when one considers the fact that most of these armies are, in essence, glorified police forces. The mere acquisition of the

Table 13
Intake of Officers in the IMA, Dehra Dun (1978–1982) by Region[31]

Province or State Agency	Number of Candidates	Percentage of Total Number of Candidates
Uttar Pradesh	721	19.11
Delhi	416	11.03
Punjab	375	9.94
Harayana	321	8.51
Maharashtra	237	6.28
Kerala	207	5.49
Bihar	196	5.20
Andhra Pradesh	138	3.66
Rajasthan	137	3.63
Himachal Pradesh	127	3.37
Madhya Pradesh	115	3.05
West Bengal	105	2.78
Tamil Nadu	103	2.73
Karnataka	100	2.65
Jammu & Kashmir	93	2.47
Orissa	92	2.44
Chandigarh	87	2.31
Gujarat	26	0.69
Assam	24	0.64
Meghalaya	6	0.16
Manipur	5	0.13
Goa, Daman & Diu	4	0.11
Sikkim	3	0.08
Arunachal Pradesh	3	0.08
Tripura	2	0.05
Nagaland	1	0.03
Podicherry	1	0.03
Nepal	9	0.24
Not settled, Not Known	118	3.13
Total:	3772	100.02

Table 14
Intake of Officers in the IMA, Dehra Dun (1983–1987) by Region[32]

Province or State Agency	Number of Candidates	Percentage of Total Number of Candidates
Andhra Pradesh	240	3.78
Arunachal Pradesh	2	0.03
Assam	35	0.55
Bihar	339	5.34
Bengal	157	2.47
Chandigarh	94	1.48
Delhi	585	9.21
Gujarat	33	0.52
Goa	4	0.06
Himachal Pradesh	237	3.73
Harayana	598	9.42
Jammu & Kashmir	189	2.97
Kerala	334	5.26
Karnataka	192	3.02
Manipur	11	0.17
Meghalaya	8	0.12
Maharashtra	268	4.22
Madhya Pradesh	247	3.89
Nagaland	5	0.07
Orissa	84	1.32
Punjab	782	12.32
Pondicherry	5	0.07
Rajasthan	275	4.33
Sikkim	-	-
Tamil Nadu	146	2.30
Tripura	1	0.01
Uttar Pradesh	1475	23.24
Total:	6346	99.9

latest jet fighters, missile boats, battle tanks, and self-propelled artillery will not transform a developing world army automatically into an effective modern fighting force. This process is almost solely dependent upon the officer corps, and it is here that many developing countries have stumbled. In the postcolonial era, it can be argued that with the exception of India no army in the developing world emerged with a viable officer corps. Many of the officer corps that sprang up in the 1950s and the 1960s (much earlier in the case of Latin America) did so lacking the foundation that India had. True, they had all the ritual and symbolic trappings of their colonial predecessors, but there were no intellectual links between the two. Worse, most, if not all, of these armies continued to be organized as internal security forces rather than conventional armies geared to combat external threats. As a result, most of these officers corps continue to search for the necessary skills and doctrine that will make them true "professional" soldiers and not just policemen.

An officer corps cannot imbibe a professional ethos and a military doctrine overnight. No amount of equipment and foreign military advice can offer a shortcut to these goals. They can be arrived at only after decades of evolution and adaption. In India this process began in the late nineteenth century with Curzon's experiments with the ICC and culminated in the late 1940s with the departure of the last of the British officers from the Indian army. Even then, a half of a century would have proven inadequate. It took the all-encompassing intensity of the Second World War to produce the seeds of a professional Indian officer corps. In the final analysis, the greatest impact of the colonial reform is yet to be seen and is still being created as the Indian army continues to evolve, in the process becoming an enduring legacy of long-forgotten generations of Indian officers, British generals, and bureaucrats.

NOTES

1. Major General Som Dutt (retired [henceforth retd.]), *Re-Organization of the Infantry Division* (New Delhi: United Services Institute of India, 1973), seminar no. 1; Lieutenant General M.L. Thapan (retd.), *Review of the Organizational Pattern of the Indian Army* (New Delhi: United Services Institute of India, 1976), seminar no. 7.

2. Indian Defence Review (IDR) Research Team, "Some Thoughts on the Evolution of Infantry Organization and Tactics" (July 1991): 47–56.

3. At Ahmednagar, next to the armored Regimental Centre, *The Times of India*, 7 February 1988.

4. Lieutenant Colonel J.K. Dutt, "Wanted: A Doctrine for Armour," *Journal of the United Services Institute of India* (henceforth *JUSII*) (October-December 1977): 45–52.

5. Brigadier R.D. Law, "The Gulf War—The Last Hundred Hours: Lessons for the Indian Mechanized Forces," *JUSII* (July-September 1991); Major Gautam Das,

"Turk-Sowar: An Indian Mechanized Force for the 21st Century," *Combat Journal* (August 1987); Lieutenant Colonel Mahesh Chahda, "Mechanized Infantry: Where Have We Gone Wrong?" *Combat Journal* (April 1989); Pradeep P. Barua, "The Evolution of the Mechanized Infantry," *Strategic Analysis*, vol. 12, no. 9 (December 1988).

6. The Indian civil bureaucracy, in fact, a maintains a very tight reign on the military, particularly in regard to financial matters. See Stephen P. Cohen, "Civilian Control of the Military in India," in Claude E. Welch (ed.), *Civilian Control of the Military: Theory and Cases from Developing Countries* (Albany, New York: States University of New York Press, 1976), 53–55.

7. Major General Pratap Narain, *Indian Arms Bazaar* (Delhi: Shipra Publications, 1994), 73–66.

8. Dilip Bobb, "The Bofors Blast," *India Today* (15 May 1987): 18.

9. Raju C. Thomas, *India's Security Policy* (Princeton, NJ: Princeton University Press, 1986), 125–32, 160; also Stephen P. Cohen, "The Military and Indian Democracy," in Atul Kohli (ed.), *India's Democracy* (Princeton, NJ: Princeton University Press, 1988), 119.

10. Major General D.K. Palit, *War in the High Himalaya: The Indian Army in Crisis, 1962* (New York: St. Martin's Press, 1991), 2–3, 21. Prior to independence, many Indian nationalists often had considered the army to be an instrument of British cultural and political imperialism. See Lloyd Rudolph and Susanne Hoeber Rudolph, "Generals and Politicians in India," in Wilson C. McWilliams (ed.), *Garrisons and Governments: Politics and the Military in New States* (San Francisco: Chandler Publishing Co. 1964), 140.

11. Manoj K. Joshi, "Directions in India's Defence and Security Policies," in Ross Babbage and Sandy Gordon (eds.), *India's Strategic Future: Regional, State, or Global Power?* (London: Macmillan, 1992), 88–89.

12. For further information on military maladministration and government meddling, see Brigadier Trigunesh Mukherjee, *Inside the Indian Army* (New Delhi: Manas Publications, 2000).

13. Sinha and Chandra, *Valour and Wisdom*, 256.

14. Rudolph and Rudolph, "Generals and Politicians," 136.

15. See Brigadier B.K. Sinha, "Career Prospects for Officers in the Armed Forces," *JUSII* (July-September 1968); Lieutenant General M.L. Thapan, "The Army as a Career," *JUSII* (July-September 1977); Captain Rajiv Kumar, "Man Management: The Present Environ," *JUSII* (January-March 1983).

16. Sinha and Chandra, *Valour and Wisdom*, 256–57.

17. Rudolf and Rudolph, "Generals and Politicians," 140.

18. R.P. Gautam, "Status of Services vis-à-vis Other Services," *JUSII* (April-June 1985): 164; R.P. Gautam, "Causes of Higher Secondary Students' Preference for Military Career," *JUSII* (October-December 1979): 380–90.

19. Cohen, *Indian Army*, 217.

20. Apurba Kundu, "Over dependence on Martial Race Officer," *IDR* (July 1991): 69–84; Sinha and Chandra, *Valour and Wisdom*, 254–55; Daljit Singh, "Military Education in India: Changes from the British Tradition," *JUSII* (July-September 1974): 227–37.

21. I recall several times as a student when recruiting officials made pointed efforts to interest graduating high school students—belonging to the underprivi-

leged "scheduled caste/tribe" communities—in an army officer's career. This includes high schools in northeast and western India.

22. The purpose for establishing these schools is not far removed from the PWRIM College established in the colonial era. Both sought to give prospective officer cadets for the military academies a firm academic and physical grounding for their new careers, something they would be unable to receive in the standard civilian schools. However, while the PWRIM was established mainly to cater to students from a princely and educated Indian middle class, the Sainik schools were created to aid students from the economically and socially underprivileged classes.

23. Lieutenant General M.L. Chibber, *Military Leadership To Prevent Military Coup* (New Delhi: Lancer International, 1986), 39–44, tables 1.1–1.3.

24. See Sinha and Chandra, *Valour and Wisdom*, 256, table 9.

25. Cohen, *Indian Army* [epilogue to 1990 edition], 214–15.

26. Ibid., Major General K.S. Bajwa, "Military Leadership and Changing Social Ethos," *JUSII* (July-September 1978): Harinder Bajewa, "Army Recruitment: Fighting Unfit," *India Today*, 28 August 2000 (electronic edition); Murali Krishnan, "The Badge of Renaissance," *Outlook*, 15 January 2001 (electronic edition); Shishir Gupta, "The Army: Changing Order," *India Today*, 14 May 2001 (electronic edition).

27. Figures from V. Longer, *Red Coats to Olive Green: A History of the Indian Army, 1600–1974* (New Delhi: Allied Publishers, 1974), 196; Kundu, "Over Dependence on Martial Races," 71.

28. Cohen, *Indian Army*, 218.

29. The exceptions and "scandals" occurred in 1975 and 1983 respectively, when junior commanders superseded senior and arguably more capable general officers to the army chief's post. Both incidents took place under Mrs. Indira Gandhi's tenure as prime minister, which leads Cohen to suggest that these actions fit into the "broader patten of her manipulative style of governance." Ibid., 221–22. See also Lieutenant General S.K. Sinha (retd.), "Preserving the Army Ethos," *IDR* (July 1992). Sinha was the senior general superseded in 1983 for the chief's position. In this remarkable article he analyzes the sorry state of relations between the army chief and the government. He notes that in 1992 there were no less than eight hundred cases pending in the Delhi High Court in which army personnel have sought redress. Omar Khalidi has argued that during the 1950s and 1960s there was a definite bias against Muslim officers. See Omar Khalidi, "Ethnic Group Recruitment in the Indian Army: The Contrasting Cases of Sikhs, Muslims, and Gurkhas," *Pacific Affairs*, vol. 74, no. 4 (Winter 2001–2002.)

30. Chibber, *Military Leadership*, 40.

31. Ibid., 41.

32. Numbers from Sinha and Chandra, *Valour and Wisdom*, 254–55, table 8.

Bibliography

UNPUBLISHED SOURCES

Private Records

British Library, India Office Records, London

Barrow Collection	Mss.Eur.E.420/9.
Birdwood Collection	Mss.Eur.D.686/31.
Birkenhead Collection	Mss.Eur.D.703/38.
Chelmsford Collection	Mss.Eur.E.264/14.
Curzon Collection	Mss.Eur.F.111/253,442,159.
Derby Collection	Mss.Eur.D.605/1,5.
Hoare Collection (Templewood Papers)	Mss.Eur.E.240/57.
Irwin Collection	Mss.Eur.C.152/21.
Kirke Collection	Mss.Eur.E.396/11,13,18.
Linlithgow Collection	Mss.Eur.F.125/28.
Montagu Collection	Mss.Eur.D.523/8.
Mountbatten Collection	Mss.Eur.F.200/6.
Reading Collection	Mss.Eur.E.238.
Rudra Collection	Mss.Eur.C.478.
S.K. Brown Collection	Mss.Eur.D.712/14. Mss.Eur.D.808/1.
Simon Collection	Mss.Eur.F.77/54.
Interviews by Gillian Wright	Mss.Eur.R.193/9.

University of Chicago Library, Chicago

Diary of Amar Singh Typescript DS485.R26R36

Government Records

British Library, India Office Records, London

Military Department:
L/MIL/1/10/39
L/MIL/3/2513
L/MIL/3/2534
L/MIL/5/844
L/MIL/5/849
L/MIL/5/857
L/MIL/5/885
L/MIL/5/886
L/MIL/5/1762
L/MIL/5/4261
L/MIL/7/10822
L/MIL/7/19006
L/MIL/8/849
L/MIL/8/885
L/MIL/9/319
L/MIL/9/357
L/MIL/17/5/1687
L/MIL/17/5/1721
L/MIL/17/5/1741
L/MIL/17/5/1742
L/MIL/17/5/1745
L/MIL/17/5/1773
L/MIL/17/5/1774
L/MIL/17/5/1778
L/MIL/17/5/1779
L/MIL/17/5/1780
L/MIL/17/5/1787
L/MIL/17/5/1800
L/MIL/17/5/1801
L/MIL/17/5/1911
L/MIL/17/5/2225

L/MIL/17/5/2281
L/MIL/17/5/2282
L/MIL/17/5/2284
L/MIL/17/5/2285
L/MIL/17/5/2290
L/MIL/17/5/2330
L/MIL/17/5/4263
L/MIL/17/5/4265
L/MIL/17/5/4266

War Staff:
WS 1934—L/WS/1/155
WS 2047—L/WS/1/164
WS 2099—L/WS/1/170
WS 5725—L/WS/1/431
WS 6385—L/WS/1/448
WS 12048—L/WS/1/616
WS 13023—L/WS/1/1523
WS 14044—L/WS/1/806
WS 14066—L/WS/1/824
WS 17089—L/WS/1/1096
WS 17069—L/WS/1/1107
WS 17169—L/WS/1/1187
WS 17169/II—L/WS/1/1188
WS 17195—L/WS/1/1217
WS 17196—L/WS/1/1217
WS 17215—L/WS/1/1234

Public Records Office, London

Cabinet Office:
CAB 2/5,6,7
CAB 4/7
CAB 5/7
CAB 6/4
CAB 16/38
CAB 23/26/72(21)
CAB 23/32/68(22)
CAB 23/26, 72, 112
CAB 24/70, 11, 287

CAB 27/65, 164
CAB 27/163
CAB 134/54

War Office:
WO 32/1285
WO 33/173
WO 73/115
WO 95/3911
WO 106/148
WO 161/82
WO 163/11
WO 201/2050

Miscellaneous

Cohen, Stephen P. interview with—Lieutenant General (retired) S.D. Verma, Midhurst, Sussex, 28 November 1963.—Lieutenant General (cashiered) B.M. Kaul, New Delhi, 19 December 1964.

Ellinwood, DeWitt C. "The Special Experiences of Amar Singh." Paper presented at the Conference on South Asia, November 1994, University of Wisconsin at Madison, 8.

Jacobsen, Mark Houston. "The Modernization of the Indian Army 1925–1939." Ph.D. dissertation (University of California, Irvine, 1979).

Rawson, J.O. "The Role of India in Imperial Defense beyond Indian Frontiers and Home Waters, 1919–1939." D. Phil. dissertation (University of Oxford, Oxford, 1976).

Rudolf, Lloyd I. "A Soldier of the Raj? Amar Singh's Military Career." Paper presented at the Conference on South Asia, November 1994, University of Wisconsin at Madison, 21.

PUBLISHED SOURCES

Government Documents

India: Legislative Assembly Debates, 2 September 1921, 1753.

Indian Army List, July-October 1906, 153–55.

Indian Sandhurst Committee: Report of the Sub-Committee which visited various military education institutions in England and other countries. Simla: Government of India Press, 1926.

India's Contribution to the Great War. Calcutta: Government of India Press, 1923.

Report of the Commissioners Appointed to Inquire into the Organization of the Indian Army [Peel Commission], Parliamentary Papers (Commons) 1859, Cmd. 2515.

Report of the Indian Military College Committee, 15 July 1931. London: HMSO, 1931.

Report of the Indian Retrenchment Committee, 1922–1923. London: HMSO, 1923.

Report of the Indian Sandhurst Committee, 14 November 1926. London: HMSO, 1927.

Report to the Combined Chiefs of Staff: By the Supreme Commander South East Asia 1943–1945. London: HMSO, 1951.

Statistics of the British Military Effort in the Great War. London: HMSO, 1922.

Books

Agar-Hamilton, J.A.I., and L.C.F. Turner. *The Sidi Rezegh Battles*. Cape Town, South Africa: Oxford University Press, 1957.

Alavi, Seema. *The Sepoys and the Company: Tradition and Transition in Northern India, 1770–1830*. New York: Oxford University Press, 1995.

Baig, M.R.A. *In Different Saddles*. Bombay and Calcutta: Asia Publishing House, 1967.

Bailey, J.B.A. *Field Artillery and Firepower*. Oxford: The Military Press, 1989.

Barnett, Corelli. *The Desert Generals*. Bloomington: Indiana University Press, 1960.

Besant, Annie. *Speeches and Writings*. Madras: G.A. Natesan, 1921.

Bienen, Henry (ed.). *The Military and Modernization*. Chicago: Aldine, Atherton, 1971.

Bond, Brian. *British Military Policy between the Two World Wars*. Oxford: Clarendon Press, 1980.

Campbell-Johnson, Allan. *Mission with Mountbatten*. London, New York: Robert Hale, 1951.

Carver, Michael. *Dilemmas of the Desert War: A New Look at the Libyan Campaign, 1940–1942*. Bloomington: Indiana University Press, 1986.

Charteris, Brigadier General John. *At GHQ*. London: Cassell, 1931.

Chibber, Lieutenant General M.L. *Military Leadership To Prevent Military Coup*. New Delhi: Lancer International, 1986.

Cohen, Stephen P. *The Indian Army: Its Contribution to the Development of a Nation*. Berkeley: University of California Press, 1971.

Connell, John. *Auchinleck, a Biography of Field-Marshall Sir Claude Auchinleck*. London: Cassell, 1959.

Das, M.N. *India Under Morley and Minto: Politics behind Revolution, Repression and Reforms*. London: George Allen & Unwin, 1964.

Denning, Major B.C. *The Future of the British Army*. London: Witherby, 1928.

Dunn, Peter M. *The First Vietnam War*. London: C. Hurst, 1985.

Dutt, Major General Som (retd.). *Re-organization of the Infantry Division*. New Delhi: United Services Institute of India, 1973, seminar no. 1.

Edwards, Captain J. Kieth. "Second (Military) Prize Winning Essay for 1927." *Journal of the Royal United Services Institute*, no. 73 (August 1928): 458–73.

Elliot, T.S. (ed.). *A Choice of Kipling's Verse*. London: Faber & Faber, 1951.

English, John A. *A Perspective on Infantry*. New York: Praeger, 1981.

Evans, Humphrey. *Thimayya of India: A Soldier's Life*. New York: Harcourt, Brace, 1960.

Fuller, J.F.C. *On Future War*. London: Sifton, Praed, 1928.

Gent, John B. (ed.). *Croydon Old and New*. South Croydon, Surrey: Southern Publishing, Brighton, 1975.

Gerth, H.H., and C. Mills. *From Max Weber: Essays in Sociology*. New York: Oxford University Press, 1946.

Gulati, Y.B. *History of the Regiment of Artillery: Indian Army* [Published under the authority of the director of artillery, Army HQ, New Delhi], London: Leo Cooper, 1972.

Hamilton, Nigel. *Monty: The Making of a General (1887–1942)*. New York: McGraw-Hill, 1981.

Hardie, Kier J. *India, Impressions and Suggestions*. London: Independent Labour Party, 1909.

Hart, B.H. Liddell. *The Defence of Britain*. London: Faber, 1939.

———. *Memoirs*. London: Cassell, 1959.

Heathcote, T.A. *The Military in British India: The Development of British Land Forces in South Asia, 1600–1947*. Manchester: Manchester University Press, 1995.

Higham, Robin. *The Military Intellectuals in Britain, 1918–1933*. New Brunswick, NJ: Rutgers University Press, 1966.

Jeffery, Keith. *The British Army and the Crisis of Empire 1918–1922*. Manchester: Manchester University Press, 1984.

Juin, Alphonse. *Memoires*, vol. 1. Paris: Fayard, 1959.

Khan, Gul Hassan. *Memoirs*. Karachi, Oxford: Oxford University Press, 1993.

Khan, Mohammad Ayub. *Friends Not Masters: A Political Autobiography*. London: Oxford University Press, 1967.

Koss, Stephen E. *John Morley and the India Office, 1905–1910*. New Haven and London: Yale University Press, 1969.

Longer, V. *Red Coats to Olive Green: A History of the Indian Army, 1600–1974*. New Delhi: Allied Publishers, 1974.

Macksey, Kenneth. *Armoured Crusader: Major General Percy Hobart*. London: Hutchinson, 1967.

Mansergh, N., E.W.R. Lumby, and Penderel Moon (eds.). *India: The Transfer of Power 1942–1947*. 12 vols. London: HMSO, 1970–1983.

Masani, Zareer. *Indian Tales from the Raj*. Berkeley, Los Angeles: University of California Press, 1987.

Mason, Phillip. *A Matter of Honor: An Account of the Indian Army, Its Officers and Men*. New York: Holt, Reinhart and Winston, 1974.

Masters, John. *Bugles and a Tiger: A Volume of Autobiography*. New York: The Viking Press, 1956.

Maurice, Sir Frederick. *The Life of General Lord Rawlinson of Trent*. London: Cassell, 1928.

Mehrotra, S.R. *India and the Commonwealth 1885–1929*. New York: Frederick R. Praeger, 1965.

Minney, R.J. *The Private Papers of Hore-Belisha*. London: Collins, 1960.

Mukherjee, Brigadier Trigunesh. *Inside the Indian Army*. New Delhi: Manas Publications, 2000.

Muthanna, I.M. *General Cariappa*. Mysore: Usha Press, 1964.

Narain, Major General Pratap. *Indian Arms Bazaar*. Delhi: Shipra Publications, 1994.

Narayan, B.K. *General J.N. Chaudhuri: An Autobiography, As Narrated to B.K. Narayan*. New Delhi: Vikas, 1978.

Omissi, David. *The Sepoy and the Raj: The Indian Army, 1860–1940*. London: Macmillan, 1994.

Palit, Major General D.K. *War in the High Himalayas: The Indian Army in Crisis, 1962*. New York: St. Martin's Press, 1991.

Parker, Geoffrey. *The Military Revolution: Military Innovation and the Rise of the West, 1500–1800*. Cambridge: Cambridge University Press, 1988.

Peers, Douglas M. *Between Mars and Mammon: Colonial Armies and the Garrison State in India, 1819–1835*. New York: Tauris Academic Press, 1995.

Pemberton, A.L. *The Development of Artillery Tactics and Equipment*. London: The War Office, 1950.

Petrie, Sir Charles. *The Life and Letters of the Right Honourable Sir Austen Chamberlain*. London: Cassell, 1940.

Playfair, I.S.O. *The Mediterranean and the Middle East*. London: HMSO, 1954–1956.

Ponnappa, Brigadier C.B. *Soldier and Citizen: And Other Writings*. Bangalore, India: Hosali Press, 1971.

Prasad, Sri Nandan (ed.). *Expansion of the Armed Forces and Defense Organization, 1939–45*. New Delhi: Combined Inter-Services Historical Section (India & Pakistan), 1956.

———. *Official History of the India Armed Forces in the Second World War: East African Campaign 1940–1941*. New Delhi: Combined Inter-Services Historical Section (India & Pakistan), 1956.

———. *Official History of the Indian Armed Forces in the Second World War: The North African Campaign 1940–1945*. New Delhi: Combined Inter-Services Historical Section (India & Pakistan), 1956.

———. *Official History of the Indian Armed Forces in the Second World War: Reconquest of Burma 1941–1942*. New Delhi: Combined Inter-Services Historical Section for (India & Pakistan), 1959.

Robb, P.G. *The Government of India and Reform: Policies towards Politics and the Constitution 1916–1921*. London: Oxford University Press, 1976.

Rommel, Erwin. *The Rommel Papers, 1891–1944*. Ed. B.H. Liddell Hart, trans Paul Findlay. New York: Harcourt, Brace, 1953.

Rudolph, Susanne Hoeber, Lloyd I. Rudolph, and Mohan Singh Kanota (eds.). *Reversing the Gaze: Amar Singh's Diary: A Colonial Subject's Narrative of Imperial India*. Boulder: Westview Press, 2002.

Sandhu, Gurcharan Singh. *The Indian Armour: History of the Indian Armoured Corps 1941–1971*. New Delhi: Vision Books, 1987.

Sastri, K.A. Nilkanta (ed.). *A Great Liberal: Speeches and Writings of Sir P.S. Sivaswamy Aiyer* (Bombay: Allied Publishers, 1965).

Saxena, K.M.L. *The Military System of India 1850–1900*. New Delhi: Sterling Publishers, 1974.

Sinha, B.P.N., and Sunil Chandra. *Valour and Wisdom: Genesis and Growth of the Indian Military Academy*. New Delhi: Oxford and IBH Publishing, 1992.

Sinha, S.K. *A Soldier Recalls*. New Delhi: Lancer International, 1992.

Singh, Mohan. *Soldier's Contribution to Indian Independence: The Epic of the Indian National Army* (New Delhi: Army Education Stores, 1974).

Stevens, G.R. *Fourth Indian Division*. Toronto: McLaren & Son, n.d.

Stokes, Eric. *The English Utilitarians in India.* London: Oxford University Press, 1959.

Strachan, Hew. *From Waterloo to Balaclava: Tactics, Technology, and the British Army, 1815–1854.* Cambridge: Cambridge University Press, 1985.

Thapan, Lieutenant General M.L. (retd.). *Review of the Organization Pattern of the Indian Army.* New Delhi: United Services Institute of India, 1976, seminar no. 7.

Thomas, Raju C. *India's Security Policy.* Princeton, NJ: Princeton University Press, 1986.

Thorat, S.P.P. *From Reveille to Retreat.* New Delhi: Allied Publishers, 1986.

Tomlinson, B.R. *The Indian National Congress and the Raj, 1929–1942: The Penultimate Phase.* London: Macmillan, 1976.

Trench, Charles Chevenix. *The Indian Army and the King's Enemies.* London: Thames & Hudson, 1988.

Tuker, General Sir Francis. *Approach to Battle.* London: Cassell, 1963.

Verma, S.D. *To Serve with Honour: My Memoirs.* Kasauli, India: Author, 1988.

Wainwright, A. Martin. *Inheritance of Empire: Britain, India and the Balance of Power in Asia, 1938–55.* Westport, Conn.: Praeger, 1994.

Wallbank, T.W. *A Short History of India and Pakistan.* New York: Scott, Foresman, 1958.

Wallerstein, Immanuel. *The Modern World System.* New York: Academic Press, 1974.

Winton, Harold R. *To Change an Army: General Sir John Burnett-Stuart and British Armored Doctrine, 1927–1938.* Lawrence, Kansas: University Press of Kansas, 1988.

Newspapers

Gazette of India

India

London

Evening News

The Statesman

The Times of India

Articles

Bajewa, Harinder. "Army Recruitment: Fighting Unfit." *India Today*, 28 August 2000 (electronic edition).

Bajwa, Major General K.S. "Military Leadership and Changing Social Ethos." *Journal of the United Services Institute of India* (July–September 1978).

Barua, Pradeep P. "The Evolution of the Mechanized Infantry." *Strategic Analysis*, vol. 12. no. 9 (December 1988).

———. "Military Developments in India, 1750–1850." *Journal of Military History*, vol. 58, no. 4 (October 1994).

———. "Inventing Race: The British and India's Martial Races." *The Historian*, vol. 58, no. 1 (Autumn 1995).

Bharucha, Major P.C. "The North African Campaign 1940–1943." In Sri Nandan

Prasad (ed.), *Official History of the Indian Armed Forces in the Second World War 1939–1945*. New Delhi: Combined Inter-Services Historical Section [India & Pakistan], 1956.

Bidwell, Brigadier R.G.S. "The Development of British Field Artillery Tactics 1940–1942." *Journal of Royal Artillery*, vol. 94 no. 2 (September 1967).

Bobb, Dilip. "The Bofors Blast." *India Today* (15 May 1987).

Bond, Brian. "The Effect of the Cardwell Reforms." *Royal United Services Institute Journal* (November 1960).

Bonerji, Sir Albion. "The Indian Attitude towards the War Aims of the Allies." *Asiatic Review*, 36 (1940).

Calvert, Brigadier Michael. "Cardwell's Army Reforms." *Army* (April 1962).

———. "Victory in Burma." In E. Bauer, ed., *The History of World War II*. London; Orbis, 1979.

Chahda, Lieutenant Colonel Mahesh. "Mechanized Infantry: Where Have We Gone Wrong?" *Combat Journal* (April 1989).

Chaudhuri, "Muchu." "Sandhurst Revisited." *Blackwood's Magazine*, vol. 306, no. 1847 (September 1969).

Chaudhuri, Nirad C. "The Martial Races of India." *The Modern Review*, no. 48 (July 1930): 41–51.

———. "The Martial Races of India." *The Modern Review*, no. 48 (September 1930): 295–307.

———. "The Martial Races of India." *The Modern Review*, no. 49 (January 1931): 215–28.

Cohen, Stephen P. "Civilian Control of the Military in India." In Claude E. Welch (ed.), *Civilian Control of the Military: Theory and Cases from Developing Countries*. Albany, New York: State University of New York Press, 1976.

———. "The Military and Indian Democracy." In Atul Kohli (ed.), *India's Democracy*. Princeton, NJ: Princeton University Press, 1988.

Cooper, Randolf G.S. "Wellington and the Marathas in 1803." *International History Review*, 11 (February 1989).

Das, Major Gautam. "Turk-Sowar: An Indian Mechanized Force for the 21st Century." *Combat Journal* (August 1987).

Dutt, Lieutenant Colonel J.K. "Wanted: A Doctrine for Armour." *Journal of the United Services Institute of India* (October-December 1997).

Garnier, Maurice G. "Changing Recruitment Patterns and Organizational Ideology: The Case of a British Military Academy." *Administrative Science Quarterly*, vol. 17, no. 4 (December 1972).

Greenhut, Jeffrey. "The Imperial Reserve: The Indian Corps on the Western Front 1914–1915." *The Journal of Imperial and Commonwealth History*, vol. 12, no. 1 (October 1983): 66–67.

———. "Sahib and Sepoy: An Inquiry into the Relationship between the British Officers and Native Soldiers of the British Indian Army." *Military Affairs* (January 1984).

Guatam, R.P. "Causes of Higher Secondary Students' Preference for Military Career." *Journal of the United Services Institute of India* (October-December 1979).

———. "Status of Services vis-à-vis other Services." *Journal of the United Services Institute of India* (April-June 1985).

Gupta, Shishir. "The Army: Changing Order." *India Today*, 14 May 2001 (electronic edition).

Gutteridge, William. "The Indianization of the Indian Army 1918–1945." *Race: Journal of the Institute of Race Relations*, vol. 4 (May 1963).

Huntington, Samuel P. "Will More Countries Become Democratic." *Political Science Quarterly*, vol. 99 (1984).

IDR Research Team. "Some Thoughts on the Evolution of Infantry Organization and Tactics." *Indian Defence Review* (July 1991).

Jalal, Ayesha. "India's Partition and the Defence of Pakistan: An Historical Perspective." *Journal of Imperial and Commonwealth History*, vol. 15, no. 3 (1987).

Joshi, Manoj K. "Directions in India's Defence and Security Policies." In Ross Babbage and Sandy Gordon (eds.), *India's Strategic Future: Regional, State, or Global Power?* London: Macmillan, 1992.

Khalidi, Omar. "Ethnic Group Recruitment in the Indian Army: The Contrasting Cases of Sikhs, Muslims, and Gurkhas." *Pacific Affairs*, vol. 74, No. 4 (Winter 2001–2002).

Krishnan, Murali. "The Badge of Renaissance." *Outlook*, 15 January 2001 (electronic edition).

Kumar, Captain Rajiv. "Man Management: The Present Environ." *Journal of the United Services Institute of India* (January-March 1983).

Kundu, Apurba. "Over Dependence and 'Martial Race' Officers." *Indian Defence Review* (July 1991).

Law, Brigadier R.D. "The Gulf War—The Last Hundred Hours: Lessons for the Indian Mechanized Forces." *Journal of the United Services Institute of India* (July-September 1991).

Lenman, Bruce P. "The Transition to European Military Ascendency in India, 1600–1800." In John Lynn (ed.), *Tools of War: Instruments, Ideas and Institutions of Warfare, 1445–1871*. Urbana: University of Illinois Press, 1990.

Mackinnon, A.C.B. "The Moplah Rebellion 1921–1922." *Army Quarterly*, no. 8 (1924): 260–77.

Martin, Gregory. "The Influence of Racial Attitudes in British Policy towards India during the First World War. *The Journal of Imperial and Commonwealth History*, vol. 47, no. 2 (January 1986): 1002–104.

Omissi, David. "Martial Races: Ethnicity and Security in Colonial India, 1858–1939." *War & Society*, vol. 9, no. 1 (May 1991): 18.

Otley, C.B. "The Social Origins of British Army Officers." *The Sociological Review*, vol. 18, no. 2 (July 1970).

Rudolph, Lloyd I. "Self as Other: Amar Singh's Diary as Reflexive 'Native' Ethnography." *Modern Asian Studies*, vol. 31, no. 1 (1997): 143–75.

Rudolph, Lloyd, and Susanne Hoeber Rudolf. "Generals and Politicians in India." In Wilson C. McWilliams (ed.), *Garrisons and Governments: Politics and the Military in New States*. San Francisco: Chandler Publishing Co., 1964.

Sharpe, Andrew. "The Indianization of the Indian Army." *History Today* (March 1986).

Singh, Anita Inder. "Imperial Defence and the Transfer of Power in India, 1946–1947." *International History Review*, vol. 4, no. 4 (1982).

———. "Keeping India in the Commonwealth: British Political and Military Aims, 1947–1949." *Journal of Contemporary History*, vol. 20, no. 3 (1985).

———. "Post Imperial British Attitudes to India: The Military Aspect, 1947–1951." *Round Table*, no. 296 (1985).

Singh, Daljit. "Military Education in India: Changes from the British Tradition." *Journal of the United Services Institute of India* (July-September 1974).

Sinha, Brigadier B.K. "Career Prospects for Officers in the Armed Forces." *Journal of the United Services Institute of India* (July-September 1968).

Sinha, Lieutenant General S.K. (retd.). "Preserving the Army Ethos." *Indian Defence Review* (July 1992).

Spangenberg, B. "The Aitchison Commission: An Introduction." In *Report of the Public Service Commission 1886–1888*. New Delhi: Concept Publishing Co., 1977 (reprint).

———. "Social Affiliations of the British Army Elites." In Jacques van Doorn (ed.), *Armed Forces and Society: Sociological Essays*. The Hague: Moutan, 1968.

Thapan, Lieutenant General M.L. "The Army as a Career." *Journal of the United Services Institute of India* (July-September 1977).

Wavell, A.P. "The Army and the Prophets." *Journal of the Royal Services Institute*, no. 75 (November 1930).

Wright, Margaret M. "The Military Papers, 1940–1948, of Field-Marshal Sir Claude Auchinleck." Bulletin of the John Rylands University Library of Manchester, vol. 70, no. 2 (Summer 1988).

Index

ABOUT THE AUTHOR

PRADEEP P. BARUA is associate professor of history at the University of Nebraska at Kearney. He has authored several articles on Indian military history in the *Journal of Military History, Journal of Imperial and Commonwealth History, Armed Forces & Society*, and *The Historian*.

6th BF/Atlantic/1195
Atlantic 1195
6th B/F